John Robinson

Proofs of a conspiracy against all the religions and governments of Europe

John Robinson

Proofs of a conspiracy against all the religions and governments of Europe

ISBN/EAN: 9783337132064

Printed in Europe, USA, Canada, Australia, Japan

Cover: Foto ©Lupo / pixelio.de

More available books at **www.hansebooks.com**

PROOFS

OF A

CONSPIRACY

AGAINST ALL THE

RELIGIONS AND GOVERNMENTS

OF

EUROPE,

CARRIED ON

IN THE SECRET MEETINGS

OF

FREE MASONS, ILLUMINATI,

AND

READING SOCIETIES.

COLLECTED FROM GOOD AUTHORITIES,

By JOHN ROBISON, A. M.

PROFESSOR OF NATURAL PHILOSOPHY, AND SECRETARY TO THE ROYAL SOCIETY OF EDINBURGH.

Nam tua res agitur paries cum proximus ardet.

The THIRD EDITION.

To which is added a POSTSCRIPT.

PHILADELPHIA:

PRINTED FOR T. DOBSON, N°. 41, SOUTH SECOND STREET, AND W. COBBET, N°. 25, NORTH SECOND STREET.

1798.

TO THE RIGHT HONOURABLE

WILLIAM WYNDHAM,

SECRETARY AT WAR, &c. &c. &c.

SIR,

It was with great satisfaction that I learned from a Friend that you coincided with me in the opinion, that the information contained in this Performance would make a useful impression on the minds of my Countrymen.

I have presumed to inscribe it with your Name, that I may publicly express the pleasure which I felt, when I found that neither a separation for thirty years, nor the pressure of the most important business, had effaced your kind remembrance of a College Acquaintance, or abated that obliging and polite attention with which you favoured me in those early days of life.

The friendship of the accomplished and the worthy is the highest honour; and to him who is cut off, by want of health, from almost every other enjoyment, it is an inestimable blessing. Accept, therefore, I pray, of my grateful acknowledgments, and of my earnest wishes for your Health, Prosperity, and increasing Honour.

With sentiments of the greatest Esteem and Respect,
  I am, SIR,
   Your most obedient,
    and most humble Servant,
      JOHN ROBISON.

EDINBURGH,
September 5, 1797.

QUOD si quis verâ vitam ratione gubernet,
Divitiæ grandes homini sunt, vivere parcè
Æquo animo: neque enim est unquam penuria parvi.
At claros se homines voluêrunt atque potentes,
Ut fundamento stabili fortuna maneret,
Et placidam possent opulenti degere vitam:
Nequicquam,—quoniam ad summum succedere honorem
Certantes, iter infestum fecêre viaï,
Et tamen è summo quasi fulmen dejicit ictos
Invidia interdum contemptim in Tartara tetra.

Ergo, Regibus occisis, subversa jacebat
Pristina majestas siliorum, et sceptra superba;
Et capitis summi præclarum insigne, cruentum,
Sub pedibus volgi magnum lugebat honorum:
Nam cupidè conculcatur nimis ante metutum.
Res itaque ad summam fæcem, turbasque redibat,
Imperium sibi cum ac summatum quisque petebat.

        LUCRETIUS, V. 1116.

INTRODUCTION.

BEING at a friend's houfe in the country during fome part of the fummer 1795, I there faw a volume of a German periodical work, called *Religions Begebenheiten*, *i. e.* Religious Occurrences: in which there was an account of the various fchifms in the Fraternity of Free Mafons, with frequent allufions to the origin and hiftory of that celebrated affociation. This account interefted me a good deal, becaufe, in my early life, I had taken fome part in the occupations (fhall I call them) of Free Mafonry; and, having chiefly frequented the Lodges on the Continent, I had learned many doctrines, and feen many ceremonials which have no place in the fimple fyftem of Free Mafonry which obtains in this country. I had alfo remarked, that the whole was much more the object of reflection and thought than I could remember it to have been among my acquaintances at home. There, I had feen a Mafon Lodge confidered merely as a pretext for paffing an hour or two in a fort of decent conviviality, not altogether void of fome rational occupation. I had fometimes heard of differences of doctrines or of ceremonies, but in terms which marked them as mere frivolities. But, on the Continent, I found them matters of ferious concern and debate.

Such

Such too is the contagion of example, that I could not hinder myself from thinking one opinion better founded, or one Ritual more appofite and fignificant than another; and I even felt fomething like an anxiety for its being adopted, and a zeal for making it a general practice. I had been initiated in a very fplendid Lodge at Liege, of which the Prince Bifhop, his Trefonciers, and the chief Nobleffe of the State were members. I vifited the French Lodges at Valenciennes, at Bruffels, at Aix-la-Chapelle, at Berlin, and Koningfberg; and I picked up fome printed difcourfes delivered by the Brother-orators of the Lodges. At St. Peterfburgh I connected myfelf with the Englifh Lodge, and occafionally vifited the German and Ruffian Lodges held there. I found myfelf received with particular refpect as a Scotch Mafon, and as an Eleve of the *Lodge de la Parfait Intelligence* at Liege. I was importuned by perfons of the firft rank to purfue my mafonic career through many degrees unknown in this country. But all the fplendor and elegance that I faw could not conceal a frivolity in every part. It appeared a bafelefs fabric, and I could not think of engaging in an occupation which would confume much time, coft me a good deal of money, and might perhaps excite in me fome of that fanaticifm, or at leaft, enthufiafm, that I faw in others, and perceived to be void of any rational fupport. I therefore remained in the Englifh Lodge, contented with the rank of Scotch Mafter, which was in a manner forced on me in a private Lodge of French Mafons, but is not given in the Englifh Lodge. My mafonic rank admitted me to a very elegant entertainment in the female *Loge de la Fidelité*, where every ceremonial was compofed in the higheft degree of elegance, and every thing conducted with the moft delicate refpect for our fair fifters, and the old fong of brotherly love was chanted in the moft refined ftrain of sentiment.

sentiment. I do not suppose that the Parisian Free Masonry of forty-five degrees could give me more entertainment. I had profited so much by it, that I had the honour of being appointed the Brother-orator. In this office I gave such satisfaction, that a worthy Brother sent me at midnight a box, which he committed to my care, as a person far advanced in masonic science, zealously attached to the order, and therefore a fit depository of important writings. I learned next day that this gentleman had found it convenient to leave the empire in a hurry, but taking with him the funds of an establishment of which her Imperial Majesty had made him the manager. I was desired to keep these writings till he should see me again. I obeyed. About ten years afterward I saw the gentleman on the street in Edinburgh, conversing with a foreigner. As I passed by him, I saluted him softly in the Russian language; but without stopping, or looking him directly in the face. He coloured, but made no return. I endeavoured, in vain, to meet with him, wishing to make a proper return for much civility and kindness which I had received from him in his own country.

I now considered the box as accessible to myself, and opened it. I found it to contain all the degrees of the *Parfait Maçon Ecossois*, with the Rituals, Catechisms, and Instructions, and also four other degrees of Free Masonry, as cultivated in the Parisian Lodges. I have kept them with all care, and mean to give them to some respectable Lodge. But as I am bound by no engagement of any kind, I hold myself at liberty to make such use of them as may be serviceable to the public, without enabling any uninitiated person to enter the Lodges of these degrees.

This acquisition might have roused my former relish for masonry, had it been merely dormant; but, after so long separation from the *Lodge de la Fidelité,* the masonic

nic spirit had evaporated. Some curiosity however remained, and some wish to trace this plastic mystery to the pit from which the clay had been dug, which has been moulded into so many different shapes, "some to "honour, and some to dishonour." But my opportunities were now gone. I have given away (when in Russia) my volumes of discourses, and some far-fetched and gratuitous histories, and nothing remained but the pitiful work of Anderson, and the *Maçonnerie Adonhiramique devoilée*, which are in every one's hands.

My curiosity was strongly roused by the accounts given in the *Religions Begebenheiten*. There I saw quotations without number; systems and schisms of which I had never heard; but what particularly struck me was a zeal and a fanaticism about what I thought trifles, which astonished me. Men of rank and fortune, and engaged in serious and honourable public employments, not only frequenting the Lodges of the cities where they resided, but journeying from one end of Germany or France to the other, to visit new Lodges, or to learn new secrets or new doctrines. I saw conventions held at Wismar, at Wisbad, at Kohlo, at Brunswick, and at Willemsbad, consisting of some hundreds of persons of respectable stations. I saw adventurers coming to a city, professing some new secret, and in a few days forming new Lodges, and instructing in a troublesome and expensive manner hundreds of brethren.

German Masonry appeared a very serious concern, and to be implicated with other subjects with which I had never suspected it to have any connection. I saw it much connected with many occurrences and schisms in the Christian church; I saw that the Jesuits had several times interfered in it; and that most of the exceptionable innovations and dissentions had arisen about the time that the order of *Loyola* was suppressed; so that it should seem, that these intriguing brethren had

attempted

attempted to maintain their influence by the help of Free Masonry. I saw it much disturbed by the mystical whims of J. Behmen and Swedenborg—by the fanatical and knavish doctrines of the modern Rosycrucians—by Magicians—Magnetisers—Exorcists, &c. And I observed that these different sects reprobated each other, as not only maintaining erroneous opinions, but even inculcating opinions which were contrary to the established religions of Germany, and contrary to the principles of the civil establishments. At the same time they charged each other with mistakes and corruptions, both in doctrine and in practice; and particularly with falsification of the first principles of Free Masonry, and with ignorance of its origin and its history; and they supported these charges by authorities from many different books which were unknown to me.

My curiosity was now greatly excited. I got from a much respected friend many of the preceding volumes of the *Religions Begebenheiten*, in hopes of much information from the patient industry of German erudition. This opened a new and very interesting scene; I was frequently sent back to England, from whence all agreed that Free Masonry had been imported into Germany. I was frequently led into France and into Italy. There, and more remarkably in France, I found that the Lodges had become the haunts of many projectors and fanatics, both in science, in religion, and in politics, who had availed themselves of the secrecy and the freedom of speech maintained in these meetings, to broach their particular whims or suspicious doctrines, which, if published to the world in the usual manner, would have exposed the authors to ridicule or to censure. These projectors had contrived to tag their peculiar nostrums to the mummery of Masonry, and were even allowed to twist the masonic emblems and ceremonies to their purpose; so that in their hands Free Masonry became a thing totally unlike, and almost in direct opposition to the system (if it may get such a name) imported from England; and some Lodges had become schools of irreligion and licentiousness.

No nation in modern times has so particularly turned its attention to the cultivation of every thing that is refined or ornamental as France, and it has long been the resort of all who hunt after entertainment in its most refined form; the French have come to consider themselves as the instructors of the world in every thing that ornaments life, and feeling themselves received as such, they have formed their manners accordingly—full of the most condescending complaisance to *all who acknowledge* their superiority. Delighted, in a high degree, with this office, they have become zealous missionaries of refinement in every department of human pursuit, and have reduced their apostolic employment to a system, which they prosecute with ardour and delight. This is not groundless declamation, but sober historical truth. It was the professed aim (and it was a magnificent and wise aim) of the great Colbert, to make the court of Louis XIV. the fountain of human refinement, and Paris the Athens of Europe. We need only look, in the present day, at the plunder of Italy by the French army, to be convinced that their low-born generals and statesmen have in this respect the same notions with the Colberts and the Richlieus.

I know no subject in which this aim at universal influence on the opinions of men, by holding themselves forth as the models of excellence and elegance, is more clearly seen than in the care that they have been pleased to take of Free Masonry. It seems indeed peculiarly suited to the talents and taste of that vain and ardent people. Baseless and frivolous, it admits of every
form

form that Gallic refinement can invent, to recommend it to the young, the gay, the luxurious; that clafs of fociety which alone deferves their care, becaufe, in one way or another, it leads all other claffes of fociety.

It has accordingly happened, that the homely Free Mafonry imported from England has been totally changed in every country of Europe either by the impofing afcendency of French brethren, who are to be found every where, ready to inftruct the world; or by the importation of the doctrines, and ceremonies, and ornaments of the Parifian Lodges. Even England, the birth-place of Mafonry, has experienced the French innovations; and all the repeated injunctions, admonitions, and reproofs of the old Lodges, cannot prevent thofe in different parts of the kingdom from admitting the French novelties, full of tinfel and glitter, and high-founding titles.

Were this all, the harm would not be great. But long before good opportunities had occurred for fpreading the refinements on the fimple Free Mafonry of England, the Lodges in France had become places of very ferious difcuffion, where opinions in morals, in religion, and in politics, had been promulgated and maintained with a freedom and a keennefs, of which we in this favoured land have no adequate notion, becaufe we are unacquainted with the reftraints which, in other countries, are laid on ordinary converfation. In confequence of this, the French innovations in Free Mafonry were quickly followed in all parts of Europe, by the admiffion of fimilar difcuffions, although in direct oppofition to a ftanding rule, and a declaration made to every newly received Brother, " that nothing touching the religion or government " fhall ever be fpoken of in the Lodge." But the Lodges in other countries followed the example of France, and have frequently become the rendezvo :s
of

of innovators in religion and politics, and other disturbers of the public peace. In short, I have found that the covert of a Mason Lodge had been employed in every country for venting and propagating sentiments in religion and politics, that could not have circulated in public without exposing the author to great danger. I found, that this impunity had gradually encouraged men of licentious principles to become more bold, and to teach doctrines subversive of all our notions of morality—of all our confidence in the moral government of the universe—of all our hopes of improvement in a future state of existence—and of all satisfaction and contentment with our present life, so long as we live in a state of civil subordination. I have been able to trace these attempts, made, through a course of fifty years, under the specious pretext of enlightening the world by the torch of philosophy, and of dispelling the clouds of civil and religious superstition which keep the nations of Europe in darkness and slavery. I have observed these doctrines gradually diffusing and mixing with all the different systems of Free Masonry; till, at last, AN ASSOCIATION HAS BEEN FORMED for the express purpose of ROOTING OUT ALL THE RELIGIOUS ESTABLISHMENTS, AND OVERTURNING ALL THE EXISTING GOVERNMENTS OF EUROPE. I have seen this Association exerting itself zealously and systematically, till it has become almost irresistible: And I have seen that the most active leaders in the French Revolution were members of this Association, and conducted their first movements according to its principles, and by means of its instructions and assistance, *formally requested and obtained:* And, lastly, I have seen that this Association still exists, still works in secret, and that not only several appearances among ourselves show that its emissaries are endeavouring to propagate their detestable doctrines

trines among us, but that the Affociation has Lodges in Britain correfponding with the mother Lodge at Munich ever fince 1784.

If all this were a matter of mere curiofity, and fufceptible of no good ufe, it would have been better to have kept it to myfelf, than to difturb my neighbours with the knowledge of a ftate of things which they cannot amend. But if it fhall appear that the minds of my countrymen are mifled in the very fame manner as were thofe of our continental neighbours—if I can fhow that the reafonings which make a very ftrong impreffion on fome perfons in this country are the fame which actually produced the dangerous affociation in Germany; and that they had this unhappy influence folely becaufe they were thought to be fincere, and the expreffions of the fentiments of the fpeakers—if I can fhow that this was all a cheat, and that the Leaders of this Affociation difbelieved *every word* that they uttered, and every doctrine that they taught; and that their real intention was to abolifh *all* religion, overturn every government, and make the world a general plunder and a wreck—if I can fhow, that the principles which the Founder and Leaders of this Affociation held forth as the perfection of human virtue, and the moft powerful and efficacious for forming the minds of men, and making them good and happy, had no influence on the Founder and Leaders themfelves, and that they were, almoft without exception, the moft infignificant, worthlefs, and profligate of men; I cannot but think, that fuch information will make my countrymen hefitate a little, and receive with caution, and even diftruft, addreffes and inftructions which flatter our felf-conceit, and which, by buoying us up with the gay profpect of what feems attainable by a change, may make us difcontented with our prefent condition, and forget that there never was a government on earth
where

where the people of a great and luxurious nation enjoyed so much freedom and security in the possession of every thing that is dear and valuable.

When we see that these boasted principles had not that effect on the Leaders which they assert to be their native, certain, and inevitable consequences, we shall distrust the fine descriptions of the happiness that should result from such a change. And when we see that the methods which were practised by this Association for the express purpose of breaking all the bands of society, were employed solely in order that the Leaders might rule the world with uncontroulable power, while all the rest, even of the associated, should be degraded in their own estimation, corrupted in their principles, and employed as mere tools of the ambition of their *unknown superiors;* surely a free-born Briton will not hesitate to reject at once, and without any farther examination, a plan so big with mischief, so disgraceful to its underling adherents, and so uncertain in its issue.

These hopes have induced me to lay before the public a short abstract of the information which I think I have received. It will be short, but I hope sufficient for establishing the fact, that *this detestable Association exists, and its emissaries are busy among ourselves.*

I was not contented with the quotations which I found in the Religions Begebenheiten, but procured from abroad some of the chief writings from which they are taken. This both gave me confidence in the quotations from books which I could not procure, and furnished me with more materials. Much, however, remains untold, richly deserving the attention of all those who *feel* themselves disposed to listen to the tales of a possible happiness that may be enjoyed in a society where all the magistrates are wise and just, and all the people are honest and kind.

I hope

I hope that I am honest and candid. I have been at all pains to give the true sense of the authors. My knowledge of the German language is but scanty, but I have had the assistance of friends whenever I was in doubt. In compressing into one paragraph what I have collected from many, I have, as much as I was able, stuck to the words of the author, and have been anxious to give his precise meaning. I doubt not but that I have sometimes failed, and will receive correction with deference. I entreat the reader not to expect a piece of good literary composition. I am very sensible that it is far from it—it is written during bad health, when I am not at ease—and I wish to conceal my name—but my motive is, without the smallest mixture of another, to do some good in the only way I am able, and I think that what I say will come with better grace, and be received with more confidence, than any anonymous publication. Of these I am now most heartily sick. I throw myself on my country with a free heart, and I bow with deference to its decision.

The association of which I have been speaking is the Order of ILLUMINATI, founded, in 1775, by Dr. Adam Weishaupt, professor of Canon law in the university of Ingolstadt, and abolished in 1786 by the Elector of Bavaria, but revived immediately after, under another name, and in a different form, all over Germany. It was again detected, and seemingly broken up; but it had by this time taken so deep root that it still subsists without being detected, and has spread into all the countries of Europe. It took its first rise among the Free Masons, but is totally different from Free Masonry. It was not, however, the mere protection gained by the secrecy of the Lodges that gave occasion to it, but it arose naturally from the corruptions that had gradually crept into that fraternity, the violence of the party spirit which pervaded
it,

it, and from the total uncertainty and darkness that hangs over the whole of that mysterious Association. It is necessary, therefore, to give some account of the innovations that have been introduced into Free Masonry from the time that it made its appearance on the continent of Europe as a mystical society, possessing secrets different from those of the mechanical employment whose name it assumed, and thus affording entertainment and occupation to persons of all ranks and professions. It is by no means intended to give a history of Free Masonry. This would lead to a very long discussion. The patient industry of German erudition has been very seriously employed on this subject, and many performances have been published, of which some account is given in the different volumes of the Religions Begebenheiten, particularly in those for 1779, 1785, and 1786. It is evident, from the nature of the thing, that they cannot be very instructive to the public; because the obligation of secrecy respecting the important matters which are the very subjects of debate, prevents the author from giving that full information that is required from an historian; and the writers have not, in general, been persons qualified for the task. Scanty erudition, credulity, and enthusiasm, appear in almost all their writings; and they have neither attempted to remove the heap of rubbish with which Anderson has disgraced his *Constitutions of Free Masonry*, (the basis of masonic history,) nor to avail themselves of informations which history really affords to a sober enquirer. Their Royal art must never forsooth appear in a state of infancy or childhood, like all other human acquirements; and therefore, when they cannot give proofs of its existence in a state of manhood, possessed of all its mysterious treasures, they suppose what they do not see, and say that they are concealed by the oath of secrecy. Of such instruction I can make

no

no ufe, even if I were difpofed to write a hiftory of the Fraternity. I fhall content myfelf with an account of fuch particulars as are admitted by all the mafonic parties, and which illuftrate or confirm my general propofition, making fuch ufe of the accounts of the higher degrees in my poffeffion as I can without admitting the profane into their Lodges. Being under no tie of fecrecy with regard to thefe, I am with-held by difcretion alone from putting the public in poffeffion of all their myfteries.

PROOFS

OF

A CONSPIRACY, &c.

CHAP. I.

Schisms in Free Masonry.

THERE is undoubtedly a dignity in the art of building, or in architecture, which no other art possesses, and this, whether we consider it in its rudest state, occupied in raising a hut, or as practised in a cultivated nation, in the erection of a magnificent and ornamented temple. As the arts in general improve in any nation, this must always maintain its pre-eminence; for it employs them all, and no man can be eminent as an architect who does not possess a considerable knowledge of almost every science and art already cultivated in his nation. His great works are undertakings of the most serious concern, connect him with the public, or with the rulers of the state, and attach to him the practitioners of other arts, who are occupied in executing his orders: His works are the objects of public attention, and are not the transient spectacles of the day, but hand down to posterity his invention,

vention, his knowledge, and his taſte. No wonder then that he thinks highly of his profeſſion, and that the public ſhould acquieſce in his pretenſions, even when in ſome degree extravagant.

It is not at all ſurpriſing, therefore, that the incorporated architects in all cultivated nations ſhould arrogate to themſelves a pre-eminence over the ſimilar aſſociations of other tradeſmen. We find traces of this in the remoteſt antiquity. The Dionyſiacs of Aſia Minor were undoubtedly an aſſociation of architects and engineers, who had the excluſive privilege of building temples, ſtadia, and theatres, under the myſterious tutelage of Bacchus, and diſtinguiſhed from the uninitiated or profane inhabitants by the ſcience which they poſſeſſed, and by many private ſigns and tokens, by which they recogniſed each other. This aſſociation came into Ionia from Syria, into which country it had come from Perſia, along with that ſtyle of architecture that we call Grecian. We are alſo certain that there was a ſimilar trading aſſociation, during the dark ages, in Chriſtian Europe, which monopolized the building of great churches and caſtles, working under the patronage and protection of the Sovereigns and Princes of Europe, and poſſeſſing many privileges. Circumſtances, which it would be tedious to enumerate and diſcuſs, continued this aſſociation later in Britain than on the Continent.

But it is quite uncertain when and why perſons who were not builders by profeſſion firſt ſought admiſſion into this Fraternity. The firſt diſtinct and unequivocal inſtance that we have of this is the admiſſion of Mr. Aſhmole, the famous antiquary, in 1648, into a Lodge at Warrington, along with his father-in law Colonel Mainwaring. It is not improbable that the covert of ſecrecy in thoſe aſſemblies had made them courted by the Royaliſts, as occaſions of meeting. Nay, the Ritual

tual of the Master's degree seems to have been formed, or perhaps twisted from its original institution, so as to give an opportunity of sounding the political principles of the candidate, and of the whole Brethren present. For it bears so easy an adaption to the death of the King, to the overturning of the venerable constitution of the English government of three orders by a mean democracy, and its re-establishment by the efforts of the loyalists, that this would start into every person's mind during the ceremonial, and could hardly fail to show, by the countenances and behaviour of the Brethren, how they were affected. I recommend this hint to the consideration of the Brethren. I have met with many particular facts, which convince me that this use had been made of the meetings of Masons, and that at this time the Jesuits interfered considerably, insinuating themselves into the Lodges, and contributing to encrease that religious mysticism that is to be observed in all the ceremonies of the order. This society is well known to have put on every shape, and to have made use of every mean that could promote the power and influence of the order. And we know that at this time they were by no means without hopes of re-establishing the dominion of the Church of Rome in England. Their services were not scrupled at by the distressed royalists, even such as were Protestants, while they were highly prized by the Sovereign. We also know that Charles II. was made a Mason, and frequented the Lodges. It is not unlikely, that besides the amusement of a vacant hour, which was always agreeable to him, he had pleasure in the meeting with his loyal friends, and in the occupations of the Lodge, which recalled to his mind their attachment and services. His brother and successor James II. was of a more serious and manly cast of mind, and had little pleasure in the frivolous ceremonies

monies of Mafonry. He did not frequent the Lodges. But, by this time, they were the refort of many perfons who were not of the profeffion, or members of the trading corporation. This circumftance, in all probability, produced the denominations of FREE and ACCEPTED. A perfon who has the privilege of working at any incorporated trade, is faid to be a *freeman* of that trade. Others were *accepted* as Brethren, and admitted to a kind of honorary freedom, as is the cafe in many other trades and incorporations, without having (as far as we can learn for certain) a legal title to earn a livelihood by the exercife of it.

The Lodges being in this manner frequented by perfons of various profeffions, and in various ranks of civil fociety, it cannot be fuppofed that the employment in thofe meetings related entirely to the oftenfible profeffion of Mafonry. We have no authentic information by which the public can form any opinion about it. It was not till fome years after this period that the Lodges made open profeffion of the cultivation of general benevolence, and that the grand aim of the Fraternity was to enforce the exercife of all the focial virtues. It is not unlikely that this was an after-thought. The political purpofes of the affociation being once obtained, the converfation and occupations of the members muft take fome particular turn, in order to be generally acceptable. The eftablifhment of a fund for the relief of unfortunate Brethren did not take place till the very end of laft century; and we may prefume that it was brought about by the warm recommendations of fome benevolent members, who would naturally enforce it by addreffes to their affembled Brethren. This is the probable origin of thofe philanthropic difcourfes which were delivered in the Lodges by one of the Brethren as an official tafk. Brotherly love was the general topic, and this, with great propriety,

priety, when we confider the object aimed at in thofe addreffes. Nor was this object altogether a novelty. For while the manners of fociety were yet but rude, Brother Mafons, who were frequently led by their employment far from home and from their friends, ftood in need of fuch helps, and might be greatly benefited by fuch an inftitution, which gave them introduction and citizenfhip wherever they went, and a right to fhare in the charitable contributions of Brethren who were ftrangers to them. Other incorporated trades had fimilar provifions for their poor. But their poor were townfmen and neighbours, well known to them. There was more perfuafion neceffary in this Fraternity, where the objects of our immediate beneficence were not of our acquaintance. But when the Lodges confifted of many who were not Mafons, and who had no particular claim to good offices from a ftranger, and their number might be great, it is evident that ftronger perfuafions were now neceffary, and that every topic of philanthropy muft now be employed. When the funds became confiderable, the effects naturally took the public eye, and recommended the Society to notice and refpect. And now the Brethren were induced to dwell on the fame topic, to join in the commendations beftowed on the Society, and to fay that univerfal beneficence was the great aim of the Order. And this is all that could be faid in public, without infringing the obligation to fecrecy. The inquifitive are always prying and teazing, and this is the only point on which a Brother is at liberty to fpeak. He will therefore do it with affectionate zeal, till perhaps he has heated his own fancy a little, and overlooks the inconfiftency of this univerfal beneficence and philanthropy with the exclufive and monopolizing fpirit of an Affociation, which not only confines its benevolence to its own Members, (like any other charitable

ritable affociation,) but hoards up in its bofom ineftimable fecrets, whofe natural tendency, they fay, is to form the heart to this generous and kind conduct, and infpire us with love to all mankind. The profane world cannot fee the beneficence of concealing from public view a principle or a motive which fo powerfully induces a Mafon to be good and kind. The Brother fays that publicity would rob it of its force, and we muft take him at his word; and our curiofity is fo much the more excited to learn what are the fecrets which have fo fingular a quality.

Thus did the Fraternity conduct themfelves, and thus were they confidered by the public, when it was carried over from England to the continent; and here it is to be particularly remarked that all our Brethren abroad profefs to have received the Myftery of Free Mafonry from Britain. This is furely a puzzle in the hiftory; and we muft leave it to others to reconcile this with the repeated affertions in Anderfon's book of Conftitutions, " That the Fraternity exifted all over the World," and the numberlefs examples which he adduces of its exertions in other countries; nay, with his repeated affertions, " that it frequently was near perifhing in " Britain, and that our Princes were obliged to fend " to France and other countries, for leading men, to " reftore it to its former energy among us." We fhall find by and by that it is not a point of mere hiftorical curiofity, but that much hinges on it.

In the mean time, let us juft remember, that the plain tale of Brotherly love had been polifhed up to proteftations of univerfal benevolence, and had taken place of loyalty and attachment to the unfortunate Family of Stuart, which was now totally forgotten in the Englifh Lodges. The Revolution had taken place, and King James, with many of his moft zealous adherents, had taken refuge in France.

But

But they took Free Masonry with them to the continent, where it was immediately received by the French, and was cultivated with great zeal in a manner suited to the taste and habits of that highly polished people. The Lodges in France naturally became the rendezvous of the adherents to the exiled King, and the means of carrying on a correspondence with their friends in England. At this time also the Jesuits took a more active hand in Free Masonry than ever. They insinuated themselves into the English Lodges, where they were caressed by the Catholics, who panted after the re-establishment of their faith, and tolerated by the Protestant royalists, who thought no concession too great a compensation for their services. At this time changes were made in some of the Masonic symbols, particularly in the tracing of the Lodge, which bear evident marks of Jesuitical interference.

It was in the Lodge held at St. Germain's that the degree of *Chevalier Maçon Ecossis* was added to the three SYMBOLICAL degrees of English Masonry. The constitution, as imported, appeared too coarse for the refined taste of our neighbours, and they must make Masonry more like the occupation of a gentleman. Therefore, the English degrees of Apprentice, Fellowcraft, and Master, were called *symbolical*, and the whole contrivance was considered either as typical of something more elegant, or as a preparation for it. The degrees afterwards superadded to this leave us in doubt which of these views the French entertained of our Masonry. But at all events, this rank of Scotch Knight was called the *first* degree of the *Maçon Parfait*. There is a device belonging to this Lodge which deserves notice. A lion, wounded by an arrow, and escaped from the stake to which he had been bound, with the broken rope still about his neck, is represented lying at the mouth of a cave, and occupied with mathematical inftruments which are lying near him. A broken crown lies at the foot of the ftake. There can be little doubt but that this emblem alludes to the dethronement, the captivity, the efcape, and the afylum of James II. and his hopes of re-eftablifhment by the help of the loyal Brethren. This emblem is worn as the gorget of the Scotch Knight. It is not very certain, however, when this degree was added, whether immediately after king James's Abdication, or about the time of the attempt to fet his fon on the Britifh Throne. But it is certain, that in 1716, this and ftill higher degrees of Mafonry were much in vogue in the Court of France. The refining genius of the French, and their love of fhow, made the humble denominations of the Englifh Brethren difgufting; and their paffion for military rank, the only character that connected them with the court of an abfolute monarch, made them adapt Free Mafonry to the fame fcale of public eftimation, and invent ranks of *Maçons Chevaliers,* ornamented with titles, and ribands, and ftars. Thefe were highly relifhed by that vain people; and the price of reception, which was very high, became a rich fund, that was generally applied to relieve the wants of the banifhed Britifh and Irifh adherents of the unfortunate Family who had taken refuge among them. Three new degrees, of *Novice, Eleve,* and *Chevalier,* were foon added, and the *Parfait Maçon* had now feven receptions to go through, for each of which a handfome contribution was made. Afterwards, when the firft beneficent purpofe of this contribution ceafed to exift, the finery that now glittered in all the Lodges made a ftill more craving demand for reception-money, and ingenuity was fet to work to invent new baits for the *Parfait Maçon.* More degrees of chivalry were added, interfperfed with degrees of *Philofophe, Pellerin, Clairvoyant,* &c. &c. till fome Parifian Lodges had forty-

five

five ranks of Masonry, having fifteen orders of chivalry. For a Knighthood, with a Riband and a Star, was a *bonne bouche*, given at every third step. For a long while these degrees of chivalry proceeded on some faint analogies with several orders of chivalry which had been erected in Europe. All of these had some reference to some myftical doctrines of the Christian church, and were, in fact, contrivances of the Church of Rome for securing and extending her influence on the laymen of rank and fortune, whom she retained in her service by these play-things. The Knights Templars of Jerusalem, and the Knights of the Desert, whose office it was to protect pilgrims, and to defend the holy city, afforded very apt models for Masonic mimicry, because the Temple of Solomon, and the Holy Sepulchre, always shared the same fate. Many contested doctrines of the theologians had also their Chevaliers to defend them.

In all this progressive mummery we see much of the hand of the Jesuits, and it would seem that it was encouraged by the church. But a thing happened which might easily have been foreseen. The Lodges had become familiar with this kind of invention; the professed object of many *real* Orders of Knighthood was often very whimsical, or very refined and far-fetched, and it required all the finesse of the clergy to give to it some slight connection with religion or morality. The Masons, protected by their secrecy, ventured to go farther. The declamations in the lodges by the Brother orator, must naturally resemble the compositions of the ancient sophifts, and consist of wire-drawn differtations on the social duties, where every thing is amplified and strained to hyperbole, in their far-fetched and fanciful explanations of the symbols of Masonry. Thus accustomed to allegory, to fiction, to finesse, and to a sort of innocent hypocrisy by which they cajoled themselves

into

into a notion that this child's-play had at bottom a ferious and important meaning, the zealous champions of Free Mafonry found no inclination to check this inventive fpirit or circumfcribe its flights. Under the protection of Mafonic fecrecy, they planned fchemes of a different kind, and inftead of more Orders of Chivalry directed againft the enemies of their faith, they formed affociations in oppofition to the ridiculous and oppreffive ceremonies and fuperftitions of the church. There can be no doubt, that in thofe hidden affemblies, a free communication of fentiment was highly relifhed and much indulged. It was foon fufpected that fuch ufe was made of the covert of a Mafon Lodge; and the church dreaded the confequences, and endeavoured to fupprefs the Lodges. But in vain. And when it was found, that even auricular confeffion, and the fpiritual threatenings of the church, could not make the Brethren break their oath of fecrecy; a full confidence in their fecurity made thefe free-thinking Brethren bring forward, with all the eagernefs of a miffionary, fuch fentiments as they were afraid to hazard in ordinary fociety. This was long fufpected; but the rigours of the church only ferved to knit the Brethren more firmly together, and provoked them to a more eager exercife of their bold criticifms. The Lodges became fchools of fcepticifm and infidelity, and the fpirit of converfion or profelytifm grew every day ftronger. Cardinal Dubois had before this time laboured with all his might to corrupt the minds of the courtiers, by patronifing, directly and indirectly, all fceptics who were otherwife men of talents. He gave the young courtiers to underftand, that if he fhould obtain the reins of government, they fhould be entirely freed from the bigotry of Louis XIV. and the oppreffion of the church, and fhould have the free indulgence of their inclinations. His own plans were
difap-

disappointed by his death; but the Regent Orleans was equally indulgent, and in a few years there was hardly a man in France who pretended knowledge and reflection, who did not laugh at all religion. Amidst the almost infinite number of publications from the French presses, there is hardly a dozen to be found where the author attempts to vindicate religion from the charges of universal superstition and falshood. And it must be acknowledged that little else was to be seen in the established religion of the kingdom. The people found nothing in Christianity but a never-ceasing round of insignificant and troublesome ceremonies, which consumed their time, and furnished a fund for supporting a set of lordly and oppressive dignitaries, who declared in the plainest manner their own disbelief of their religion, by their total disregard of common decency, by their continual residence at court, and by absolute neglect, and even the most haughty and oppressive treatment of the only part of their order that took any concern about the religious sentiments of the nation, namely the Curés or parish-priests. The monks appeared only as lazy drones; but the parish-priests instructed the people, visited the sick, reconciled the offender and the offended, and were the great mediators between the landlords and their vassals, an office which endeared them more to the people than all the other circumstances of their profession. And it is remarkable, that in all the licentious writings and bitter satirical tales of the philosophic freethinkers, such as Voltaire, who never fails to have a taunting hit at the clergy, the Curé is generally an amiable personage, a charitable man, a friend to the poor and unfortunate, a peace-maker, and a man of piety and worth. Yet these men were kept in a state of the most slavish and cruel subjection by the higher orders of the clergy, and all hopes of advancement cut off. Rarely, hardly

hardly ever, does it happen, that a Curé becomes a Bishop. The Abbés step into every line of preferment. When such procedure is observed by a whole nation, what opinion can be formed but that the whole is a vile cheat? This however was the case in France, and therefore infidelity was almost universal. Nor was this overstrained freedom or licentiousness confined to religious opinions. It was perhaps more naturally directed to the restraints arising from civil subordination. The familiar name of Brother could not but tickle the fancy of those of inferior rank, when they found themselves side by side with persons whom they cannot approach out of doors but with cautious respect; and while these men of rank have their pride lulled a little, and perhaps their hearts a little softened by the hackneyed cant of sentimental declamation on the topic of Brotherly love and Utopian felicity, the others begin to fancy the happy days arrived, and the light of philanthropy beaming from the east and illuminating the Lodge. The Garret Pamphleteer enjoys his fancied authority as Senior Warden, and conducts with affectionate solemnity the young nobleman, who pants for the honour of Mastership, and he praises the trusty Brother who has guarded him in his perilous journies round the room. What topic of declamation can be more agreeable than the equality of the worthy Brethren? and how naturally will the Brother Orator in support of this favourite topic, slide into all the common-place pictures of human society, freed from all the anxieties attending civil distinction, and passing their days in happy simplicity and equality. From this state of the fancy, it is hardly a step to descant on the propriety, the expediency, and at last, the justice of such an arrangement of civil society; and in doing this, one cannot avoid taking notice of the great obstructions to human felicity which we see in every

quarter,

quarter, proceeding from the abuses of those distinctions of rank and fortune which have arisen in the world : and as the mischiefs and horrors of superstition are topics of continual declamation to those who wish to throw off the restraints of religion; so the oppression of the rulers of this world, and the sufferings of talents and worth in inferior stations, will be no less greedily listened to by all whose notions of morality are not very pure, and who would be glad to have the enjoyments of the wealthy without the trouble of labouring for them. Free Masonry may be affirmed to have a natural tendency to foster such levelling wishes; and we cannot doubt but that great liberties are taken with those subjects in the Lodges, especially in countries where the distinctions of rank and fortune are strongly expressed and noticed.

But it is not a matter of mere probability that the Mason Lodges were the seminaries of these libertine instructions. We have distinct proof of it, even in some of the French degrees. In the degree called the *Chevalier de Soleil*, the whole instruction is aimed against the established religion of the kingdom. The professed object is the emancipation from error and the discovery of truth. The inscription in the east is *Sagesse*, that in the north is *Liberté*, that in the south is *Fermeté*, and in the west it is *Caution;* terms which are very significant. The *Tres Vénerable* is Adam; the Senior Warden is Truth, and all the Brethren are Children of Truth. The process of reception is very well contrived: the whole ritual is decent and circumspect, and nothing occurs which can alarm the most timid. Brother Truth is asked, What is the hour? He informs Father Adam, that among men it is the hour of darkness, but that it is mid-day in the Lodge. The candidate is asked, Why he has knocked at the door, and what is become of his eight companions (he is one of the

the *Elus*)? He says, that the world is in darkness, and his companions and he have lost each other; that *Hesperus*, the star of Europe, is obscured by clouds of incense, offered up by superstition to despots, who have made themselves gods, and have retired into the inmost recesses of their palaces, that they may not be recognised to be men, while their priests are deceiving the people, and causing them to worship these divinities. This and many similar sentiments are evident allusions to the pernicious doctrine of the book called *Origine du Despotisme Oriental*, where the religion of all countries is considered as a mere engine of state; where it is declared that reason is the only light which nature has given to man: that our anxiety about futurity has made us imagine endless torments in a future world; and that princes, taking advantage of our weakness, have taken the management of our hopes and fears, and directed them so as to suit their own purposes; and emancipation from the fear of death is declared to be the greatest of all deliverances. Questions are put to the candidate, tending to discover whether and how far he may be trusted, and what sacrifices he is willing to make in search after truth.

This shape given to the plastic mysteries of Masonry was much relished, and in a very short time this new path was completely explored, and a new series of degrees was added to the list, viz. the *Novice*, and the *Elu de la Verité*, and the *Sublime Philosophe*. In the progress through these degrees, the Brethren must forget that they have formerly been *Chevaliers de l'Orient*, *Chevaliers de l'Aigle*, when the symbols were all explained as typical of the life and immortality brought to light by the gospel. Indeed they are taught to class this among the other clouds which have been dispelled by the sun of reason. Even in the *Chevalerie de l'Aigle* there is a twofold explanation given of the symbols, by which

which a lively imagination may conceive the whole history and peculiar doctrines of the New Testament, as being typical of the final triumph of reason and philosophy over error. And perhaps this degree is the very first step in the plan of ILLUMINATION.

We are not to suppose that this was carried to extremity at once. But it is certain, that before 1743, it had become universal, and that the Lodges of Free Masons had become the places for making proselytes to every strange and obnoxious doctrine. *Theurgy, Cosmogony, Cabala,* and many whimsical and mystical doctrines which have been grafted on the distinguishing tenets and the pure morality of the Jews and Christians, were subjects of frequent discussion in the Lodges. The celebrated Chevalier Ramsay had a great share in all this business. Affectionately attached to the family of Stuart, and to his native country, he had co-operated heartily with those who endeavoured to employ Masonry in the service of the Pretender, and, availing himself of the pre-eminence given (at first perhaps as a courtly compliment) to Scotch Masonry, he laboured to shew that it existed, and indeed arose, during the Crusades, and that there really was either an order of chivalry whose business it was to rebuild the Christian churches destroyed by the Saracens, or that a fraternity of Scotch Masons were thus employed in the east, under the protection of the Knights of St. John of Jerusalem. He found some facts which were thought sufficient grounds for such an opinion, such as the building of the college of these Knights in London, called the Temple, which was actually done by the public Fraternity of Masons who had been in the holy wars. It is chiefly to him that we are indebted for that rage of Masonic chivalry which distinguishes the French Free Masonry. Ramsay was as eminent for his piety as he was for his enthusiasm, but his opinions were fingular. His eminent learning, his elegant talents, his amiable character, and particularly his eftimation at court, gave great influence to every thing he said on a fubject which was merely a matter of fafhion and amufement. Whoever has attended much to human affairs, knows the eagernefs with which men propagate all fingular opinions, and the delight which attends their favourable reception. None are more zealous than the apoftles of infidelity and atheifm. It is in human nature to catch with greedinefs any opportunity of doing what lies under general reftraint. And if our apprehenfions are not completely quieted, in a cafe where our wifhes lead us ftrongly to fome favourite but hazardous object, we are confcious of a kind of felf bullying. This naturally gets into our difcourfe, and in our eagernefs to get the encouragement of joint adventurers, we enforce our tenets with an energy, and even a violence, that is very inconfiftent with the fubject in hand. If I am an Atheift, and my neighbour a Theift, there is furely nothing that fhould make me violent in my endeavours to rid him of his error. Yet how violent were the people of this party in France.

These facts and obfervations fully account for the zeal with which all this patch-work addition to the fimple Free Mafonry of England was profecuted in France. It furprifes us Britons, who are accuftomed to confider the whole as a matter of amufement for young men, who are glad of any pretext for indulging in conviviality. We generally confider a man advanced in life with lefs refpect, if he fhows any ferious attachment to fuch things. But in France, the civil and religious reftraints in converfation made thefe fecret affemblies very precious; and they were much frequented by men of letters, who there found an opportunity of expreffing in fafety their diffatisfaction

with

with thofe reftraints, and with that inferiority of rank and condition to which they were fubjected, and which appeared to themfelves fo inadequate to their own talents and merits. The *Avocats au Parlement*, the unbeneficed Abbés, the young men of no fortune, and the *foidifant* philofophers, formed a numerous band, frequented the Lodges, and there difcuffed every topic of religion and politics. Specimens of this occupation appeared from time to time in Collections of Difcourfes delivered by the *Frere Orateur*. I once had in my poffeffion two volumes of thefe difcourfes, which I now regret that I left in a Lodge on the continent, when my relifh for Free Mafonry had forfaken me. One of thefe is a difcourfe by Brother Robinet, delivered in the *Loge des Chevaliers Bienfaifants de la Sainte Cité* at Lyons, at a vifitation by the Grand Mafter the *Duc de Chartres*, afterwards *Orleans* and *Egalité*. In this difcourfe we have the germ and fubftance of his noted work, *La Nature, ou l'Homme moral et phyfique*.* In another difcourfe, delivered by Brother Condorcet in the *Loge des Philalethes* at Strafbourg, we have the outlines of his pofthumous work, *Le Progres de l'Efprit humain*; and in another, delivered by Mirabeau in the *Loge des Chevaliers Bienfaifants* at Paris, we have a great deal of the levelling principles, and cofmopolitifm,† which he thundered from the tribunes of the National Affembly. But the moft remarkable performances of this kind are, the *Archives Myftico-Hermetiques*, and the *Des Erreurs, et de la Verité*. The firft is confidered as an account, hiftorical and dogmatical, of the procedure and fyftem of the *Loge des Chevaliers Bienfaifants* at

---

* And I may add the *Syfteme de la Nature* of Diderot, who corrected the crude whims of Robinet by the more refined mechanifm of Hartley.

† Citizenfhip of the World, from the Greek words *Cofmos*, world, and *Polis*, a city.

at Lyons. This was the moſt zealous and ſyſtematical of all the coſmopolitical Lodges in France. It worked long under the patronage of its Grand Maſter the *Duc des Chartres*, afterwards *Orleans*, and at laſt *Ph. Egalité*. It ſent out many affiliated Lodges, which were erected in various parts of the French dominions. The daughter Lodges at Paris, Straſbourg, Lille, Thoulouſe, took the additional title of *Philalethes*. There aroſe ſome ſchiſms, as may be expected, in an Aſſociation where every man is encouraged to broach and to propagate any the moſt ſingular opinion. Theſe ſchiſms were continued with ſome heat, but were in a great meaſure repaired in Lodges which took the name of *Amis reunis de la Verité*. One of this denomination at Paris became very eminent. The mother Lodge at Lyons extended its correſpondence into Germany, and other foreign countries, and ſent conſtitutions or ſyſtems, by which the Lodges conducted their operations.

I have not been able to trace the ſteps by which this Lodge acquired ſuch an aſcendancy; but I ſee, that in 1769 and 1770, all the refined or philoſophical Lodges in Alſace and Lorraine united, and in a convention at Lyons, formally put themſelves under the patronage of this Lodge, cultivated a continual correſpondence, and conſidered themſelves as profeſſing one Maſonic Faith, ſufficiently diſtinguiſhable from that of other Lodges. What this was we do not very diſtinctly know. We can only infer it from ſome hiſtorical circumſtances. One of its favourite daughters, the Lodge *Theodor von der guten Rath*, at Munich, became ſo remarkable for diſcourſes dangerous to church and ſtate, that the Elector of Bavaria, after repeated admonitions during a courſe of five or ſix years, was obliged to ſuppreſs it in 1786. Another of its ſuffragan Lodges at Regenſburgh became exceedingly obnoxious to the
ſtate,

ſtate, and occaſioned ſeveral commotions and inſurrections. Another, at Paris, gradually refined into the Jacobin club—And in the year 1791, the Lodges in Alſace and Lorraine, with thoſe of Spire and Worms, invited Cuſtine into Germany, and delivered Mentz into his hands.

When we reflect on theſe hiſtorical facts, we get ſome key to the better underſtanding of the two performances which I mentioned as deſcriptive of the opinions and occupations of this Sect of Free-Maſons. The *Archives Myſtico-Hermetiques* exhibit a very ſtrange mixture of Myſticiſm, Theoſophy, Cabaliſtic whim, real Science, Fanaticiſm, and Freethinking, both in religion and politics. They muſt not be conſidered as an account of any ſettled ſyſtem, but rather as annals of the proceedings of the Lodge, and abſtracts of the ſtrange doctrines which made their ſuceſſive appearance in it. But if an intelligent and cautious reader examine them attentively, he will ſee, that the book is the work of one hand, and that all the wonders and oddities are caricatured, ſo as to engroſs the general attention, while they alſo are twiſted a little, ſo that in one way or another they accord with a general ſpirit of licentiouſneſs in morals, religion, and politics. Although every thing is expreſſed decently, and with ſome caution and moderation, atheiſm, materialiſm, and diſcontent with civil ſubordination, pervade the whole. It is a work of great art. By keeping the ridicule and the danger of ſuperſtition and ignorance continually in view, the mind is captivated by the relief which free enquiry and communication of ſentiment ſeems to ſecure, and we are put off our guard againſt the riſk of deluſion, to which we are expoſed when our judgment is warped by our paſſions.

The other book, " Des Erreurs et de la Verité," came from the ſame ſchool, and is a ſort of holy ſcripture,

ture, or at leaſt a Talmud among the Free Maſons of France. It is intended only for the initiated, and is indeed a myſtery to any other reader. But as the object of it was to ſpread the favourite opinions of ſome enthuſiaſtic Brethren, every thing is ſaid that does not directly betray the ſecrets of the Order. It contains a ſyſtem of Theoſophy that has often appeared in the writings of philoſophers, both in ancient and modern times. " All the intelligence and moral ſentiment
" that appears in the univerſe, either directly, as in
" the minds of men, or indirectly, as an inference
" from the marks of deſign that we ſee around us, ſome
" of which ſhow us that men have acted, and many
" more that ſome other intelligence has acted, are con-
" ſidered as parts or portions of a general maſs of in-
" telligence which exiſts in the univerſe, in the ſame
" manner as matter exiſts in it. This intelligence has
" an inſcrutable connection with the material part of
" the univerſe, perhaps reſembling the connection,
" equally unſearchable, that ſubſiſts between the mind
" and body of man ; and it may be conſidered as the
" *Soul of the World.* It is this ſubſtance, the natural
" object of wonder and reſpect, that men have called
" God, and have made the object of religious wor-
" ſhip. In doing ſo they have fallen into groſs miſ-
" takes, and have created for themſelves numberleſs
" unfounded hopes and fears, which have been the
" ſource of ſuperſtition and fanaticiſm, the moſt def-
" tructive plagues that have ever afflicted the human
" race. The Soul of Man is ſeparated from the ge-
" neral maſs of intelligence by ſome of the operations
" of nature, which we ſhall never underſtand, juſt as
" water is raiſed from the ground by evaporation, or
" taken up by the root of a plant. And as the water,
" after an unſearchable train of changes, in which it
" ſometimes makes part of a flower, ſometimes part

" of

"of an animal, &c. is at laſt reunited, in its original
"form, to the great maſs of waters, ready to run over
"the ſame circle again; ſo the Soul of Man, after
"performing its office, and exhibiting all that train
"of intellectual phenomena that we call human life,
"is at laſt ſwallowed up in the great ocean of intelli-
"gence." The author then may ſing

> "Felix qui potuit rerum cognoſcere cauſas,
> "Atque metus omnes et inexorabile fatum
> "Subjecit pedibus, ſtrepitumque Acherontis avari."

For he has now got to his aſylum. This deity of his may be the object of wonder, like every thing great and incomprehenſible, but not of worſhip, as the moral Governor of the univerſe. The hopes are at end, which reſt on our notions of the immortality and individuality of the human ſoul, and on the encouragement which religion holds forth to believe, that improvement of the mind in the courſe of this life, by the exerciſe of wiſdom and of virtuous diſpoſitions, is but the beginning of an endleſs progreſs in all that can give delight to the rational and well-diſpoſed mind. No relation now ſubſiſts between man and Deity that can warm the heart. But, as this is contrary to ſome natural propenſity in the human mind, which in all ages and nations has panted after ſome connection with Deity, the author ſtrives to avail himſelf of ſome cold principles of ſymmetry in the works of nature, ſome ill-ſupported notions of propriety, and other ſuch conſiderations, to make this *anima mundi* an object of love and reſpect. This is done in greater detail in another work, *Tableau, des rapports entre l'Homme, Dieu, et l'Univers,* which is undoubtedly by the ſame hand. But the intelligent reader will readily ſee, that ſuch incongruous things cannot be reconciled, and that we can expect nothing here but ſophiſtry. The author
proceeds,

proceeds, in the next place, to confider man as related to man, and to trace out the path to happinefs in this life. Here we have the fame overftrained morality as in the other work, the fame univerfal benevolence, the fame lamentations over the miferable ftate of mankind, refulting from the oppreffion of the powerful, the great ones of the earth, who have combined againft the happinefs of mankind, and have fucceeded, by debafing their minds, fo that they have become willing flaves. This could not have been brought about without the affiftance of fuperftition. But the princes of this world enlifted into their fervice the priefts, who exerted themfelves in darkening the underftandings of men, and filled their minds with religious terrors. The altar became the chief pillar of the throne, and men were held in complete fubjection. Nothing can recover them from this abject ftate but knowledge. While this difpels their fears, it will alfo fhow them their rights, and the way to attain them.

It deferves particularly to be remarked, that this fyftem of opinions (if fuch an inconfiftent mafs of affertions can be called a fyftem) bears a great refemblance to a performance of Toland's, publifhed in 1720, called *Pantheifticon, feu Celebratio Sodalitii Socratici*. It is an account of the principles of a Fraternity which he calls Socratica, and the Brothers Pantheiftæ. They are fuppofed to hold a Lodge, and the author gives a ritual of the procedure in this Lodge; the ceremonies of opening and fhutting of the Lodge, the admiffion of Members into its different degrees, &c. Reafon is the Sun that illuminates the whole, and Liberty and Equality are the objects of their occupations.

'We fhall fee afterwards that this book was fondly pufhed into Germany, tranflated, commented upon, and fo mifreprefented, as to call off the attention from the

the real spirit of the book, which is intentionally wrapped up in cabala and enigma. Mirabeau was at much pains to procure it notice; and it must therefore be considered as a treasure of the cosmo-political opinions of the Association of *Chevaliers Bienfaisants*, *Philalethes*, and *Amis Reunis*, who were called the *improved* Lodges, working under the D. de Chartres—of these there were 266 in 1784. This will be found a very important remark. Let it also be recollected afterwards, that this Lodge of Lyons sent a deputy to a grand Convention in Germany in 1772, viz. Mr. Willermooz, and that the business was thought of such importance, that he remained there two years.

The book *Des Erreurs et de la Verité*, must therefore be considered as a classical book of these opinions. We know that it originated in the *Loge des Chev. Bienfaisants* at Lyons. We know that this Lodge stood as it were at the head of French Free Masonry, and that the fictitious Order of Masonic Knights Templars was formed in this Lodge, and was considered as the model of all the rest of this mimic chivalry. They proceeded so far in this mummery, as even to have the clerical tonsure. The Duke of Orleans, his son, the Elector of Bavaria, and some other German Princes, did not scruple at this mummery in their own persons. In all the Lodges of reception, the Brother Orator never failed to exclaim on the topics of superstition, blind to the exhibition he was then making, or indifferent as to the vile hypocrisy of it. We have, in the lists of Orators and Office-bearers, many names of persons, who have had an opportunity at last of proclaiming their sentiments in public. The Abbé Sieyes was of the Lodge of Philalethes at Paris, and also at Lyons. Lequinio, author of the most profligate book that ever disgraced a press, the *Prejuges vaincus par la Raison*, was Warden in the Lodge *Compacte Sociale*.

F   Despremenil,

Defpremenil, Bailly, Fauchet, Maury, Mounier, were of the fame fyftem, though in different Lodges. They were called Martinifts, from a St. Martin, who formed a fchifm in the fyftem of the *Chevaliers Bienfaifants*, of which we have not any very precife account. Mercier gives fome account of it in his *Tableau de Paris*, and in his *Anné* 2440. The breach alarmed the Brethren, and occafioned great heats. But it was healed, and the Fraternity took the name of *Mifa du Renis*, which is an anagram of *des Amis Reunis*. The Bifhop of Autun, the man fo bepraifed as the benevolent Citizen of the World, the friend of mankind and of good order, was Senior Warden of another Lodge at Paris, eftablifhed in 1786, (I think chiefly by Orleans and himfelf,) which afterwards became the Jacobin Club. In fhort, we may affert with confidence, that the Mafon Lodges in France were the hot-beds, where the feeds were fown, and tenderly reared, of all the pernicious doctrines which foon after choaked every moral or religious cultivation, and have made the Society worfe than a wafte, have made it a noifome marfh of human corruption, filled with every rank and poifonous weed.

These Lodges were frequented by perfons of all ranks, and of every profeffion. The idle and the frivolous found amufement, and glittering things to tickle their fatiated fancies. There they became the dupes of the declamations of the crafty and licentious Abbés, and writers of every denomination. Mutual encouragement in the indulgence of hazardous thoughts and opinions which flatter our wifhes or propenfities is a lure which few minds can refift. I believe that moft men have felt this in fome period of their lives. I can find no other way of accounting for the company that I have fometimes feen in a Mafon Lodge. The Lodge *de la Parfaite Intelligence* at Liege, contained, in December

December 1770, the Prince Bifhop, and the greateft part of his Chapter, and all the Office-bearers were dignitaries of the church; yet a difcourfe given by the Brother Orator was as poignant a fatire on fuperftition and credulity, as if it had been written by Voltaire. It was under the aufpices of this Lodge that the collection of difcourfes, which I mentioned above, was publifhed, and there is no fault found with Brother Robinet, nor Brother Condorcet. Indeed the Trefonciers of Liege were proverbial, even in Brabant, for their Epicurifm in the moft extenfive fenfe of the word.

Thus was corruption fpread over the kingdom under the mafk of moral inftruction. For thefe difcourfes were full of the moft refined and ftrained morality, and florid paintings of Utopian felicity, in a ftate where all are Brothers and citizens of the world. But alas! thefe wire-drawn principles feem to have had little influence on the hearts, even of thofe who could beft difplay their beauties. Read the tragedies of Voltaire, and fome of his grave performances in profe—What man is there who feems better to know his Mafter's will? No man expreffes with more propriety, with more exactnefs, the feelings of a good mind. No man feems more fenfible of the immutable obligation of juftice and of truth. Yet this man, in his tranfactions with his bookfellers, with the very men to whom he was immediately indebted for his affluence and his fame, was repeatedly, nay inceffantly, guilty of the meaneft, the vileft tricks. When he fold a work for an enormous price to one bookfeller, (even to Cramer, whom he really refpected,) he took care that a furreptitious edition fhould appear in Holland, almoft at the fame moment. Proof-fheets have been traced from Ferney to Amfterdam. When a friend of Cramer's expoftulated with Voltaire on the injuftice of this conduct, he faid, grinning, *Oh le bon Cramer—eh bien—il n'a n'a que d' etre du parti*—he may take a share—he will not give me a livre the lefs for the firſt piece I offer him. Where ſhall we ſee more tenderneſs, more honour, more love of every thing that is good and fair, than in Diderot's *Pere de Famille?*—Yet this man did not ſcruple to ſell to the Empreſs of Ruſſia an immenſe library, which he did not poſſeſs, for an enormous price, having got her promiſe that it ſhould remain in his poſſeſſion in Paris during his life. When her ambaſſador wanted to ſee it, after a year or two's payments, and the viſitation could be no longer ſtaved off, Diderot was obliged to ſet off in a hurry, and run through all the bookſellers ſhops in Germany, to help him to fill his empty ſhelves. He had the good fortune to ſave appearances—but the trick took air, becauſe he had been niggardly in his attention to the ambaſſador's ſecretary. This, however, did not hinder him from honouring his Imperial pupil with a viſit. He expected adoration, as the light of the world, and was indeed received by the Ruſſian courtiers with all the childiſh fondneſs that they feel for every Pariſian mode. But they did not underſtand him, and as he did not like to loſe money at play, they did not long court his company. He found his pupil too clear ſighted. *Ces philoſophes*, ſaid ſhe, *ſont beaux, vûs de loin; mais de plus près, le diamant parait cryſtal.* He had contrived a poor ſtory, by which he hoped to get his daughter married in parade, and portioned by her Majeſty—but it was ſeen through, and he was diſappointed.

When we ſee the inefficacy of this refined humanity on theſe two apoſtles of philoſophical virtue, we ſee ground for doubting of the propriety and expediency of truſting entirely to it for the peace and happineſs of a ſtate, and we ſhould be on our guard when we liſten to the florid ſpeeches of the Brother Orator, and his congratulations on the emancipation from superstition and oppression, which will in a short time be effectuated by the *Chevaliers Bienfaisants*, the *Philalethes*, or any other sect of cosmo-political Brethren.

I do not mean by all this to maintain, that the Mason Lodges were the sole corrupters of the public mind in France.—No.—In all nations that have made much progress in cultivation, there is a great tendency to corruption, and it requires all the vigilance and exertions of magistrates, and of moral instructors, to prevent the spreading of licentious principles and maxims of conduct. They arise naturally of themselves, as weeds in a rich soil; and, like weeds, they are pernicious, only because they are, where they should not be, in a cultivated field. Virtue is the cultivation of the human soul, and not the mere possession of good dispositions; all men have these in some degree, and occasionally exhibit them. But virtue supposes exertion; and, as the husbandman must be incited to his laborious task by some cogent motive, so must man be prompted to that exertion which is necessary on the part of every individual for the very existence of a great society: For man is indolent, and he is luxurious; he wishes for enjoyment, and this with little trouble. The less fortunate envy the enjoyments of others, and repine at their own inability to obtain the like. They see the idle in affluence. Few, even of good men, have the candour, nay, I may call it the wisdom, to think on the activity and the labour which had procured those comforts to the rich or to their ancestors; and to believe that they are idle only because they are wealthy, but would be active if they were needy.— Such spontaneous reflexions cannot be expected in persons who are engaged in unceasing labour, to procure a very moderate share (in their estimation at least) of the comforts of life. Yet such reflexions would, in the

the main, be juft, and furely they would greatly tend to quiet the minds of the unfuccefsful.

This excellent purpofe may be greatly forwarded by a national eftablifhment for moral inftruction and admonition; and if the public inftructors fhould add all the motives to virtuous moderation which are fuggefted by the confiderations of genuine religion, every advice would have a tenfold influence. Religious and moral inftructions are therefore, in their own nature, unequivocal fupports to that moderate exertion of the authority arifing from civil fubordination, which the moft refined philanthropift or cofmo-polite acknowledges to be neceffary for the very exiftence of a great and cultivated fociety. I have never feen a fcheme of Utopian happinefs that did not contain fome fyftem of education, and I cannot conceive any fyftem of education of which moral inftruction is not a principal part. Such eftablifhments are dictates of nature, and obtrude themfelves on the mind of every perfon who begins to form plans of civil union. And in all exifting focieties they have indeed been formed, and are confidered as the greateft corrector and foother of thofe difcontents that are unavoidable in the minds of the unfuccefsful and the unfortunate. The magiftrate, therefore, whofe profeffional habits lead him frequently to exert himfelf for the maintenance of public peace, cannot but fee the advantages of fuch ftated remembrancers of our duty. He will therefore fupport and cherifh this public eftablifhment, which fo evidently affifts him in his beneficent and important labours.

But all the evils of fociety do not fpring from the difcontents and the vices of the poor. The rich come in for a large and a confpicuous fhare. They frequently abufe their advantages. Pride and haughty behaviour on their part rankle in the breafts, and affect the tempers of their inferiors, already fretted by
the

the hardships of their own condition. The rich also are luxurious; and are often needy. Grasping at every mean of gratification, they are inattentive to the rights of inferiors whom they despise, and, despising, oppress. Perhaps their own superiority has been acquired by injustice. Perhaps most sovereignties have been acquired by oppression. Princes and Rulers are but men; as such, they abuse many of their greatest blessings. Observing that religious hopes make the good resigned under the hardships of the present scene, and that its terrors frequently restrain the bad; they avail themselves of these observations, and support religion as an engine of state, and a mean of their own security. But they are not contented with its real advantages; and they are much more afraid of the resentment and the crimes of the offended profligate, than of the murmurs of the suffering worthy. Therefore they encourage superstition, and call to their aid the vices of the priesthood. The priests are men of like passions as other men, and it is no ground of peculiar blame that they also frequently yield to the temptations of their situation. They are encouraged to the indulgence of the love of influence natural to all men, and they heap terror upon terror, to subdue the minds of men, and darken their understandings. Thus the most honourable of all employments, the moral instruction of the state, is degraded to a vile trade, and is practised with all the deceit and rapacity of any other trade; and religion, from being the honour and the safeguard of nation, becomes its greatest disgrace and curse.

When a nation has fallen into this lamentable state, it is extremely difficult to reform. Although nothing would so immediately and so completely remove all ground of complaint, as the re-establishing private virtue, this is of all others the least likely to be adopted. The really worthy, who see the mischief where it
actually

actually is, but who view this life as the school of improvement, and know that man is to be made perfect through suffering, are the last persons to complain. The worthless are the most discontented, the most noisy in their complaints, and the least scrupulous about the means of redress. Not to improve the nation, but to advance themselves, they turn the attention to the abuses of power and influence. And they begin their attack where they think the place most defenceless, and where perhaps they expect assistance from a discontented garrison. They attack superstition, and are not at all solicitous that true religion shall not suffer along with it. It is not perhaps, with any direct intention to ruin the state, but merely to obtain indulgence for themselves and the co-operation of the wealthy. They expect to be listened to by many who wish for the same indulgence; and thus it is that religious free-thinking is generally the first step of anarchy and revolution. For in a corrupted state, persons of all ranks have the same licentious wishes, and if superstitious fear be really an ingredient of the human mind, it requires some *struggle* to shake it off. Nothing is so effectual as mutual encouragement, and therefore all join against priest-craft; even the rulers forget their interest, which should lead them to support it. In such a state, the pure morality of true religion vanishes from the sight. There is commonly no remains of it in the religion of the nation, and therefore all goes together.

Perhaps there never was a nation where all these co-operating causes had acquired greater strength than in France. Oppressions of all kinds were at a height. The luxuries of life were enjoyed exclusively by the upper classes, and this in the highest degree of refinement; so that the desires of the rest were whetted to the utmost. Religion appeared in its worst form, and seemed calculated

culated solely for procuring establishments for the younger sons of the insolent and useless noblesse. The morals of the higher orders of the clergy and of the laity were equally corrupted. Thousands of literary men were excluded by their station from all hopes of advancement to the more respectable offices in the church. These vented their discontents as far as there was safety, and were encouraged by many of the upper classes, who joined them in their satires on the priesthood. The clergy opposed them, it is true, but feebly, because they could not support their opposition by examples of their own virtuous behaviour, but were always obliged to have recourse to the power of the church, the very object of hatred and disgust. The whole nation became infidel; and when in a few instances a worthy Curé uttered the small still voice of true religion, it was not heard amidst the general noise of satire and reproach. The misconduct of administration, and the abuse of the public treasures, were every day growing more impudent and glaring, and exposed the government to continual criticism. But it was still too powerful to suffer this to proceed to extremities; while therefore infidelity and loose sentiments of morality passed unpunished, it was still very hazardous to publish any thing against the state. It was in this respect, chiefly, that the Mason Lodges contributed to the dissemination of dangerous opinions, and they were employed for this purpose all over the kingdom. This is not an assertion hazarded merely on account of its probability. Abundant proof will appear by and by, that the most turbulent characters in the nation frequented the Lodges. We cannot doubt, but that under this covert they indulged their factious dispositions; nay, we shall find the greatest part of the Lodges of France, converted, in the course of a very few weeks, into corresponding political societies.

G But

But it is now time to turn our eyes to the progress of Free Masonry in Germany and the north of Europe; there it took a more serious turn. Free Masonry was imported into Germany somewhat later than into France. The first German Lodge that we have any account of is that at Cologne, erected in 1716, but very soon suppressed. Before the year 1725 there were many, both in Protestant and Catholic Germany. Those of Wetzlar, Frankfort on the Mayne, Brunswick, and Hamburg, are the oldest, and their priority is doubtful. All of them received their institution from England, and had patents from a mother Lodge in London. All seem to have got the mystery through the same channel, the banished friends of the Stuart family. Many of these were Catholics, and entered into the service of Austria and the Catholic princes.

The true hospitality, that is no where more conspicuous than in the character of the Germans, made this institution a most agreeable and useful passport to these gentlemen; and as many of them were in military stations, and in garrison, they found it a very easy matter to set up Lodges in all parts of Germany. These afforded a very agreeable pastime to the officers, who had little to occupy them, and were already accustomed to a subordination which did not affect their vanity on account of family distinctions. As the Ensign and the General were equally gentlemen, the allegory or play of universal Brotherhood was neither novel nor disgusting. Free Masonry was then of the simplest form, consisting of the three degrees of Apprentice, Fellow-craft, and Master. It is remarkable, that the Germans had been long accustomed to the word, the sign, and the gripe of the Masons, and some other handicraft trades. In many parts of Germany there was a distinction of operative Masons into Wort-
Maurers

Maurers and Schrift-Maurers. The Wort-Maurers had no other proof to give of their having been regularly brought up to the trade of builders, but the word and signs; the Schrift-Maurers had written indentures to shew. There are extant and in force, borough-laws, enjoining the Masters of Masons to give employment to journeymen who had the proper words and sign. In particular it appears, that some cities had more extensive privileges in this respect than others. The word given at Wetzlar, the seat of the great council of revision for the empire, entitled the possessor to work over the whole empire. We may infer from the processes and decisions in some of those municipal courts, that a master gave a word and token for each year's progress of his apprentice. He gave the word of the incorporated Imperial city or borough on which he depended, and also a word peculiar to himself, by which all his own pupils could recognise each other. This mode of recognisance was probably the only document of education in old times, while writing was confined to a very small part of the community. When we reflect on the nature of the German empire, a confederation of small independent states, we see that this profession cannot keep pace with the other mechanic arts, unless its practitioners are invested with greater privileges than others. Their great works exceed the strength of the immediate neighbourhood, and the workmen must be brought together from a distance. Their association must therefore be more cared for by the public.*

When English Free Masonry was carried into Germany, it was hospitably received. It required little effort

* Note. The Wort or Grüfs-Maurer were abolished by an Imperial edict in 1731, and none were intitled to the privileges of the corporation but such as could shew written indentures.

effort to give it respectability, and to make it the occupation of a gentleman, and its secrets and mysteries were not such novelties as in France. It spread rapidly, and the simple topic of Brotherly love was sufficient for recommending it to the honest and hospitable Germans. But it soon took a very different turn. The German character is the very opposite of frivolity. It tends to seriousness, and requires serious occupation. The Germans are eminent for their turn for investigation; and perhaps they indulge this to excess. We call them plodding and dull, because we have little relish for enquiry for its own sake. But this is surely the occupation of a rational nature, and deserves any name but stupidity. At the same time it must be acknowledged, that the spirit of enquiry requires regulation as much as any propensity of the human mind. But it appears that the Germans are not nice in their choice of their objects; it appears that singularity, and wonder, and difficulty of research, are to them irresistible recommendations and incitements. They have always exhibited a strong predilection for every thing that is wonderful, or solemn, or terrible; and in spite of the great progress which men have made in the course of these two last centuries, in the knowledge of nature, a progress too in which we should be very unjust if we did not acknowledge that the Germans have been generally in the foremost ranks, the gross absurdities of magic, exorcism, witchcraft, fortune-telling, transmutation of metals, and universal medicine, have always had their zealous partizans, who have listened with greedy ears to the nonsense and jargon of fanatics and cheats; and though they every day saw examples of many who had been ruined or rendered ridiculous by their credulity, every new pretender to secrets found numbers ready to listen to him, and to run over the same course.

Free

Free Masonry, professing mysteries, instantly roused all these people, and the Lodges appeared to the adventurers who wanted to profit by the enthusiasm or the avarice of their dupes, the fittest places in the world for the scene of their operations. The Rosycrucians were the first who availed themselves of the opportunity. This was not the Society which had appeared formerly under that name, and was now extinct, but a set of Alchymists, pretenders to the transmutation of metals and the universal medicine, who, the better to inveigle their votaries, had mixed with their own tricks a good deal of the absurd superstitions of that sect, in order to give a greater air of mystery to the whole, to protract the time of instruction, and to afford more room for evasions, by making so many difficult conditions necessary for perfecting the grand work, that the unfortunate gull, who had thrown away his time and his money, might believe that the failure was owing to his own incapacity or unfitness for being the possessor of the grand secret. These cheats found it convenient to make Masonry one of their conditions, and by a small degree of art, persuaded their pupils that they were the only true Masons. These Rosycrucian Lodges were soon established, and became numerous, because their mysteries were addressed, both to the curiosity, the sensuality, and the avarice of men. They became a very formidable band, adopting the constitution of the Jesuits, dividing the Fraternity into circles, each under the management of its own superior, known to the president, but unknown to the individuals of the Lodges. These superiors were connected with each other in a way known only to themselves, and the whole was under one General. At least this is the account which they wish to be believed. If it be just, nothing but the absurdity of the ostensible motives of their occupations could have prevented

vented this combination from carrying on schemes big with hazard to the peace of the world. But the Rosycrucian Lodges have always been considered by other Free Masons as bad Societies, and as gross schismatics. This did not hinder, however, their alchymical and medical secrets from being frequently introduced into the Lodges of simple Free Masonry; and in like manner, exorcism, or ghost-raising, magic, and other gross superstitions, were often held out in their meetings as attainable mysteries, which would be immense acquisitions to the Fraternity, without any necessity of admitting along with them the religious deliriums of the Rosycrucians.

In 1743, Baron Hunde, a gentleman of honourable character and independent fortune, was in Paris, where he said he had got acquainted with the Earl of Kilmarnock and some other gentlemen who were about the Pretender, and learned from them that they had some wonderful secrets in their Lodges. He was admitted, through the medium of that nobleman, and of a Lord Clifford, and his Masonic patent was signed *George* (said to be the signature of Kilmarnock). Hunde had attached himself to the fortunes of the Pretender, in hopes (as he says himself) of rising in the world under his protection. The mighty secret was this.
" When the Order of Knights Templars was abolish-
" ed by Philip the Fair, and cruelly persecuted, some
" worthy persons escaped, and took refuge in the
" Highlands of Scotland, where they concealed them-
" selves in caves. These persons possessed the true
" secrets of Masonry, which had always been in that
" Order, having been acquired by the Knights, du-
" ring their services in the East, from the pilgrims
" whom they occasionally protected or delivered. The
" *Chevaliers de la Rose-Croix* continued to have the
" same duties as formerly, though robbed of their
" emolu-

" emoluments. In fine, every true Mason is a Knight
" Templar." It is very true that a clever fancy can
accommodate the ritual of reception of the *Chevalier de
l'Epée*, &c. to something like the institution of the
Knights Templars, and perhaps this explanation of
young Zerobabel's pilgrimage, and of the rebuilding
of the Temple by Ezra, is the most significant explanation that has been given of the meagre symbols of
Free Masonry.

When Baron Hunde returned to Germany, he exhibited to some friends his extensive powers for propagating this system of Masonry, and made a few
Knights. But he was not very active. Probably the
failure of the Pretender's attempt to recover the throne
of his ancestors had put an end to Hunde's hopes of
making a figure. In the mean time Free Masonry
was cultivated with zeal in Germany, and many adventurers found their advantage in supporting particular schisms.

But in 1756, or 1757, a complete revolution took
place. The French officers who were prisoners at
large in Berlin, undertook, with the assurance peculiar
to their nation, to instruct the simple Germans in every
thing that embellishes society. They said, that the
homespun Free Masonry, which had been imported
from England, was fit only for the unpolished minds
of the British; but that in France it had grown into
an elegant system, fit for the profession of Gentlemen.
Nay, they said, that the English were ignorant of true
Masonry, and possessed nothing but the introduction
to it; and even this was not understood by them.
When the ribbands and stars, with which the French
had ornamented the Order, were shown to the Germans, they could not resist the enchantment. A Mr.
Rosa, a French commissary, brought from Paris a
complete waggon load of Masonic ornaments, which

were

were all diftributed before it had reached Berlin, and he was obliged to order another, to furnifh the Lodges of that city. It became for a while a moft profitable bufinefs to many French officers and commiffaries difperfed over Germany, having little elfe to do. Every body gaped for inftruction, and thefe kind teachers were always ready to beftow it. In half a year Free Mafonry underwent a complete revolution all over Germany, and Chevaliers multiplied without number. The Rofaic fyftem was a gofpel to the Mafons, and the poor Britifh fyftem was defpifed. But the new Lodges of Berlin, as they had been the teachers of the whole empire, wanted alfo to be the governors, and infifted on complete fubjection from all the others. This ftartled the Free Mafons at a diftance, and awakened them from their golden dreams. Now began a ftruggle for dominion and for independency. This made the old Lodges think a little about the whole affair. The refult of this was a counter revolution. Though no man could pretend that he underftood the true meaning of Free Mafonry, its origin, its hiftory, or its real aim, all faw that the interpretations of their hieroglyphics, and the rituals of the new degrees imported from France, were quite gratuitous. It appeared, therefore, that the fafeft thing for them was an appeal to the birth-place of Mafonry. They fent to London for inftructions. There they learned, that nothing was acknowledged for genuine unfophifticated Mafonry but the three degrees; and that the mother Lodge of London alone could, by her inftructions, prevent the moft dangerous fchifms and innovations. Many Lodges, therefore, applied for patents and inftructions. Patents were eafily made out, and moft willingly fent to the zealous Brethren; and thefe were thankfully received and paid for. But inftruction was not fo eafy a matter. At that time we had nothing

but

but the book of conſtitutions, drawn up about 1720, by Anderſon and Deſaguilliers, two perſons of little education, and of low manners, who had aimed at little more than making a pretext, not altogether contemptible, for a convivial meeting. This, however, was received with reſpect. We are apt to ſmile at grave men's being ſatisfied with ſuch coarſe and ſcanty fare. But it was of uſe, merely becauſe it gave an oſtenſible reaſon for reſiſting the deſpotiſm of the Lodges of Berlin. Several reſpectable Lodges, particularly that of Frankfort on the Mayne, that of Brunſwick, that of Wetzlar, and the Royal York of Berlin, reſolutely adhered to the Engliſh ſyſtem, and denied themſelves all the enjoyment of the French degrees, rather than acknowledge the ſupremacy of the Roſaic Lodges of Berlin.

About the year 1764 a new revolution took place. An adventurer, who called himſelf Johnſon, and paſſed himſelf for an Engliſhman, but who was really a German or Bohemian named Leucht, ſaid that he was ambaſſador from the Chapter of Knights Templars at Old Aberdeen in Scotland, ſent to teach the Germans what was true Maſonry. He pretended to tranſmute metals, and ſome of the Brethren declared that they had ſeen him do it repeatedly. This reached Baron Hunde, and brought back all his former enthuſiaſm. There is ſomething very dark in this part of the hiſtory; for in a little Johnſon told his partiſans that the only point he had to inform them of was, that Baron Hunde was the Grand Maſter of the 7th province of Maſonry, which included the whole of Germany, and the royal dominions of Pruſſia. He ſhowed them a map of the Maſonic Empire arranged into provinces, each of which had diſtinguiſhing emblems. Theſe are all taken from an old forgotten and inſignificant book, *Typotii Symbola Divina et Humana*, publiſhed in 1601. There is not the leaſt trace in this book either of Maſonry of Templars,

plars, and the emblems are taken out without the smallest ground of selection. Some inconsistency with the former magnificent promises of Johnson startled them at first, but they acquiesced and submitted to Baron Hunde as Grand Master of Germany. Soon after Johnson turned out to be a cheat, escaped, was taken, and put in prison, where he died. Yet this seems not to have ruined the credit of Baron Hunde. He erected Lodges, gave a few simple instructions, all in the system of English Masonry, and promised, that when they had approved themselves as good Masons, he would then impart the mighty secret. After two or three years of noviciate, a convention was held at Altenberg; and he told them that his whole secret was, *that every true Mason was a Knight Templar.* They were astonished, and disappointed; for they expected in general that he would teach them the philosopher's stone, or ghost-raising, or magic. After much discontent, falling out, and dispute, many Lodges united in this system, made somewhat moderate and palatable, under the name of the STRICT DISCIPLINARIANS, *Strickten Observanz.* It was acceptable to many, because they insisted that they were really Knights, properly consecrated, though without temporalities; and they seriously set themselves about forming a fund which should secure the Order in a landed property and revenue, which would give them a respectable civil existence. Hunde declared that his whole estate should devolve on the Order. But the vexations which he afterwards met with, and his falling in love with a lady who prevailed on him to become Roman Catholic, made him alter his intention. The Order went on, however, and acquired considerable credit by the serious regularity of their proceedings; and, although in the mean time a new apostle of Mysteries, a Dr. Zinzendorff, one of the *Strict Observanz,* introduced a new system,

fyftem, which he faid was from Sweden, diftinguifhed
by fome of the myftical doctrines of the Swedenborgh
fect, and though the fyftem obtained the Royal patronage, and a National Lodge was eftablifhed at Berlin
by patent, ftill the *Tempelorden,* or *Orden des Stricten
Obfervanz,* continued to be very refpectable. The
German gentry were better pleafed with a Grand Mafter of their own choofing, than with any impofed on
them by authority.

During this ftate of things, one Stark, a Proteftant
divine, well known in Germany by his writings, made
another trial of public faith. One Gugomos, (a private gentleman, but who would pafs for fon to a King
of Cyprus), and one Schropfer, keeper of a coffee-
houfe at Nuremberg, drew crowds of Free Mafons
around them, to learn ghoft-raifing, exorcifm, and al-
chymy. Numbers came from a great diftance to
Weifbad to fee and learn thefe myfteries, and Free Mafonry was on the point of another revolution. Dr.
Stark was an adept in all thefe things, and had contended
with Caglioftro in Courland for the palm of fuperiority.
He faw that this deception could not long ftand its
ground. He therefore came forward, at a convention
at Braunfchweig in 1772, and faid to the Strict Dif-
ciplinarians or Templars, That he was of their Order,
but of the fpiritual department, and was deputed by
the Chapter of K—m—d—t in Scotland, where he
was Chancellor of the Congregation, and had the name
of Archidemides, *Eques ab Aquila fulva:* That this
Chapter had the fuperintendance of the Order: That
they alone could confecrate the Knights, or the unknown fuperiors; and that he was deputed to inftruct
them in the real principles of the Order, and impart its
ineftimable fecrets, which could not be known to Baron Hunde, as he would readily acknowledge when he
fhould converfe with him. Johnfon, he faid, had been
a cheat,

a cheat, and probably a murderer. He had got some knowledge from papers which he must have stolen from a missionary, who had disappeared, and was probably killed. Gugomos and Schropfer must have had some similar information; and Schropfer had even deceived him for a time. He was ready to execute his commission, upon their coming under the necessary obligations of secrecy and of submission. Hunde (whose name in the Order was the *Eques ab Ense*) acquiesced at once, and proposed a convention, with full powers to decide and accept. But a Schubart, a gentleman of character, who was treasurer to the Templar Masons, and had an employment which gave him considerable influence in the Order, strongly dissuaded them from such a measure. The most unqualified submission to unknown superiors, and to conditions equally unknown, was required previous to the smallest communication, or any knowledge of the powers which Archidemides had to treat with them. Many meetings were held, and many attempts were made to learn something of this spiritual court, and of what they might expect from them. Dr. Stark, Baron Weggenfak, Baron von Raven, and some others of his coadjutors in the Lodges at Koningsberg in Prussia, and at Wismar, were received into the Order. But in vain—nothing was obtained from these ghostly Knights but some insignificant ceremonials of receptions and consecrations. Of this kind of novelties they were already heartily sick; and though they all panted after the expected wonders, they were so much frightened by the unconditional submission, that they could come to no agreement, and the secrets of the Scotch Congregation of K—m—d—t still remain with Dr. Stark. They did, however, a sensible thing; they sent a deputation to Old Aberdeen, to enquire after the caves where their venerable mysteries were known, and their treasures were hid. They had

had, as they thought, merited some more confidence; for they had remitted annual contributions to these unknown superiors, to the amount of some thousands of rix dollars. But alas! their ambassadors found the Free Masons of Old Aberdeen ignorant of all this, and as eager to learn from the ambassadors what was the true origin and meaning of Free Masonry, of which they knew nothing but the simple tale of Old Hiram. This broke Stark's credit; but he still insisted on the reality of his commission, and said that the Brethren at Aberdeen were indeed ignorant, but that he had never said otherwise; their expectations from that quarter had rested on the scraps purloined by Johnson. He reminded them of a thing well known to themselves; that one of them had been sent for by a dying nobleman to receive papers on this subject, and that his visit having been delayed a few hours by an unavoidable accident, he found all burnt but a fragment of a capitulary, and a thing in cypher, part of which he (Dr. Stark) had explained to them. They had employed another gentleman, a H. Wachter, to make similar enquiries in Italy, where Schropfer and others (even Hunde) had told them great secrets were to be obtained from the Pretender's secretary Approfi, and others. Wachter told them, that all this was a fiction, but that he had seen at Florence some Brethren from the Holy Land, who really possessed wonderful secrets, which he was willing to impart, on proper conditions. These, however, they could not accede to; but they were cruelly tortured by seeing Wachter, who had left Germany in sober circumstances, now a man of great wealth and expence. He would not acknowledge that he had got the secret of gold-making from the Asiatic Brethren; but said that no man had any right to ask him how he had come by his fortune. It was enough that he behaved hono-
rably,

rably, and owed no man any thing. He broke off all connections with them, and left them in great diſtreſs about their Order, and panting after his ſecrets. *Riſum teneatis amici?*

Stark, in revenge for the oppoſition he had met with from Schubart, left no ſtone unturned to hurt him with his Brethren, and ſucceeded, ſo that he left them in diſguſt. Hunde died about this time. A book appeared, called, *The Stumbling Block and Rock of Offence,* which betrayed (by their own confeſſion) the whole ſecrets of the Order of Templars, and ſoon made an end of it, as far as it went beyond the ſimple Engliſh Maſonry.

Thus was the faith of Free Maſons quite unhinged in Germany. But the rage for myſteries and wonder was not in the leaſt abated; and the habits of theſe ſecret Aſſemblies were becoming every day more craving. Diſſenſion and ſchiſm was multiplying in every quarter; and the Inſtitution, inſtead of being an incitement to mutual complaiſance and Brotherly love, had become a ſource of contention, and of bitter enmity. Not ſatisfied with defending the propriety of its own Inſtitutions, each Syſtem of Free Maſonry was buſy in enticing away the partiſans of other Syſtems, ſhut their Lodges againſt each other, and proceeded even to vilify and perſecute the adherents of every Syſtem but their own.

Theſe animoſities aroſe chiefly from the quarrels about precedency, and the arrogance (as it was thought) of the patent Lodge of Berlin, in pretending to have any authority in the other parts of the empire. But theſe pretenſions were not the reſult of mere vanity. The French importers of the new degrees, always true to the glory of their nation, hoped by this means to ſecure the dependence even of this frivolous ſociety; perhaps they might foreſee political uſes and benefits

which

which might arife from it. One thing is worth notice: The French Lodges had all emanated from the great Confederation under the Duke de Chartres; and, even if we had no other proof, we might prefume that they would cultivate the fame principles that characterifed that Sect. But we are certain that infidelity and laxity of moral principles were prevalent in the Rofaic Lodges, and that the obfervation of this corruption had offended many of the fober old-fafhioned Lodges, and was one great caufe of any check that was given to the brilliant Mafonry of France. It is the obfervation of this circumftance, in which they all refembled, and which foon ceafed to be a diftinction, becaufe it pervaded the other Lodges, that has induced me to expatiate more on this hiftory of Free Mafonry in Germany, than may appear to my readers to be adequate to the importance of Free Mafonry in the general fubject-matter of thefe pages. But I hope that it will appear in the courfe of my narration that I have not given it a greater value than it deferves.

About this very time there was a great revolution of the public mind in Germany, and fcepticifm, infidelity, and irreligion, not only were prevalent in the minds and manners of the wealthy and luxurious, and of the profligate of lower ranks, but began to appear in the productions of the prefs. Some circumftances, peculiar to Germany, occafioned thefe declenfions from the former acquiefcence in the faith of their forefathers to become more uniform and remarkable than they would otherwife have been. The confeffions of Germany are the Roman Catholic, the Lutheran, (which they call Proteftant,) and the Calvinift, (which they call Reformed). Thefe are profeffed in many fmall contiguous principalities, and there is hardly one of them in which all the three have not free exercife. The defire of making profelytes is natural to all ferious profeffors fessors of a rational faith, and was frequently exercised. The Roman Catholics are supposed by us to be particularly zealous, and the Protestants (Lutherans and Calvinists) were careful to oppose them by every kind of argument, among which those of ridicule and reproach were not spared. The Catholics accused them of infidelity respecting the fundamental doctrines of Christianity which they professed to believe, and even with respect to the doctrines of natural religion. This accusation was long very slightly supported; but, of late, by better proofs. The spirit of free enquiry was the great boast of the Protestants, and the only support against the Catholics, securing them both in their religious and civil rights. It was therefore encouraged by their governments. It is not to be wondered at that it should be indulged to excess, or improperly, even by serious men, liable to error, in their disputes with the Catholics. In the progress of this contest, even their own Confessions did not escape criticism, and it was asserted that the Reformation which those Confessions express was not complete. Further Reformations were proposed. The Scriptures, the foundation of our faith, were examined by clergymen of very different capacities, dispositions, and views, till by explaining, correcting, allegorising, and otherwise twisting the Bible, men's minds had hardly any thing left to rest on as a doctrine of revealed religion. This encouraged others to go farther, and to say that revelation was a solecism, as plainly appeared by the irreconcileable differences among those Enlighteners (so they were called) of the public, and that man had nothing to trust to but the dictates of natural reason. Another set of writers, proceeding from this as a point already settled, proscribed all religion whatever, and openly taught the doctrines of materialism and atheism. Most of these innovations were the work of Protestant

divines

divines, from the caufes that I have mentioned. Teller, Semler, Eberhardt, Leffing, Bahrdt, Riem, and Shultz, had the chief hand in all thefe innovations. But no man contributed more than Nicholai, an eminent and learned bookfeller in Berlin. He has been for many years the publifher of a periodical work, called the General German Library, *(Algemein deutfche Bibliothek,)* confifting of original differtations, and reviews of the writings of others. The great merit of this work, on account of many learned differtations which appear in it, has procured it much influence on that clafs of readers whofe leifure or capacity did not allow them a more profound kind of reading. This is the bulk of readers in every country. Nicholai gives a decided preference to the writings of the Enlighteners, and in his reviews treats them with particular notice, makes the public fully acquainted with their works, and makes the moft favourable comments; whereas the performances of their opponents, or more properly fpeaking, the defenders of the National Creeds, are neglected, omitted, or barely mentioned, or they are criticifed with every feverity of ridicule and reproach. He fell upon a very fure method of rendering the orthodox writers difagreeable to the public, by reprefenting them as the abetters of fuperftition, and as fecret Jefuits. He afferted, that the abolition of the Order of *Loyola* is only apparent. The Brethren ftill retained their connection, and moft part of their property, under the fecret patronage of Catholic Princes. They are, therefore, in every corner, in every habit and character, working with unwearied zeal for the reftoration of their empire. He raifed a general alarm, and made a journey through Germany, hunting for Jefuits, and for this purpofe, became Free Mafon and Rofycrucian, being introduced by his friends Gedicke and Biefter,

clergymen,

clergymen, publishers of the *Berlin Monatschrift*, and most zealous promoters of the new doctrines. This favour he has repaid at his return, by betraying the mysteries of the Lodges, and by much bitter satire. His journey was published in several volumes, and is full of frightful Jesuitisms. This man, as I have said, found the greatest success in his method of slandering the defenders of Bible-Christianity, by representing them as concealed Jesuits. But, not contented with open discussion, he long ago published a sort of romance, called *Sebaldus Nothanker*, in which these divines are introduced under feigned names, and made as ridiculous and detestable as possible. All this was a good trading job; for sceptical and free-thinking writings have every where a good market; and Nicholai was not only reviewer, but publisher, having presses in different cities of the Empire. The immense literary manufacture of Germany, far exceeding that of any nation of Europe, is carried on in a very particular way. The books go in sheets to the great fairs of Leipsic and Frankfort, twice a-year. The booksellers meet there, and see at one glance the state of literature; and having speculated and made their bargains, the books are instantly dispersed through every part of the Empire, and appear at once in all quarters. Although every Principality has an officer for licensing, it is impossible to prevent the currency of a performance, although it may be prohibited; for it is to be had by the carrier at three or four miles distance in another state. By this mode of traffic, a plot may be formed, and actually has been formed, for giving any particular turn to the literature of the country. There is an excellent work printed at Bern by the author Heinzmann, a bookseller, called, *Appeal to my Country, concerning a Combination of Writers, and Booksellers, to rule the Literature of Germany, and form*

the

the Public Mind into a Contempt for the Religion and Civil Eſtabliſhments of the Empire. It contains a hiſtorical account of the publications in every branch of literature for about thirty years. The author ſhows, in the moſt convincing manner, that the prodigious change from the former ſatisfaction of the Germans on thoſe ſubjects to their preſent diſcontent and attacks from every quarter, is neither a fair picture of the prevailing ſentiments, nor has been the ſimple operation of things, but the reſult of a combination of trading Infidels.

I have here ſomewhat anticipated, (for I hope to point out the ſources of this combination,) becauſe it helps to explain or illuſtrate the progreſs of infidelity and irreligion that I was ſpeaking of. It was much accelerated by another circumſtance. One *Baſedow*, a man of talents and learning, ſet up, in the Principality of Anhalt-Deſſau, a PHILANTHROPINE, or academy of general education, on a plan extremely different from thoſe of the Univerſities and Academies. By this appellation, the founder hoped to make parents expect that much attention would be paid to the morals of the pupils; and indeed the programs or advertiſements by which Baſedow announced his inſtitution to the public, deſcribed it as the profeſſed ſeminary of practical Ethics. Languages, ſciences, and the ornamental exerciſes, were here conſidered as mere acceſſories, and the great aim was to form the young mind to the love of mankind and of virtue, by a plan of moral education which was very ſpecious and unexceptionable. But there was a circumſtance which greatly obſtructed the wide proſpects of the founder. How were the religious opinions of the youth to be cared for? Catholics, Lutherans, and Calviniſts, were almoſt equally numerous in the adjoining Principalities; and the excluſion of any two of theſe communions would prodigiouſly limit the propoſed uſefulneſs

of

of the inftitution. Bafedow was a man of talents, a good fcholar, and a perfuafive writer. He framed a fet of rules, by which the education fhould be conducted, and which, he thought, fhould make every parent eafy; and the plan is very judicious and manly. But none came but Lutherans. His zeal and intereft in the thing made him endeavour to intereft others; and he found this no hard matter. The people of condition, and all fenfible men, faw that it would be a very great advantage to the place, could they induce men to fend their children from all the neighbouring ftates. What we wifh, we readily believe to be the truth; and Bafedow's plan and reafonings appeared complete, and had the fupport of all claffes of men. The moderate Calvinifts, after fome time, were not averfe from them, and the literary manufacture of Germany was foon very bufy in making pamphlets, defending, improving, attacking, and reprobating the plans. Innumerable were the projects for moderating the differences between the three Chriftian communions of Germany, and making it poffible for the members of them all, not only to live amicably among each other, and to worfhip God in the fame church, but even to communicate together. This attempt naturally gave rife to much fpeculation and refinement; and the propofals for amendment of the formulas and the inftructions from the pulpit were profecuted with fo much keennefs, that the ground-work, Chriftianity, was refined and refined, till it vanifhed altogether, leaving Deifm, or Natural, or, as it was called, Philofophical Religion, in its place. I am not much miftaken as to hiftorical fact, when I fay, that the aftonifhing change in religious doctrine which has taken place in Proteftant Germany within thefe laft thirty years was chiefly occafioned by this fcheme of Bafedow's. The predifpofing caufes exifted, indeed, and

were

were general and powerful, and the diforder had already broken out. But this fpecious and enticing object firft gave a title to Proteftant clergymen to put to their hand without rifk of being cenfured.

Bafedow corrected, and corrected again, but not one Catholic came to the Philanthropine. He feems to have thought that the beft plan would be, to banifh all pofitive religion whatever, and that he would then be fure of Catholic fcholars. Cardinal Dubois was fo far right with refpect to the firft Catholic pupil of the church. He had recommended a man of his own ftamp to Louis XIV. to fill fome important office. The monarch was aftonifhed, and told the Cardinal, that " that would never do, for the man was a Janfe- " nift; *Eh! que non, Sire,*" faid the Cardinal, " *il* " *n'eft qu' Athée;*" all was fafe, and the man got the priory. But though all was in vain, Bafedow's Philanthropine at Deffau got a high character. He publifhed many volumes on education that have much merit.

It were well had this been all. But moft unfortunately, though moft naturally, writers of loofe moral principles and of wicked hearts were encouraged by the impunity which the fceptical writers experienced, and ventured to publifh things of the vileft tendency, inflaming the paffions and juftifying licentious manners. Thefe maxims are congenial with irreligion and Atheifm, and the books found a quick market. It was chiefly in the Pruffian States that this went on. The late King was, to fay the beft of him, a naturalift, and, holding this life for his all, gave full liberty to his fubjects to write what they pleafed, provided they did not touch on ftate matters. He declared, however, to a minifter of his court, long before his death, that " he " was extremely forry that his indifference had pro- " duced fuch effects; that he was fenfible it had greatly
" contri-

" contributed to hurt the peace and mutual good treat-
" ment of his fubjects;" and he faid, " that he would
" willingly give up the glory of his beft-fought battle,
" to have the fatisfaction of leaving his people in the
" fame ftate of peace and fatisfaction with their reli-
" gious eftablifhments, that he found them in at his
" acceffion to the throne." His fucceffor Frederick
William found that things had gone much too far, and
determined to fupport the church-eftablifhment in the
moft peremptory manner; but at the fame time to allow perfect freedom of thinking and converfing to the
profeffors of every Chriftian faith, provided it was enjoyed without difturbing the general peace, or any
encroachment on the rights of thofe already fupported
by law. He publifhed an edict to this effect, which
is really a model worthy of imitation in every country.
This was the epoch of a ftrange revolution. It was
attacked from all hands, and criticifms, fatires, flanders, threatenings, poured in from every quarter. The
independency of the neighbouring ftates, and the monarch's not being a great favourite among feveral of
his neighbours, permitted the publication of thofe
pieces in the adjoining principalities, and it was impoffible to prevent their circulation even in the Pruffian States. His edict was called an unjuftifiable tyranny over the confciences of men; the dogmas fupported by it were termed abfurd fuperftitions; the
King's private character, and his opinions in religious
matters, were treated with little reverence, nay, were
ridiculed and fcandaloufly abufed. This field of difcuffion being thus thrown open, the writers did not
confine themfelves to religious matters. After flatly
denying that the prince of any country had the fmalleft
right to prefcribe, or even direct the faith of his fubjects, they extended their difcuffions to the rights of
princes in general; and now they fairly opened their
trenches,

trenches, and made an attack in form on the conftitutions of the German confederacy, and, after the ufual approaches, they fet up the ftandard of univerfal citizenfhip on the very ridge of the glacis, and fummoned the fort to furrender. The moft daring of thefe attacks was a collection of anonymous letters on the conftitutution of the Pruffian States. It was printed (or faid to be fo) at Utrecht; but by comparing the faults of fome types with fome books printed in Berlin, it was fuppofed by all to be the production of one of Nicholai's preffes. It was thought to be the compofition of Mirabeau. It is certain that he wrote a French tranflation, with a preface and notes, more impudent than the work itfelf. The monarch is declared to be a tyrant; the people are addreffed as a parcel of tame wretches crouching under oppreffion. The people of Silefia are reprefented as ftill in a worfe condition, and are repeatedly called to roufe themfelves, and to rife up and affert their rights. The King is told, that there is a combination of philofophers (*conjuration*) who are leagued together in defence of truth and reafon, and which no power can withftand; that they are to be found in every country, and are connected by mutual and folemn engagement, and will put in practice every mean of attack. Enlightening, inftruction, was the general cry among the writers. The triumph of reafon over error, the overthrow of fuperftition and flavifh fear, freedom from religious and political prejudices, and the eftablifhment of liberty and equality, the natural and unalienable rights of man, were the topics of general declamation; and it was openly maintained, that fecret focieties, where the communication of fentiment fhould be free from every reftraint, was the moft effectual means for inftructing and enlightening the world.

And

And thus it appears, that Germany has experienced the same gradual progress, from Religion to Atheism, from decency to dissoluteness, and from loyalty to rebellion, which has had its course in France. And I must now add, that this progress has been effected in the same manner, and by the same means; and that one of the chief means of seduction has been the Lodges of the Free Masons. The French, along with their numerous chevaleries, and stars, and ribands, had brought in the custom of haranguing in the Lodges, and as human nature has a considerable uniformity every where, the same topics became favourite subjects of declamation that had tickled the ear in France; there were the same corruptions of sentiments and manners among the luxurious or profligate, and the same incitements to the utterance of these sentiments, wherever it could be done with safety; and I may say, that the zealots in all these tracts of freethinking were more serious, more grave, and fanatical. These are not assertions *a priori*. I can produce proofs. There was a Baron Knigge residing at that time in the neighbourhood of Frankfort, of whom I shall afterwards have occasion frequently to speak. This man was an enthusiast in Masonry from his youth, and had run through every possible degree of it. He was dissatisfied with them all, and particularly with the frivolity of the French chivalry; but he still believed that Masonry contained invaluable secrets. He imagined that he saw a glimse of them in the cosmo-political and sceptical discourses in their Lodges; he sat down to meditate on these, and soon collected his thoughts, and found that those French orators were right without knowing it; and that Masonry was pure natural religion and universal citizenship, and that this was also true Christianity. In this faith he immediately began his career of Brotherly love, and published three volumes of sermons;

the

the firſt and third publiſhed at Frankfort, and the ſecond at Heidelberg, but without his name. He publiſhed alſo a popular ſyſtem of religion. In all theſe publications, of which there are extracts in the *Religions Begebenheiten,* Chriſtianity is conſidered as a mere allegory, or a Maſonic type of natural religion; the moral duties are ſpun into the common-place declamations of univerſal benevolence; and the attention is continually directed to the abſurdities and horrors of ſuperſtition, the ſufferings of the poor, the tyranny and oppreſſion of the great, the tricks of the prieſts, and the indolent ſimplicity and patience of the laity and of the common people. The happineſs of the patriarchal life, and ſweets of univerſal equality and freedom, are the burden of every paragraph; and the general tenor of the whole is to make men diſcontented with their condition of civil ſubordination, and the reſtraints of revealed religion.

All the proceedings of Knigge in the Maſonic ſchiſms ſhow that he was a zealous apoſtle of coſmo-politiſm, and that he was continually dealing with people in the Lodges who were aſſociated with him in propagating thoſe notions among the Brethren; ſo that we are certain that ſuch converſations were common in the German Lodges.

When the reader conſiders all theſe circumſtances, he will abate of that ſurpriſe which naturally affects a Briton, when he reads accounts of conventions for diſcuſſing and fixing the dogmatic tenets of Free Maſonry. The perfect freedom, civil and religious, which we enjoy in this happy country, being familiar to every man, we indulge it with calmneſs and moderation, and ſecret aſſemblies hardly differ from the common meetings of friends and neighbours. We do not forget the expediency of civil ſubordination, and of thoſe diſtinctions which ariſe from ſecure poſſeſſion

K of

of our rights, and the gradual accumulation of the comforts of life in the families of the sober and industrious. These have, by prudence and a respectable œconomy, preserved the acquisitions of their ancestors. Every man feels in his own breast the strong call of nature to procure for himself and his children, by every honest and commendable exertion, the means of public consideration and respect. No man is so totally without spirit, as not to think the better of his condition when he is come of creditable parents, and has creditable connections; and without thinking that he is in any respect generous, he presumes that others have the same sentiments, and therefore allows the moderate expression of them, without thinking it insolence or haughtiness. All these things are familiar, are not thought of, and we enjoy them as we enjoy ordinary health, without perceiving it. But in the same manner as a young man who has been long confined by sickness, exults in returning health, and is apt to riot in the enjoyment of what he so distinctly feels; so those who are under continual check in open society, feel this emancipation in those hidden assemblies, and indulge with eagerness in the expression of sentiments which in public they must smother within their own breast. Such meetings, therefore, have a zest that is very alluring, and they are frequented with avidity. There is no country in Europe where this kind of enjoyment is so poignant as in Germany. Very insignificant principalities have the same rank in the General Federation with very extensive dominions. The internal constitution of each petty state being modelled in nearly the same manner, the official honours of their little courts become ludicrous and even farcical. The Geheim Hofrath, the Hofmareschal, and all the Kammerhers of a Prince, whose dominions do not equal the estates

of

of many English Squires, cause the whole to appear like the play of children, and must give frequent occasion for discontent and ridicule. Mason Lodges even keep this alive. The fraternal equality professed in them is very flattering to those who have not succeeded in the scramble for civil distinctions. Such persons become the most zealous Masons, and generally obtain the active offices in the Lodges, and have an opportunity of treating with authority persons whom in public society they must look up to with some respect.

These considerations account, in some measure, for the importance which Free Masonry has acquired in Germany. For a long while the hopes of learning some wonderful secret made a German Baron think nothing of long and expensive journies in quest of some new degree. Of late, the cosmo-political doctrines encouraged and propagated in the Lodges, and some hopes of producing a Revolution in society, by which men of talents should obtain the management of public affairs, seem to be the cause of all the zeal with which the order is still cherished and promoted. In a periodical work, published at Neuwied, called *Algemein Zeitung der Freymaurerey*, we have the list of the Lodges in 1782, with the names of the Office-bearers. Four-fifths of these are clergymen, professors, persons having offices in the common law-courts, men of letters by trade, such as reviewers and journalists, and other pamphleteers; a class of men, who generally think that they have not attained that rank in society to which their talents entitle them, and imagine that they could discharge the important offices of the state with reputation to themselves and advantage to the public.

The miserable uncertainty and instability of the Masonic faith, which I described above, was not altogether the effect of mere chance, but had been greatly accelerated by the machinations of Baron Knigge, and
some

some other cosmo-political Brethren whom he had called to his assistance. Knigge had now formed a scheme for uniting the whole Fraternity, for the purpose of promoting his Utopian plan of universal benevolence in a state of liberty and equality. He hoped to do this more readily by completing their embarrassment, and showing each system how infirm its foundation was, and how little chance it had of obtaining a general adherence. The *Stricten Observanz* had now completely lost its credit, by which it had hoped to get the better of all the rest. Knigge therefore proposed a plan to the Lodges of Frankfort and Wetzlar, by which all the systems might, in some measure, be united, or at least be brought to a state of mutual forbearance and intercourse. He proposed that the English system should be taken for the ground-work, and to receive all and only those who had taken the three symbolical degrees, as they were now generally called. After thus guarding this general point of faith, he proposed to allow the validity of every degree or rank which should be received in any Lodge, or be made the character of any particular system. These Lodges having secured the adherence of several others, brought about a general convention at Willemsbad in Hainault, where every different system should communicate its peculiar tenets. It was then hoped, that after an examination of them all, a constitution might be formed, which should comprehend every thing that was most worthy of selection, and therefore be far better than the accommodating system already described. By this he hoped to get his favourite scheme introduced into the whole Order, and Free Masons made zealous Citizens of the World. I believe he was sincere in these intentions, and did not wish to disturb the public peace. The convention was accordingly held, and lasted a

long

long while, the deputies confulting about the frivolities of Mafonry, with all the ferioufnefs of ftate ambaffadors. But there was great fhynefs in their communications; and Knigge was making but fmall progrefs in his plan, when he met with another Mafon, the Marquis of Conftanza, who in an inftant converted him, and changed all his meafures, by fhowing him that he (Knigge) was only doing by halves what was already accomplifhed by another Society, which had carried it to its full extent. They immediately fet about undoing what he had been occupied with, and heightened as much as they could the diffentions already fufficiently great, and, in the mean time, got the Lodges of Frankfort and Wetzlar, and feveral others, to unite, and pick out the beft of the things they had obtained by the communications from the other fyftems, and they formed a plan of what they called, the *Eclectic or Syncritic Mafonry of the United Lodges* of Germany. They compofed a conftitution, ritual, and catechifm, which has merit, and is indeed the completeft body of Free Mafonry that we have.

Such was the ftate of this celebrated and myfterious Fraternity in Germany in 1776. The fpirit of innovation had feized all the Brethren. No man could give a tolerable account of the origin, hiftory, or object of the Order, and it appeared to all as a loft or forgotten myftery. The fymbols feemed to be equally fufceptible of every interpretation, and none of thefe feemed entitled to any decided preference.

CHAP.

CHAP. II.

The Illuminati.

I HAVE now arrived at what I should call the great epoch of Cosmo-politism, the scheme communicated to Baron Knigge by the *Marchese di Constanza*. This obliges me to mention a remarkable Lodge of the Eclectic Masonry, erected at Munich in Bavaria in 1775, under the worshipful Master, Professor Baader. It was called *The Lodge Theodore of Good Counsel*. It had its constitutional patent from the Royal York at Berlin, but had formed a particular system of its own, by instructions from the *Loge des Chevaliers Bienfaisants* at Lyons, with which it kept up a correspondence. This respect to the Lodge at Lyons had arisen from the preponderance acquired in general by the French party in the convention at Willemsbad. The deputies of the Rosaic Lodges, as well as the remains of the Templars, and *Stricten Observanz*, all looking up to this as the mother Lodge of what they called the *Grand Orient de la France*, consisting in (in 1782) of 266 improved Lodges united under the *D. de Chartres*. Accordingly the Lodge at Lyons sent Mr. Wilermooz as deputy to this convention at Willemsbad. Refining gradually on the simple British Masonry, the Lodge had formed a system of practical morality, which it asserted to be the aim of genuine Masonry, saying,

saying, that a true mason, and a man of upright heart and active virtue, are synonimous characters, and that the great aim of Free Masonry is to promote the happiness of mankind by every mean in our power. In pursuance of these principles, the Lodge Theodore professedly occupied itself with œconomical, statistical, and political matters, and not only published from time to time discourses on such subjects by the Brother Orator, but the Members considered themselves as in duty bound to propagate and inculcate the same doctrines out of doors.

Of the zealous members of the Lodge Theodore the most conspicuous was Dr. Adam Weishaupt, Professor of Canon Law in the University of Ingolstadt. This person had been educated among the Jesuits; but the abolition of their order made him change his views, and from being their pupil, he became their most bitter enemy. He had acquired a high reputation in his profession, and was attended not only by those intended for the practice in the law-courts, but also by young gentlemen at large in their course of general education; and he brought numbers from the neighbouring states to this university, and gave a *ton* to the studies of the place. He embraced with great keenness this opportunity of spreading the favorite doctrines of the Lodge, and his auditory became the seminary of Cosmo-politism. The engaging pictures of the possible felicity of a society where every office is held by a man of talents and virtue, and where every talent is set in a place fitted for its exertion, forcibly catches the generous and unsuspecting minds of youth, and in a Roman Catholic state, far advanced in the habits of gross superstition (a character given to Bavaria by its neighbours) and abounding in monks and idle dignitaries, the opportunities must be frequent for observing the inconsiderate dominion of the clergy, and

and the abject and indolent submission of the laity. Accordingly Professor Weishaupt says, in his Apology for Illuminatism, that Deism, Infidelity, and Atheism are more prevalent in Bavaria than in any country he was acquainted with. Discourses, therefore, in which the absurdity and horrors of superstition and spiritual tyranny were strongly painted, could not fail of making a deep impression. And during this state of the minds of the auditory the transition to general infidelity and irreligion is so easy, and so inviting to sanguine youth, prompted perhaps by a latent wish that the restraints which religion imposes on the expectants of a future state might be found, on enquiry, to be nothing but groundless terrors, that I imagine it requires the most anxious care of the public teacher to keep the minds of his audience impressed with the reality and importance of the great truths of religion, while he frees them from the shackles of blind and absurd superstition. I fear that this celebrated instructor had none of this anxiety, but was satisfied with his great success in the last part of this task, the emancipation of his young hearers from the terrors of superstition. I suppose also that this was the more agreeable to him, as it procured him the triumph over the Jesuits, with whom he had long struggled for the direction of the university.

This was in 1777. Weishaupt had long been scheming the establishment of an Association or Order, which, in time, should govern the world. In his first fervour and high expectations, he hinted to several Ex-Jesuits the probability of their recovering, under a new name, the influence which they formerly possessed, and of being again of great service to society, by directing the education of youth of distinction, now emancipated from all civil and religious prejudices. He prevailed on some to join him, but they all retracted

ted but two. After this disappointment Weishaupt became the implacable enemy of the Jesuits; and his sanguine temper made him frequently lay himself open to their piercing eye, and drew on him their keenest resentment, and at last made him the victim of their enmity.

The Lodge Theodore was the place where the above-mentioned doctrines were most zealously propagated. But Weishaupt's emissaries had already procured the adherence of many other Lodges; and the Eclectic Masonry had been brought into vogue chiefly by their exertions at the Willemsbad convention. The Lodge Theodore was perhaps less guarded in its proceedings, for it became remarkable for the very bold sentiments in politics and religion which were frequently uttered in their harangues; and its members were noted for their zeal in making proselytes. Many bitter pasquinades, satires, and other offensive pamphlets were in secret circulation, and even larger works of very dangerous tendency, and several of them were traced to that Lodge. The Elector often expressed his disapprobation of such proceedings, and sent them kind messages, desiring them to be careful not to disturb the peace of the country, and particularly to recollect the solemn declaration made to every entrant into the Fraternity of Free Masons, " That no subject " of religion or politics shall ever be touched on in " the Lodge;" a declaration which alone could have procured his permission of any secret assembly whatever, and on the sincerity and honour of which he had reckoned when he gave his sanction to their establishment. But repeated accounts of the same kind increased the alarms, and the Elector ordered a judicial enquiry into the proceedings of the Lodge Theodore.

It was then discovered that this and several associated Lodges were the nursery or preparation school for another

other Order of Masons, who called themselves the ILLUMINATED, and that the express aim of this Order was to abolish Christianity, and overturn all civil government. But the result of the enquiry was very imperfect and unsatisfactory. No illuminati were to be found. They were unknown in the Lodge. Some of the members occasionally heard of certain candidates for illumination called MINERVALS, who were sometimes seen among them. But whether these had been admitted, or who received them, was known only to themselves. Some of these were examined in private by the Elector himself. They said that they were bound by honour to secrecy: But they assured the Elector, on their honour, that the aim of the Order was in the highest degree praise-worthy, and useful both to church and state. But this could not allay the anxiety of the profane public; and it was repeatedly stated to the Elector, that members of the Lodge Theodore had unguardedly spoken of this Order as one that in time must rule the world. He therefore issued an order forbidding, during his pleasure, all secret assemblies, and shutting up the Mason Lodges. It was not meant to be rigorously enforced, but was intended as a trial of the deference of these Associations for civil authority. The Lodge Theodore distinguished itself by pointed opposition, continuing its meetings; and the members, out of doors, openly reprobated the prohibition as an absurd and unjustifiable tyranny.

In the beginning of 1783, four professors of the Marianen Academy, founded by the widow of the late Elector, viz. Utschneider, Cossandey, Renner, and Grunberger, with two others, were summoned before the Court of Enquiry, and questioned, on their allegiance, respecting the Order of the Illuminati. They acknowledged that they belonged to it, and when more

more closely examined, they related several circumstances of its constitution and principles. Their declarations were immediately published, and were very unfavourable. The Order was said to abjure Christianity, and to refuse admission into the higher degrees to all who adhered to any of the three confessions. Sensual pleasures were restored to the rank they held in the Epicurean philosophy. Self-murder was justified on Stoical principles. In the Lodges death was declared an eternal sleep; patriotism and loyalty were called narrow-minded prejudices, and incompatible with universal benevolence; continual declamations were made on liberty and equality as the unalienable rights of man. The baneful influence of accumulated property was declared an insurmountable obstacle to the happiness of any nation whose chief laws were framed for its protection and increase. Nothing was so frequently discoursed of as the propriety of employing, for a good purpose, the means which the wicked employed for evil purposes; and it was taught, that the preponderancy of good in the ultimate result consecrated every mean employed; and that wisdom and virtue consisted in properly determining this balance. This appeared big with danger, because it seemed evident that nothing would be scrupled at, if it could be made appear that the Order would derive advantage from it, because the great object of the Order was held as superior to every consideration. They concluded by saying that the method of education made them all spies on each other and on all around them. But all this was denied by the Illuminati. Some of these tenets were said to be absolutely false; and the rest were said to be mistakes. The apostate professors had acknowledged their ignorance of many things. Two of them were only Minervals, another was an Illuminatus of the lowest class, and the fourth was but one step

farther

farther advanced. Pamphlets appeared on both sides, with very little effect. The Elector called before him one of the superiors, a young nobleman, who denied those injurious charges, and said that they were ready to lay before his Highness their whole archives and all constitutional papers.

Notwithstanding all this, the government had received such an impression of the dangerous tendency of the Order, that the Elector issued another edict, forbidding all hidden assemblies; and a third, expressly abolishing the Order of Illuminati. It was followed by a search after their papers. The Lodge Theodore was immediately searched, but none were to be found. They said now that they burnt them all, as of no use, since that Order was at an end.

It was now discovered, that Weishaupt was the head and founder of the Order. He was deprived of his Professor's chair, and banished from the Bavarian States; but with a pension of 800 florins, which he refused. He went to Regensburgh, on the confines of Switzerland. Two Italians, the Marquis Constanza and Marquis Savioli, were also banished, with equal pensions, (about L. 40,) which they accepted. One Zwack, a counsellor, holding some law-office, was also banished. Others were imprisoned for some time. Weishaupt went afterwards into the service of the D. of Saxe Gotha, a person of a romantic turn of mind, and whom we shall again meet with. Zwack went into the service of the Pr. de Salms, who soon after had so great a hand in the disturbances in Holland.

By destroying the papers, all opportunity was lost for authenticating the innocence and usefulness of the Order. After much altercation and paper war, Weishaupt, now safe in Regensburg, published an account of the Order, namely, the account which was given to every *Novice* in a discourse read at his reception.

To

To this were added the statutes and the rules of proceeding, as far as the degree of *Illuminatus Minor*, included. This account he affirmed to be conformable to the real practice of the Order. But this publication did by no means satisfy the public mind. It differed exceedingly from the accounts given by the four professors. It made no mention of the higher degrees, which had been most blamed by them. Besides, it was alleged, that it was all a fiction, written in order to lull the suspicions which had been raised (and this was found to be the case, except in respect of the very lowest degree). The real constitution was brought to light by degrees, and shall be laid before the reader, in the order in which it was gradually discovered, that we may the better judge of things not fully known by the conduct of the leaders during the detection. The first account given by Weishaupt is correct, as far as I shall make use of it, and shows clearly the methods that were taken to recommend the Order to strangers.

The Order of ILLUMINATI appears as an accessory to Free Masonry. It is in the Lodges of Free Masons that the Minervals are found, and there they are prepared for Illumination. They must have previously obtained the three English degrees. The founder says more. He says that his doctrines are the only true Free Masonry. He was the chief promoter of the *Eclectic System*. This he urged as the best method for getting information of all the explanations which have been given of the Masonic Mysteries. He was also a *Strict Observanz*, and an adept Rosycrucian. The result of all his knowledge is worthy of particular remark, and shall therefore be given at large.

" I declare," says he, " and I challenge all man-
" kind to contradict my declaration, that no man can
" give

" give any account of the Order of Free Mafonry, of
" its origin, of its hiftory, of its object, nor any ex-
" planation of its myfteries and fymbols, which does
" not leave the mind in total uncertainty on all thefe
" points. Every man is entitled, therefore, to give
" any explanation of the fymbols, and any fyftem of
" the doctrines, that he can render palatable. Hence
" have fprung up that variety of fyftems which for
" twenty years have divided the Order. The fim-
" ple tale of the Englifh, and the fifty degrees of
" the French, and the Knights of Baron Hunde, are
" equally authentic, and have equally had the fupport
" of intelligent and zealous Brethren. Thefe fyftems
" are in fact but one. They have all fprung from the
" Blue Lodge of Three degrees; take thefe for their
" ftandard, and found on thefe all the improvements
" by which each fyftem is afterwards fuited to the par-
" ticular object which it keeps in view. There is no
" man, nor fyftem, in the world, which can fhow by
" undoubted fucceffion that it fhould ftand at the head
" of the Order. Our ignorance in this particular frets
" me. Do but confider our fhort hiftory of 120 years.
" —Who will fhow me the Mother Lodge? Thofe
" of London we have difcovered to be felf-erected in
" 1716. Afk for their archives. They tell you they
" were burnt. They have nothing but the wretched
" fophiftications of the Englifhman Anderfon, and
" the Frenchman Defaguilliers. Where is the Lodge
" of York, which pretends to the priority, with their
" King Bouden, and the archives that he brought from
" the Eaft? Thefe too are all burnt. What is the
" Chapter of Old Aberdeen, and its Holy Clericate?
" Did we not find it unknown, and the Mafon Lodges
" there the moft ignorant of all the ignorant, gaping
" for inftruction from our deputies? Did we not find
" the fame thing at London? and have not their
" miffionaries

"missionaries been among us, prying into our myste-
"ries, and eager to learn from us what is true Free
"Masonry? It is in vain, therefore, to appeal to
"judges; they are no where to be found; all claim
"for themselves the sceptre of the Order; all indeed
"are on an equal footing. They obtained followers,
"not from their authenticity, but from their condu-
"civeness to the end which they proposed, and from
"the importance of that end. It is by this scale that
"we must measure the mad and wicked explanations
"of the Rosycrucians, the Exorcists, and Cabalists.
"These are rejected by all good Masons, because in-
"compatible with social happiness. Only such systems
"as promote this are retained. But alas, they are all
"sadly deficient, because they leave us under the do-
"minion of political and religious prejudices; and
"they are as inefficient as the sleepy dose of an ordi-
"nary sermon.

"But I have contrived an explanation which has
"every advantage; is inviting to Christians of every
"communion; gradually frees them from all religious
"prejudices; cultivates the social virtues; and ani-
"mates them by a great, a feasible, and *speedy* prospect
"of universal happiness, in a state of liberty and mo-
"ral equality, freed from the obstacles which subordi-
"nation, rank, and riches, continually throw in our
"way. My explanation is accurate, and complete,
"my means are effectual, and irresistible. Our secret
"Association works in a way that nothing can with-
"stand, *and man shall soon be free and happy.*

"This is the great object held out by this Associa-
"tion, and the means of attaining it is Illumination,
"enlightening the understanding by the sun of reason,
"which will dispel the clouds of superstition and of pre-
"judice. The proficients in this Order are therefore
"justly named the Illuminated. And of all Illumina-

"tion

" tion which human reafon can give, none is compara-
" ble to the difcovery of what we are, our nature, our
" obligations, what happinefs we are capable of, and
" what are the means of attaining it. In comparifon
" with this, the moft brilliant fciences are but amufe-
" ments for the idle and luxurious. To fit man by
" Illumination for active virtue, to engage him to it
" by the ftrongeft motives, to render the attainment
" of it eafy and certain, by finding employment for
" every talent, and by placing every talent in its pro-
" per fphere of action, fo that all, without feeling any
" extraordinary effort, and in conjunction with and
" completion of ordinary bufinefs, fhall urge forward,
" with united powers, the general tafk. This indeed
" will be an employment, fuited to noble natures;
" grand in its views, and delightful in its exercife.

" And what is this general object ? THE HAPPINESS
" OF THE HUMAN RACE. Is it not diftreffing to a
" generous mind, after comtemplating what human
" nature is capable of, to fee how little we enjoy ?
" When we look at this goodly world, and fee that
" every man *may* be happy, but that the happinefs of
" one depends on the conduct of another; when we
" fee the wicked fo powerful and the good fo weak ;
" and that it is in vain to ftrive fingly and alone, againft
" the general current of vice and oppreffion: the wifh
" naturally arifes in the mind, that it were poffible to
" form a durable combination of the moft worthy
" perfons, who fhould work together in removing the
" obftacles to human happinefs, become terrible to
" the wicked, and give their aid to all the good with-
" out diftinction, and fhould, by the moft powerful
" means, firft fetter, and by fettering, leffen vice ;
" means which at the fame time fhould promote virtue,
" by rendering the inclination to rectitude hitherto fo
feeble,

CHAP. II. THE ILLUMINATI.

" feeble, more powerful and engaging. Would not
" such an association be a blessing to the world?
" But where are the proper persons, the good, the
" generous, and the accomplished, to be found; and
" how, and by what strong motives, are they to be
" induced to engage in a task so vast, so incessant, so
" difficult, and so laborious? This Association must
" be gradual. There *are* some such persons to be
" found in every society. Such noble minds will be
" engaged by the heart-warming object. The first task
" of the Association must therefore be to form the
" young members. As these multiply and advance,
" they become the apostles of beneficence, and the
" work is now on foot, and advances with a speed en-
" creasing every day. The slightest observation shows
" that nothing will so much contribute to increase the
" zeal of the members as secret union. We see with
" what keenness and zeal the frivolous business of
" Free Masonry is conducted, by persons knit toge-
" ther by the secrecy of their union. It is needless to
" enquire into the causes of this zeal which secrecy
" produces. It is an universal fact, confirmed by the
" history of every age. Let this circumstance of our
" constitution therefore be directed to this noble pur-
" pose, and then all the objections urged against it by
" jealous tyranny and affrighted superstition will vanish.
" The order will thus work silently, and securely;
" and though the generous benefactors of the human
" race are thus deprived of the applause of the world,
" they have the noble pleasure of seeing their work
" prosper in their hands."

Such is the aim, and such are the hopes of the Order of the Illuminated. Let us now see how these were
to be accomplished. We cannot judge with perfect
certainty of this, because the account given of the constitution of the Order by its founder includes only the
M lowest

lowest degree, and even this is liable to great suspicion. The accounts given by the four Professors, even of this part of the Order, make a very different impression on the mind, although they differ only in a few particulars.

The only ostensible members of the Order were the Minervals. They were to be found only in the Lodges of Free Masons. A candidate for admission must make his wish known to some Minerval; he reports it to a Superior, who, by a channel to be explained presently, intimates it to the Council. No notice is farther taken of it for some time. The candidate is carefully observed in silence, and if thought unfit for the Order, no notice is taken of his solicitation. But if otherwise, the candidate receives privately an invitation to a conference. Here he meets with a person unknown to him, and, previous to all further conference, he is required to peruse and to sign the following oath:

"I, N. N. hereby bind myself, by mine honour
"and good name, forswearing all mental reservation,
"never to reveal, by hint, word, writing, or in any
"manner whatever, even to my most trusted friend,
"any thing that shall now be said or done to me re-
"specting my wished-for reception, and this whether
"my reception shall follow or not, I being previously
"assured that it shall contain nothing contrary to reli-
"gion, the state, nor good manners. I promise, that
"I shall make no intelligible extract from any papers
"which shall be shewn me now or during my novi-
"ciate. All this I swear, as I am, and as I hope to
"continue, a Man of Honour."

The urbanity of this protestation must agreeably impress the mind of a person who recollects the dreadful imprecations which he made at his reception into the different ranks of Free Masonry. The candidate is then introduced to an *Illuminatus Dirigens*, whom perhaps

perhaps he knows, and is told that this person is to be his future inftructor. There is now prefented to the candidate, what they call a table, in which he writes his name, place of birth, age, rank, place of refidence, profeffion, and favourite ftudies. He is then made to read feveral articles of this table. It contains, 1*ſt*, a very concife account of the Order, its connection with Free Mafonry, and its great object, the promoting the happinefs of mankind by means of inftruction and confirmation in virtuous principles. 2*d*, Several queftions relative to the Order. Among thefe are, "What advantages he hopes to derive from being a "member? What he moft particularly wifhes to "learn? What delicate queftions relative to the life, "the profpects, the duties of man, as an individual, "and as a citizen, he wifhes to have particularly dif- "cuffed to him? In what refpects he thinks he can "be of ufe to the Order? Who are his anceftors, re- "lations, friends, correfpondents, or enemies? Whom "he thinks proper perfons to be received into the "Order, or whom he thinks unfit for it, and the rea- "fons for both opinions?" To each of thefe queftions he muft give fome anfwer in writing.

The Novice and his Mentor are known only to each other; perhaps nothing more follows upon this; if otherwife, the Mentor appoints another conference, and begins his inftructions, by giving him in detail certain portions of the conftitution, and of the fundamental rules of the Order. Of thefe the Novice muft give a weekly account in writing. He muft alfo read, in the Mentor's houfe, a book containing more of the inftructions of the Order; but he muft make no extracts. Yet from this reading he muft derive all his knowledge; and he muft give an account in writing of his progrefs. All writings received from his Superiors muft be returned with a ftated punctuality.—

Thefe

These writings confist chiefly of important and delicate queſtions, ſuited, either to the particular inclination, or to the peculiar taſte which the candidate had diſcovered in his ſubſcriptions of the articles of the table, and in his former reſcripts, or to the direction which the Mentor wiſhes to give to his thoughts.

Enlightening the underſtanding, and the rooting out of prejudices, are pointed out to him as the principal taſks of his noviciate. The knowledge of himſelf is conſidered as preparatory to all other knowledge. To diſcloſe to him, by means of the calm and unbiaſſed obſervation of his inſtructor, what is his own character, his moſt vulnerable ſide, either in reſpect of temper, paſſions, or prepoſſeſſions, is therefore the moſt eſſential ſervice that can be done him. For this purpoſe there is required of him ſome account of his own conduct on occaſions where he doubted of its propriety; ſome account of his friendſhips, of his differences of opinion, and of his conduct on ſuch occaſions. From ſuch relations the Superior learns his manner of thinking and judging, and thoſe propenſities which require his chief attention.

Having made the candidate acquainted with himſelf, he is appriſed that the Order is not a ſpeculative, but an active aſſociation, engaged in doing good to others. The knowledge of human character is therefore of all others the moſt important. This is acquired only by obſervation, aſſiſted by the inſtructions of his teacher. Characters in hiſtory are propoſed to him for obſervation, and his opinion is required. After this he is directed to look around him, and to notice the conduct of other men; and part of his weekly reſcripts muſt conſiſt of accounts of all intereſting occurrences in his neighbourhood, whether of a public or private nature. Coſſandey, one of the four Profeſſors, gives a particular account of the inſtructions relating to this kind

of

of science. "The Novice must be attentive to tri-
"fles: For in frivolous occurrences a man is indolent,
"and makes no effort to act a part, so that his real
"character is then acting alone. Nothing will have
"such influence with the Superiors in promoting the
"advancement of a candidate as very copious narra-
"tions of this kind, because the candidate, if promo-
"ted, is to be employed in an active station, and it
"is from this kind of information only that the Supe-
"riors can judge of his fitness. These characteristic
"anecdotes are not for the instruction of the Superi-
"ors, who are men of long experience, and familiar
"with such occupation. But they inform the Order
"concerning the talents and proficiency of the young
"member. Scientific instruction, being connected
"by system, is soon communicated, and may in ge-
"neral be very completely obtained from the books
"which are recommended to the Novice, and acqui-
"red in the public seminaries of instruction. But
"knowledge of character is more multifarious and
"more delicate. For this there is no college, and it
"must therefore require longer time for its attainment.
"Besides, this assiduous and long continued study of
"men, enables the possessor of such knowledge to act
"with men, and by his knowledge of their character,
"to influence their conduct. For such reasons this
"study is continued, and these rescripts are required,
"during the whole progress through the Order, and
"attention to them is recommended as the only mean
"of advancement. Remarks on Physiognomy in
"these narrations are accounted of considerable va-
"lue." So far Mr. Cossandey.

During all this trial, which may last one, two, or three years, the Novice knows no person of the Order but his own instructor, with whom he has frequent meetings, along with other Minervals. In these conversations

versations he learns the importance of the Order, and the opportunities he will afterwards have of acquiring much hidden science. The employment of his unknown Superiors naturally causes him to entertain very high notions of their abilities and worth. He is counselled to aim at a resemblance to them by getting rid by degrees of all those prejudices or prepossessions which checked his own former progress; and he is assisted in this endeavour by an invitation to a correspondence with them. He may address his Provincial Superior, by directing his letter *Soli*, or the General by *Primo*, or the Superiors in general by *Quibus licet*. In these letters he may mention whatever he thinks conducive to the advancement of the Order; he may inform the Superiors how his instructor behaves to him; if assiduous or remiss, indulgent or severe. The Superiors are enjoined by the strongest motives to convey these letters wherever addressed. None but the General and Council know the result of all this; and all are enjoined to keep themselves and their proceedings unknown to all the world.

If three years of this Noviciate have elapsed without further notice, the Minerval must look for no further advancement; he is found unfit, and remains a Free Mason of the highest class. This is called a *Sta bene*.

But should his Superiors judge more favourably of him, he is drawn out of the general mass of Free Masons, and becomes *Illuminatus Minor*. When called to a conference for this purpose, he is told in the most serious manner, that " it is vain for him to hope
" to acquire wisdom by mere systematic instruction;
" for such instruction the Superiors have no leisure.
" Their duty is not to form speculators, but active
" men, whom they must *immediately* employ in the
" service of the Order. He must therefore grow wise
" and

"and able entirely by the unfolding and exertion of
"his own talents. His Superiors have already difco-
"vered what thefe are, and know what fervice he may
"be capable of rendering the Order, provided he
"now heartily acquiefces in being thus honourably
"employed. They will affift him in bringing his ta-
"lents into action, and will place him in the fitua-
"tions moft favourable for their exertion, fo that he
"may be *affured* of fuccefs. Hitherto he has been a
"mere fcholar, but his firft ftep farther carries him
"into action; he muft therefore now confider himfelf
"as an inftrument in the hands of his Superiors, to
"be ufed for the nobleft purpofes." The aim of the order is now more fully told him. It is, in one fentence, "to make of the human race, without any
"diftinction of nation, condition, or profeffion, one
"good and happy family." To this aim, demonftrably attainable, every fmaller confideration muft give way. This may fometimes require facrifices which no man ftanding alone has fortitude to make; but which become light, and a fource of the pureft enjoyment, when fupported and encouraged by the countenance and co-operation of the united wife and and good, fuch as are the Superiors of the Order. If the candidate, warmed by the alluring picture of the poffible happinefs of a virtuous Society, fays that he is fenfible of the propriety of this procedure, and ftill wifhes to be of the Order, he is required to fign the following obligation.

"I, N. N. proteft before you, the worthy Pleni-
"potentiary of the venerable Order into which I wifh
"to be admitted, that I acknowledge my natural
"weaknefs and inability, and that I, with all my pof-
"feffions, rank, honours, and titles which I hold in
"political fociety, am, at bottom, only a man; I
"can enjoy thefe things only through my fellow-men,
                                                     "and

"and through them also I may lose them. The approbation and consideration of my fellow-men are indispensably necessary, and I must try to maintain them by all my talents. These I will never use to the prejudice of universal good, but will oppose, with all my might, the enemies of the human race, and of political society. I will embrace every opportunity of saving mankind, by improving my understanding and my affections, and by imparting all important knowledge, as the good and statutes of this Order require of me. I bind myself to perpetual silence and unshaken loyalty and submission to the Order, in the persons of my Superiors; here making a faithful and complete surrender of my private judgment, my own will, and every narrow-minded employment of my power and influence. I pledge myself to account the good of the Order as my own, and am ready to serve it with my fortune, my honour, and my blood. Should I, through omission, neglect, passion, or wicknedness, behave contrary to this good of the Order, I subject myself to what reproof or punishment my Superiors shall enjoin. The friends and enemies of the Order shall be my friends and enemies; and with respect to both I will conduct myself as directed by the Order, and am ready, in every lawful way, to devote myself to its increase and promotion, and therein to employ all my ability. All this I promise, and protest, without secret reservation, according to the intention of the Society which require from me this engagement. This I do as I am, and as I hope to continue, a Man of Honour."

A drawn sword is then pointed at his breast, and he is asked, Will you be obedient to the commands of your Superiors? He is threatened with unavoidable vengeance, from which no potentate can defend him,

if

if he should ever betray the Order. He is then asked, 1. What aim does he wish the Order to have ? 2. What means he would choose to advance this aim ? 3. Whom he wishes to keep out of the Order ? 4. What subjects he wishes not to be discussed in it?

Our candidate is now ILLUMINATUS MINOR. It is needless to narrate the mummery of reception, and it is enough to say, that it nearly resembles that of the *Masonic Chevalier du Soleil,* known to every one much conversant in Masonry. Weishaupt's preparatory discourse of reception is a piece of good composition, whether considered as argumentative, (from topics indeed, that are very gratuitous and fanciful,) or as a specimen of that declamation which was so much practised by Libanius and the other Sophists, and it gives a distinct and captivating account of the professed aim of the Order.

The *Illuminatus Minor* learns a good deal more of the Order, but by very sparing morsels, under the same instructor. The task has now become more delicate and difficult. The chief part of it is the rooting out of prejudices in politics and religion; and Weishaupt has shown much address in the method which he has employed. Not the most hurtful, but the most easily refuted were the first subjects of discussion, so that the pupil gets into the habits of victory; and his reverence for the systems of either kind is diminished when they are found to have harboured such untenable opinions. The proceedings in the Eclectic Lodges of Masonry, and the harangues of the Brother Orators, teemed with the boldest sentiments both in politics and religion. Enlightening, and the triumph of reason, had been the *ton* of the country for some time past, and every institution, civil and religious, had been the subject of the most free criticism. Above all, the Cosmopolitism, imported from France, where it had been the favourite topic of the enthufiaftical œconomifts, was now become a general theme of difcuffion in all focieties that had any pretenfions to cultivation. It was a fubject of eafy and agreeable declamation; and the Literati found in it a fubject admirably fitted for fhewing their talents, and ingratiating themfelves with the young men of fortune, whofe minds, unfufpicious as yet and generous, were fired with the fair profpects fet before them of univerfal and attainable happinefs. And the pupils of the Illuminati were ftill more warmed by the thought that they were to be the happy inftruments of accomplifhing all this. And though the doctrines of univerfal liberty and equality, as imprefcriptible rights of man, might fometimes ftartle thofe who poffeffed the advantage of fortune, there were thoufands of younger fons, and of men of talents without fortune, to whom thefe were agreeable founds. And we muft particularly obferve, that thofe who were now the pupils were a fet of picked fubjects, whofe characters and peculiar biafes were well known by their conduct during their noviciate as Minervals. They were therefore fuch as, in all probability, would not boggle at very free fentiments. We might rather expect a partiality to doctrines which removed fome reftraints which formerly checked them in the indulgence of youthful paffions. Their inftructors, who have thus relieved their minds from feveral anxious thoughts, muft appear men of fuperior minds. This was a notion moft carefully inculcated; and they could fee nothing to contradict it; for, except their own Mentor, they knew none; they heard of Superiors of different ranks, but never faw them; and the fame mode of inftruction that was practifed during their noviciate was ftill retained. More particulars of the Order were flowly unfolded to them, and they were taught that their Superiors were men of diftinguifhed talents,

talents, and were Superiors for this reason alone. They were taught, that the great opportunities which the Superiors had for observation, and their habits of continually occupying their thoughts with the great objects of this Order, had enlarged their views, even far beyond the narrow limits of nations and kingdoms, which they hoped would one day coalesce into one great Society, where consideration would attach to talents and worth alone, and that pre-eminence in these would be invariably attended with all the enjoyments of influence and power. And they were told that they would gradually become acquainted with these great and venerable Characters, as they advanced in the Order. In earnest of this, they were made acquainted with one or two Superiors, and with several Illuminati of their own rank. Also, to whet their zeal, they are now made instructors of one or two Minervals, and report their progress to their Superiors. They are given to understand that nothing can so much recommend them as the success with which they perform this task. It is declared to be the best evidence of their usefulness in the great designs of the Order.

The baleful effects of general superstition, and even of any peculiar religious prepossession, are now strongly inculcated, and the discernment of the pupils in these matters is learned by questions which are given them from time to time to discuss. These are managed with delicacy and circumspection, that the timid may not be alarmed. In like manner, the political doctrines of the Order are inculcated with the utmost caution. After the mind of the pupil has been warmed by the pictures of universal happiness, and convinced that it is a possible thing to unite all the inhabitants of the earth in one great society; and after it has been made out, in some measure to the satisfaction

of the pupil, that a great addition of happiness would be gained by the abolition of national distinctions and animosities; it may frequently be no hard task to make him think that patriotism is a narrow-minded monopolising sentiment, and even incompatible with the more enlarged views of the Order; namely, the uniting the whole human race into one great and happy society. Princes are a chief feature of national distinction. Princes, therefore, may now be safely represented as unnecessary. If so, loyalty to Princes loses much of its sacred character; and the so frequent enforcing of it in our common political discussions may now be easily made to appear a selfish maxim of rulers, by which they may more easily enslave the people; and thus, it may at last appear, that religion, the love of our particular country, and loyalty to our Prince, should be resisted, if, by these partial or narrow views, we prevent the accomplishment of that Cosmo-political happiness which is continually held forth as the great object of the Order. It is in this point of view that the terms of devotion to the Order, which are inserted in the oath of admission, are now explained. The authority of the ruling powers is therefore represented as of inferior moral weight to that of the Order. "These
" powers are despots, when they do not conduct them-
" selves by its principles; and it is therefore our duty
" to surround them with its members, so that the
" profane may have no access to them. Thus we are
" able most powerfully to promote its interests. If
" any person is more disposed to listen to Princes
" than to the Order, he is not fit for it, and must rise
" no higher. We must do our utmost to procure the
" advancement of Illuminati into all important civil
" offices."

Accordingly the Order laboured in this with great zeal and success. A correspondence was discovered,

in

in which it is plain, that by their influence, one of the greateſt eccleſiaſtical dignities was filled up in oppoſition to the right and authority of the Archbiſhop of Spire, who is there repreſented as a tyrannical and bigoted prieſt. They contrived to place their Members as tutors to the youth of diſtinction. One of them, Baron Leuchtſenring, took the charge of a young prince without any ſalary. They inſinuated themſelves into all public offices, and particularly into courts of juſtice. In like manner, the chairs in the Univerſity of Ingolſtadt were (with only two exceptions) occupied by Illuminati. "Rulers who are members muſt be
" promoted through the ranks of the Order only in
" proportion as they acknowledge the goodneſs of its
" great object, and manner of procedure. Its object
" may be ſaid to be the checking the tyranny of
" princes, nobles, and prieſts, and eſtabliſhing an
" univerſal equality of condition and of religion."
The pupil is now informed, " that ſuch a religion is
" contained in the Order, is the perfection of Chriſ-
" tianity, and will be imparted to him in due time."

Theſe and other principles and maxims of the Order are partly communicated by the verbal inſtruction of the Mentor, partly by writings, which muſt be punctually returned, and partly read by the pupil at the Mentor's houſe, (but without taking extracts,) in ſuch portions as he ſhall direct. The reſcripts by the pupil muſt contain diſcuſſions on theſe ſubjects, and anecdotes and deſcriptions of living characters; and theſe muſt be zealouſly continued, as the chief mean of advancement. All this while the pupil knows only his Mentor, the Minervals, and a few others of his own rank. All mention of degrees, or other buſineſs of the Order, muſt be carefully avoided, even in the meetings with other members : " For the Or-
" der wiſhes to be ſecret, and to work in ſilence; for
                                            " thus

"thus it is better secured from the oppression of the ruling powers, and because this secrecy gives a greater zest to the whole."

This short account of the *Noviciate*, and of the lowest class of illuminati, is all we can get from the authority of Mr. Weishaupt. The higher degrees were not published by him. Many circumstances appear suspicious, are certainly susceptible of different turns, and may easily be pushed to very dangerous extremes. The accounts given by the four professors confirm these suspicions. They declare upon oath, that they make all these accusations in consequence of what they heard in the meetings, and of what they knew of the Higher Orders.

But since the time of the suppression by the Elector, discoveries have been made which throw great light on the subject. A collection of original papers and correspondence was found by searching the house of one Zwack (a Member) in 1786. The following year a much larger collection was found at the house of Baron Bassus; and since that time Baron Knigge, the most active Member next to Weishaupt, published an account of some of the higher degrees, which had been formed by himself. A long while after this were published, *Neueste Arbeitung des Spartacus und Philo in der Illuminaten Orden*, and *Hohere Graden des Illum. Ordens*. These two works give an account of the whole secret constitution of the Order, its various degrees, the manner of conferring them, the instructions to the intrants, and an explanation of the connection of the Order with Free Masonry, and a critical history. We shall give some extracts from such of these as have been published.

Weishaupt was the founder in 1776. In 1778 the number of Members was considerably increased, and the Order was fully established. The Members took

antique

antique names. Thus Weishaupt took the name of Spartacus, the man who headed the insurrection of slaves, which in Pompey's time kept Rome in terror and uproar for three years. Zwack was called Cato. Knigge was Philo. Bassus was Hannibal. Hertel was Marius. Marquis Constanza was Diomedes.— Nicolai, an eminent and learned bookseller in Berlin, and author of several works of reputation, took the name of Lucian, the great scoffer at all religion. Another was Mahomet, &c. It is remarkable, that except Cato and Socrates, we have not a name of any ancient who was eminent as a teacher and practiser of virtue. On the contrary, they seem to have affected the characters of the free-thinkers and turbulent spirits of antiquity. In the same manner they gave ancient names to the cities and countries of Europe. Munich was Athens, Vienna was Rome, &c.

Spartacus to Cato, Feb. 6, 1778.

" *Mon but est de faire valoir la raison.* As a subor-
" dinate object I shall endeavour to gain security to
" ourselves, a backing in case of misfortunes, and as-
" sistance from without. I shall therefore press the
" cultivation of science, especially such sciences as
" may have an influence on our reception in the world,
" and may serve to remove obstacles out of the way.
" We have to struggle with pedantry, with intole-
" rance, with divines and statesmen, and above all,
" princes and priests are in our way. Men are unfit
" as they are, and must be formed; each class must
" be the school of trial for the next. This will be te-
" dious, because it is hazardous. In the last classes I
" propose academics under the direction of the Order.
" This will secure us the adherence of the Literati.
" Science

" Science shall here be the lure. Only those who are
" assuredly proper subjects shall be picked out from
" among the inferior classes for the higher mysteries,
" which contain the first principles and means of pro-
" moting a happy life. No religionist must, on any
" account, be admitted into these: For here we work
" at the discovery and extirpation of superstition and
" prejudices. The instructions shall be so conducted
" that each shall disclose what he thinks he conceals
" within his own breast, what are his ruling propensi-
" ties and passions, and how far he has advanced in
" the command of himself. This will answer all the
" purposes of auricular confession. And, in particu-
" lar, every person shall be made a spy on another
" and on all around him. Nothing can escape our
" sight; by these means we shall readily discover who
" are contented, and receive with relish the peculiar
" state-doctrines and religious opinions that are laid
" before them; and, at last, the trust-worthy alone
" will be admitted to a participation of the whole
" maxims and political constitution of the Order. In
" a council composed of such members we shall labour
" at the contrivance of means to drive by degrees the
" enemies of reason and of humanity out of the world,
" and to establish a peculiar morality and religion fit-
" ted for the great Society of Mankind.

" But this is a ticklish project, and requires the ut-
" most circumspection. The squeamish will start at
" the sight of religious or political novelties; and
" they must be prepared for them. We must be par-
" ticularly careful about the books which we recom-
" mend; I shall confine them at first to moralists and
" reasoning historians. This will prepare for a patient
" reception, in the higher classes, of works of a bolder
" flight, such as Robinet's *Systeme de la Nature—Poli-*
" *tique Naturelle—Philosophie de la Nature—Systeme So-*
                                                   " *cial—*

" *cial*—The writings of Mirabaud, &c. Helvetius
" is fit only for the strongest stomachs. If any one
" has a copy already, neither praise nor find fault with
" him. Say nothing on such subjects to intrants, for
" we don't know how they will be received—folks are
" not yet prepared. Marius, an excellent man, must
" be dealt with. His stomach, which cannot yet di-
" gest such strong food, must acquire a better tone.
" The allegory on which I am to found the mysteries
" of the Higher Orders is *the fire-worship of the Magi.*
" We must have some worship, and none is so apposite.
" LET THERE BE LIGHT, AND THERE SHALL BE
" LIGHT. This is my motto, and is my fundamental
" principle. The degrees will be *Feuer Orden, Parsen
" Orden**; all very practicable. In the course through
" these there will be no STA BENE (this is the answer
" given to one who solicits preferment, and is refused).
" For I engage that none shall enter this class who has
" not laid aside his prejudices. No man is fit for our
" Order who is not a Brutus or a Catiline, and is not
" ready to go every length.—Tell me how you like
" this?"

Spartacus to Cato, March 1778.

" To collect unpublished works, and information
" from the archives of States, will be a most useful ser-
" vice. We shall be able to show in a very ridiculous
" light the claims of our despots. Marius (keeper of
" the archives of the Electorate) has ferreted out a no-
" ble document, which we have got. He makes it,
" forsooth, a case of conscience—how silly that—since

* This is evidently the *Mystere du Mithras* mentioned by Barruel, in his History of Jacobinism, and had been carried into France by Bede and Busche.

" only

" only that is *fin* which is *ultimately* productive of mischief. In this cafe, where the advantage far exceeds the hurt, it is meritorious virtue. It will do more good in our hands than by remaining for 1000 years on the dufty fhelf."

There was found in the hand-writing of Zwack a project for a Sifterhood, in fubferviency to the defigns of the Illuminati. In it are the following paffages:

" It will be of great fervice, and procure us both much information *and money*, and will fuit charmingly the tafte of many of our trueft members, who are lovers of the fex. It fhould confift of two claffes, the virtuous and the freer hearted (i. e. thofe who fly out of the common track of prudifh manners); they muft not know of each other, and muft be under the direction of men, but without knowing it. Proper books muft be put into their hands, and fuch (but fecretly) as are flattering to their paffions."

There are, in the fame hand-writing, Defcription of a ftrong box, which, if forced open, fhall blow up and deftroy its contents—Several receipts for procuring abortion—A compofition which blinds or kills when fpurted in the face—A fheet, containing a receipt for fympathetic ink—Tea for procuring abortion—*Herbæ quae habent qualitatem deleteream*—A method for filling a bed-chamber with peftilential vapours—How to take off impreffions of feals, fo as to ufe them afterwards as feals—A collection of fome hundreds of fuch impreffions, with a lift of their owners, princes, nobles, clergymen, merchants, &c.—A receipt *ad excitandum furorem uterinum,*—A manufcript intitled, " Better than Horus." It was afterwards printed and diftributed at Leipzig fair, and is an attack and bitter fatire on all religion. This is in the hand-writing of Ajax. As alfo a differtation on fuicide.—N. B. His fifter-in-law threw herfelf from the top of a tower. There was alfo a fet of portraits,

portraits, or characters of eighty-five ladies in Munich; with recommendations of some of them for members of a Lodge of Sifter Illuminatæ; alfo injunctions to all the Superiors to learn to write with both hands; and that they should use more than one cypher.

Immediately after the publication of these writings, many defences appeared. It was said that the dreadful medical apparatus were with propriety in the hands of Counsellor Zwack, who was a judge of a criminal court, and whose duty it was therefore to know such things. The same excuse was offered for the collection of seals; but how came these things to be put up with papers of the Illuminati, and to be in the handwriting of one of that Order? Weishaupt says, "These "things were not carried into effect—only spoken of, "and are justifiable when taken in proper connec- "tion." This however he has not pointed out; but he appeals to the account of the Order, which he had published at Regensburg, and in which neither these things are to be found, nor any possibility of a connection by which they may be justified. "All men," says he, "are subject to errors, and the best man is he "who best conceals them. I have never been guilty "of any such vices or follies: for proof, I appeal to "the whole tenor of my life, which my reputation, "and my struggles with hostile cabals, had brought "completely into public view long before the institu- "tion of this Order, without abating any thing of that "flattering regard which was paid to me by the first "persons of my country and its neighbourhood; a re- "gard well evinced by their confidence in me as the "best instructor of their children." In some of his private letters, we learn the means which he employed to acquire this influence among the youth, and they are such as could not fail. But we must not anticipate. "It is well known that I have made the chair which I
"occupied

" occupied in the university of Ingolstadt, the resort
" of the first class of the German youth; whereas for-
" merly it had only brought round it the low-born
" practitioners in the courts of law. I have gone
" through the whole circle of human enquiry. I have
" exorcised spirits—raised ghosts—discovered trea-
" sures—interrogated the Cabala—*hatte Loto gespielt*—I
" have never transmuted metals."—(A very pretty
and respectable circle indeed, and what vulgar spirits
would scarcely have included within the pale of their
curiosity.)—" The Tenor of my life has been the op-
" posite of every thing that is vile; and no man can
" lay any such thing to my charge. I have reason to
" rejoice that these writings have appeared; they are a
" vindication of the Order and of my conduct. I can
" and must declare to God, and I do it now in the
" most solemn manner, that in my whole life I never
" saw or heard of the so much condemned secret wri-
" tings; and in particular, respecting these abomina-
" ble means, such as poisoning, abortion, &c. was it
" ever known to me in any case, that any of my friends
" or acquaintances ever even thought of them, advis-
" ed them, or made any use of them. I was indeed
" always a schemer and projector, but never could en-
" gage much in detail. My general plan is good,
" though in the detail there may be faults. I had my-
" self to form. In another situation, and in an active
" station in life, I should have been keenly occupied,
" and the founding an Order would never have come
" into my head. But I would have executed much
" greater things, had not government always opposed
" my exertions, and placed others in the situations
" which suited my talents. It was the full conviction
" of this and of what could be done, if every man were
" placed in the office for which he was fitted by nature
" and a proper education, which first suggested to me
                                                  " the

"the plan of Illumination." Surely Mr. Weishaupt had a very serious charge, the education of youth; and his encouragement in that charge was the most flattering that an Illuminatus could wish for; because he had brought round him the youth whose influence in society was the greatest, and who would most of all contribute to the diffusing good principles, and exciting to good conduct through the whole state. "I did not," says he, " bring deism into Bavaria more than into " Rome. I found it here, in great vigour, more a- " bounding than in any of the neighbouring Protestant " states. I am proud to be known to the world as " the founder of the Order of Illuminati; and I repeat " my wish to have for my epitaph,

" *Hic situs est Phæthon, currús auriga paterni,*
" *Quem si non tenuit, magnis tamen excidit ausis.*"

The second discovery of secret correspondence at Sanderstorff, the seat of Baron Batz, (Hannibal,) contains still more interesting facts.

Spartacus to Cato.

" What shall I do? I am deprived of all help. So-
" crates, who would insist on being a man of conse-
" quence among us, and is really a man of talents,
" and of a *right way of thinking*, is eternally besotted.
" Augustus is in the worst estimation imaginable. Al-
" cibiades sits the day long with the vintner's pretty
" wife, and there he sighs and pines. A few days
" ago, at Corinth, Tiberius attempted to ravish the
" wife of Democides, and her husband came in upon
" them. Good heavens! what *Areopagitæ* I have got.
" When the worthy man Marcus Aurelius comes to
" Athens, (Munich,) what will he think? What a
                                                              " meeting

" meeting of diffolute, immoral wretches, whoremaf-
" ters, liars, bankrupts, braggarts, and vain fools!
" When he fees all this, what will he think? He will
" be afhamed to enter into an Affociation," (obferve
Reader, that Spartacus writes this in Auguft 1783, in
the very time that he would have murdered Cato's fifter, as we fhall fee,) "where the chiefs raife the
" higheft expectations, and exhibit fuch wretched ex-
" amples; and all this from felf-will, from fenfuality.
" Am I not in the right—that this man—that any
" fuch worthy man—whofe name alone would give us
" the felection of all Germany, will declare that the
" whole province of Grecia, (Bavaria,) innocent and
" guilty, muft be excluded. I tell you, we may ftu-
" dy, and write, and toil till death. We may facri-
" fice to the Order, our health, our fortune, and our
" reputation, (alas, the lofs!) and thefe Lords, fol-
" lowing their own pleafures, will whore, cheat, fteal,
" and drive on like fhamelefs rafcals; and yet muft
" be *Areopagitæ*, and interfere in every thing. In-
" deed, my deareft friend, we have only enflaved
" ourfelves."

In another part of this fine correfpondence, Diomedes has had the good fortune to intercept a Q. L.
(*Quibus Licet,*) in which it is faid, and fupported by
proofs, that Cato had received 250 florins as a bribe
for his fentence in his capacity of a judge in a criminal
court (the end had furely fanctified the means.) In
another, a Minerval complains of his Mentor for having by lies occafioned the difmiffion of a phyfician
from a family, by which the Mentor obtained, in the
fame capacity, the cuftom of the houfe and free accefs,
which favour he repaid by debauching the wife; and
he prays to be informed whether he may not get another Mentor, faying that although that man had always
given him the moft excellent inftructions, and he
                                                doubted

doubted not would continue them, yet he felt a difguſt at the hypocriſy, which would certainly diminiſh the impreſſion of the moſt ſalutary truths. (Is it not diſtreſſing to think, that this promiſing youth will by and by laugh at his former ſimplicity, and follow the ſteps and not the inſtructions of his phyſician.) In another place, Spartacus writes to Marius, (in confidence,) that another worthy Brother, an *Areopagita*, had ſtolen a gold and a ſilver watch, and a ring, from Brutus, *(Savioli,)* and begs Marius, in another letter, to try, while it was yet poſſible, to get the things reſtored, becauſe the culprit was a moſt *excellent man*, *(Vortrefflich,)* and of vaſt uſe to the Order, having the direction of an eminent ſeminary of young *gentlemen*; and becauſe Savioli was much in good company, and did not much care for the Order, except in ſo far as it gave him an opportunity of knowing and leading ſome of them, and of ſteering his way at court.

I cannot help inſerting here, though not the moſt proper place, a part of a provincial report from Knigge, the man of the whole *Aeropagitæ* who ſhows any thing like urbanity or gentleneſs of mind.

"Of my whole colony, (Weſtphalia,) the moſt brilliant is Claudiopolis *(Neuwied)*. There they work, and direct, and do wonders."

If there ever was a ſpot upon earth where men may be happy in a ſtate of cultivated ſociety, it was the little principality of Neuwied. I ſaw it in 1770. The town was neat, and the palace handſome and in good taſte. But the country was beyond conception delightful; not a cottage that was out of repair, not a hedge out of order; it had been the hobby (pardon me the word) of the Prince, who made it his *daily* employment to go through his principality regularly, and aſſiſt every houſholder, of whatever condition, with his advice,

and

and with his purse; and, when a freeholder could not of himself put things into a thriving condition, the Prince sent his workmen and did it for him. He endowed schools for the common people, and two academies for the gentry and the people of business. He gave little portions to the daughters, and prizes to the well-behaving sons of the labouring people. His own houshold was a pattern of elegance and economy; his sons were sent to Paris to learn elegance, and to England to learn science and agriculture. In short, the whole was like a romance (and was indeed romantic). I heard it spoken of with a smile at the table of the Bishop of Treves, at Ehrenbretstein, and was induced to see it next day as a curiosity: And yet even here, the fanaticism of Knigge would distribute his poison, and tell the blinded people, that they were in a state of sin and misery, that their Prince was a despot, and that they would never be happy till he was made to fly, and till they were all made equal.

They got their wish; the swarm of French locusts sat down on Neuwied's beautiful fields in 1793, and entrenched themselves; and in three months, Prince and farmers houses, and cottages, and schools, and academies—all had vanished; and all the subjects were made equal. But when they complained to the French General (René le Grand) of being plundered by his soldiers, he answered, with a contemptuous and cutting laugh, " All is ours—we have left you your eyes " to cry."—(*Report to the Convention*, 13*th June* 1795.)

Discite justitiam moniti, et non temnere divos!

To proceed:

Spartacus to Cato.

" By this plan we shall direct all mankind. In this manner, and by the simplest means, we shall set all in motion and in flames. The occupations must be so allotted and contrived, that we may, in secret, influence all political transactions." N. B. This alludes to a part that is with-held from the public, because it contained the allotment of the most rebellious and profligate occupations to several persons whose common names could not be traced. " I have considered," says Spartacus, " every thing, and so prepared it, that if the Order should this day go to ruin, I shall in a year re-establish it more brilliant than ever." Accordingly it got up again in about this space of time, under the name of the GERMAN UNION, appearing in the form of READING SOCIETIES. One of these was set up in Zwack's house; and this raising a suspicion, a visitation was made at Landshut, and the first set of the private papers were found. The scheme was, however, zealously prosecuted in other parts of Germany, as we shall see by and by. " Nor," continues Spartacus, " will it signify though all should be betrayed and printed. I am so certain of success, in spite of all obstacles, (for the springs are in every heart,) that I am indifferent, though it should involve my life and my liberty. What! have thousands thrown away their lives about *homoios* and *homoiousios* and shall not this cause warm even the heart of a coward? But I have the art to draw advantage even from misfortune; and when you would think me sunk to the bottom, I shall rise with new vigour. Who would have thought, that a professor at Ingol-
" stadt

" stadt was to become the teacher of the professors of
" Gottingen, and of the greatest men in Germany?"

Spartacus to Cato.

" Send me back my degree of *Illuminatus Minor*;
" it is the wonder of all men here (I may perhaps find
" time to give a translation of the discourse of recep-
" tion, which contains all that can be said of this As-
" sociation to the public); as also the two last sheets
" of my degree, which is in the keeping of Marius,
" and Celsus, under 100 locks, which contains my
" history of the lives of the Patriarchs." N. B. Nothing very particular has been discovered of these lives
of the Patriarchs. He says, that there were above
sixty sheets of it. To judge by the care taken of it,
it must be a favourite work, very hazardous, and very
catching.

In another letter to Cato, we have some hints of the
higher degrees, and concerning a peculiar morality,
and a popular religion, which the Order was one day
to give the world. He says, " There must *(a la Je-*
" *suite)* not a single purpose ever come in sight that is
" ambiguous, and that may betray our aims against
" religion and the state. One must speak sometimes
" one way and sometimes another, but so as never to
" contradict ourselves, and so that, with respect to
" our true way of thinking, we may be impenetrable.
" When our strongest things chance to give offence,
" they must be explained as attempts to draw answers
" which discover to us the sentiments of the person
" we converse with." N. B. This did not always succeed with him.

Spartacus says, speaking of the priests degree, " One
" would almost imagine, that this degree, as I have ma-
" naged

"naged it, is genuine Christianity, and that its end
"was to free the Jews from flavery. I fay, that Free
"Mafonry is concealed Chriftianity. My explanation
"of the hieroglyphics, at leaft, proceeds on this fup-
"pofition; and as I explain things, no man need be
"afhamed of being a Chriftian. Indeed I afterwards
"throw away this name, and fubftitute *Reafon*. But
"I affure you this is no fmall affair; a new religion,
"and a new ftate-government, which fo happily ex-
"plain one and all of thefe fymbols, and combine
"them in one degree. You may think that this is
"my chief work; but I have three other degrees,
"all different, for my clafs of higher myfteries, in
"comparifon with which this is but child's play; but
"thefe I keep for myfelf as General, to be beftowed
"by me only on the *Benemeritiſſimi*," (furely fuch as
Cato, his deareft friend, and the poffeffor of fuch pretty fecrets, as abortives, poifons, peftilential vapours,
&c.). "The promoted may be Areopagites or not.
"Were you here I fhould give you this degree with-
"out hefitation. But it is too important to be intruf-
"ted to paper, or to be beftowed otherwife than from
"my own hand. It is the key to hiftory, to religion,
"and to every ftate-government in the world."*

"Spartacus proceeds, "There fhall be but three
"copies for all Germany. You can't imagine what
"refpect and curiofity my prieft-degree has raifed;
"and, which is wonderful, a famous Proteftant di-
"vine, who is now of the Order, is perfuaded that
                                                                "the

---

* I obferve, in other parts of his correfpondence where he fpeaks of this, feveral fingular phrafes, which are to be found in two books; *Antiqueté devoilée par fes Ufages*, and *Origine du Defpotifme Oriental*. Thefe contain indeed much of the maxims inculcated in the reception difcourfe of the degree *Illumanitus Minor*. Indeed I have found, that Weifhaupt is much lefs an inventor than he is generally thought.

"the religion contained in it is the true sense of Chris"tianity. O MAN, MAN! TO WHAT MAY'ST THOU NOT BE PERSUADED. Who would imagine that I was to be the founder of a new religion?"

In this scheme of Masonic Christianity, Spartacus and Philo laboured seriously together. Spartacus sent him the materials, and Philo worked them up. It will therefore illustrate this capital point of the constitution of the Order, if we take Philo's account of it.

Philo to Cato.

" We must consider the ruling propensities of every
" age of the world. At present the cheats and tricks
" of the priests have roused all men against them, and
" against Christianity. But, at the same time, super-
" stition and fanaticism rule with unlimited dominion,
" and the understanding of man really seems to be
" going backwards. Our task, therefore, is doubled.
" We must give such an account of things, that fana-
" tics should not be alarmed, and that shall, notwith-
" standing, excite a spirit of free enquiry. We must
" not throw away the good with the bad, the child
" with the dirty water; but we must make the secret
" doctrines of Christianity be received as the secrets
" of genuine Free Masonry. But farther, we have to
" deal with the despotism of Princes. This increases
" every day. But then, the spirit of freedom breathes
" and sighs in every corner; and, by the assistance of
" hidden schools of wisdom, Liberty and Equality,
" the natural and imprescriptible rights of man, warm
" and glow in every breast. We must therefore unite
" these extremes. We proceed in this manner.

" Jesus Christ established no new Religion; he
" would only set Religion and Reason in their ancient
" rights.

" rights. For this purpose he would unite men in a
" common bond. He would fit them for this by
" spreading a just morality, by enlightening the un-
" derstanding, and by assisting the mind to shake off
" all prejudices. He would teach all men, in the first
" place, to govern themselves. Rulers would then
" be needless, and equality and liberty would take
" place without any revolution, by the natural and
" gentle operation of reason and expediency. This
" great Teacher allows himself to explain every part
" of the Bible in conformity to these purposes; and
" he forbids all wrangling among his scholars, because
" every man may there find a reasonable application
" to his peculiar doctrines. Let this be true or false, it
" does not signify. This was a simple Religion, and
" it was so far inspired; but the minds of his hearers
" were not fitted for receiving these doctrines. I told
" you, says he, but you could not bear it. Many
" therefore were called, but few were chosen. To
" this elect were entrusted the most important secrets;
" and even among them there were degrees of infor-
" mation. There was a seventy, and a twelve. All
" this was in the natural order of things, and accord-
" ing to the habits of the Jews, and indeed of all an-
" tiquity. The Jewish Theosophy was a mystery;
" like the Eleusinian, or the Pythagorean, unfit for
" the vulgar. And thus the doctrines of Christianity
" were committed to the *Adepti*, in a *Disciplina Arcani*.
" By these they were maintained like the Vestal Fire.—
" They were kept up only in hidden societies, who
" handed them down to posterity; and they are now
" possessed by the genuine Free Masons."

N. B. This explains the origin of many anonymous pamphlets which appeared about this time in Germany, showing that Free Masonry was Christianity.— They have doubtless been the works of Spartacus and
his

his partisans among the Eclectic Masons. Nicholai, the great apostle of infidelity, had given very favourable reviews of these performances, and having always shewn himself an advocate of such writers as depreciated Christianity, it was natural for him to take this opportunity of bringing it still lower in the opinion of the people. Spartacus therefore conceived a high opinion of the importance of gaining Nicholai to the Order. He had before this gained Leuchtsenring, a hotheaded fanatic, who had spied Jesuits in every corner, and set Nicholai on his journey through Germany, to hunt them out. This man finding them equally hated by the Illuminati, was easily gained, and was most zealous in their cause. He engaged Nicholai, and Spartacus exults exceedingly in the acquisition, saying, " that he was an unwearied champion, *et quidem conten-* " *tissimus.*" Of this man Philo says, " that he had
" spread this Christianity into every corner of Ger-
" many. I have put meaning," says Philo, " to all
" these dark symbols, and have prepared both de-
" grees, introducing beautiful ceremonies, which I
" have selected from among those of the ancient com-
" munions, combined with those of the Rosaic Ma-
" sonry; and now," says he, " it will appear that *we*
" are the only true Christians. We shall now be in a
" condition to say a few words to Priests and Princes.
" I have so contrived things, that I would admit even
" Popes and Kings, after the trials which I have pre-
" fixed; and they would be glad to be of the Order."

But how is all this to be reconciled with the plan of Illumination, which is to banish Christianity altogether? Philo himself in many places says, " that it is " only a cloak, to prevent squeamish people from " starting back." This is done pretty much in the same way that was practised in the French Masonry. In one of their Rituals the Master's degree is made

typical

typical of the death of Jesus Christ, the preacher of Brotherly love. But, in the next step, the *Chevalier du Soleil*, it is Reason that has been destroyed and entombed, and the Master in this degree, the *Sublime Philosophe*, occasions the discovery of the place where the body is hid; Reason rises again, and superstition and tyranny disappear, and all becomes clear; man becomes free and happy.

Let us hear Spartacus again.

Spartacus, in another place.

" We must, 1*st*, gradually explain away all our preparatory pious frauds. And when persons of discernment find fault, we must desire them to consider the end of all our labour. This sanctifies our means, which at any rate are harmless, and have been useful, even in this case, because they procured us a patient hearing, when otherwise men would have turned away from us like petted children. This will convince them of our sentiments in all the intervening points; and our ambiguous expressions will then be interpreted into an endeavour to draw answers of any kind, which may show us the minds of our pupils. 2*d*, We must unfold, from history and other writings, the origin and fabrication of all religious lies whatever; and then, 3*d*, We give a critical history of the Order. But I cannot but laugh, when I think of the ready reception which all this has met with from the grave and learned divines of Germany and of England; and I wonder how their William failed when he attempted to establish a Deistical Worship in London, (what can this mean?) for, I am certain, that it must have been most acceptable to that learned and free people. But
" they

"they had not the enlightening of our days." I may here remark, that Weishaupt is presuming too much on the ignorance of his friend, for there was a great deal of this enlightening in England at the time he speaks of, and if I am not mistaken, even this celebrated Professor of Irreligion has borrowed most of his scheme from this kingdom. This to be sure is nothing in our praise. But the PANTHEISTICON of Toland resembles Weishaupt's Illumination in every thing but its rebellion and its villainy. Toland's Socratic Lodge is an elegant pattern for Weishaupt, and his Triumph of Reason, his Philosophic Happiness, his God, or *Anima Mundi*, are all so like the harsh system of Spartacus, that I am convinced that he has copied them, stamping them with the roughness of his own character. But to go on; Spartacus says of the English:

" Their poet Pope made his Essay on Man a system
" of pure naturalism, without knowing it, as Brother
" Chrysippus did with my Priest's Degree, and was
" equally astonished when this was pointed out to him.
" Chrysippus is religious, but not superstitious. Bro-
" ther Lucian (Nicolai, of whom I have already said
" so much) says, that the grave Zolikofer now allows
" that it would be a very proper thing to establish a
" Deistical Worship at Berlin. I am not afraid but
" things will go on very well. But Philo, who was
" entrusted with framing the Priest's Degree, has de-
" stroyed it without any necessity; it would, forsooth,
" startle those who have a hankering for Religion. But
" I always told you that Philo is fanatical and prudish.
" I gave him fine materials, and he has stuffed it full
" of ceremonies and child's play, and as Minos says,
" *c'est jouer la religion*. But all this may be corrected
" in the revision by the *Areopagitæ*."

N. B. I have already mentioned Baron Knigge's conversion to Illuminatism by the M. de Costanza, whose name in the Order was Diomedes. Knigge (henceforth Philo) was, next to Spartacus, the most serviceable man in the Order, and procured the greatest number of members. It was chiefly by his exertions among the Masons in the Protestant countries, that the *Eclectic System* was introduced, and afterwards brought under the direction of the Illuminati. This conquest was owing entirely to his very extensive connections among the Masons. He travelled like a philosopher from city to city, from Lodge to Lodge, and even from house to house, before his Illumination, trying to unite the Masons, and he now went over the same ground to extend the *Eclectic System*, and to get the Lodges put under the direction of the Illuminati, by their choice of the Master and Wardens. By this the Order had an opportunity of noticing the conduct of individuals; and when they had found out their manner of thinking, and that they were fit for their purpose, they never quitted them till they had gained them over to their party. We have seen, that he was by no means void of religious impressions, and we often find him offended with the atheism of Spartacus. Knigge was at the same time a man of the world, and had kept good company. Weishaupt had passed his life in the habits of a college: therefore he knew Knigge's value, and communicated to him all his projects, to be dressed up by him for the taste of society. Philo was of a much more affectionate disposition, with something of a devotional turn, and was shocked at the hard indifference of Spartacus. After labouring four years with great zeal, he was provoked with the disingenuous tricks of Spartacus, and he broke off all connection with the Society in 1784, and some time after published a declaration of all that he had done in it. This is a most excellent account of the plan and principles of the Order, (at least as he conceived it,

Q for

for Spartacus had much deeper views,) and shows that the aim of it was to abolish Christianity, and all the state-governments in Europe, and to establish a great republic. But it is full of romantic notions and enthusiastic declamation, on the hackneyed topics of universal citizenship, and liberty and equality. Spartacus gave him line, and allowed him to work on, knowing that he could discard him when he chose. I shall after this give some extracts from Philo's letters, from which the reader will see the vile behaviour of Spartacus, and the nature of his ultimate views. In the mean time we may proceed with the account of the principles of the system.

Spartacus to Cato.

" Nothing would be more profitable to us than a
" right history of mankind. Despotism has robbed
" them of their liberty. How can the weak obtain
" protection? Only by union; but this is rare. No-
" thing can bring this about but hidden societies.
" Hidden schools of wisdom are the means which will
" one day free men from their bonds. These have in
" all ages been the archives of nature, and of the
" rights of men; and by them shall human nature be
" raised from her fallen state. Princes and nations
" shall vanish from the earth. The human race will
" then become one family, and the world will be the
" dwelling of rational men.

" Morality alone can do this. The Head of every
" family will be what Abraham was, the patriarch, the
" priest, and the unlettered lord of his family, and
" Reason will be the code of laws to all mankind.
" This," says Spartacus, " is our GREAT SECRET.
" True, there may be some disturbance; but by and
" by

CHAP. II.   THE ILLUMINATI.   123

"by the unequal will become equal; and after the
"storm all will be calm. Can the unhappy conse-
"quences remain when the grounds of diffension are
"removed? Rouse yourselves therefore, O men! af-
"sert your rights; and then will Reason rule with un-
"perceived sway; and ALL SHALL BE HAPPY.*

"Morality will perform all this; and morality is
"the fruit of Illumination; duties and rights are reci-
"procal. Where Octavius has no right, Cato owes
"him no duty. Illumination shews us our rights, and
"Morality follows; that Morality which teaches us
"to be *of age*, to be *out of wardenship*, to be *full grown*,
"and to *walk without the leading strings of priests and
"princes.*"

"Jesus of Nazareth, the Grand Master of our Or-
"der, appeared at a time when the world was in the
"utmost disorder, and among a people who for ages
"had groaned under the yoke of bondage. He taught
"them the lessons of Reason. To be more effective,
"he took in the aid of Religion—of opinions which
"were current—and, in *a very clever manner*, he com-
"bined his secret doctrines with the popular religion,
"and with the customs which lay to his hand. In
"these he wrapped up his lessons—he taught by para-
"bles. Never did any prophet lead men so easily and
"so securely along the road of liberty. He concealed
"the precious meaning and consequences of his doc-
"trines; but fully disclosed them to a chosen few. He
"speaks of a kingdom of the upright and faithful; his
"Father's kingdom, whose children we also are. Let
"us only take Liberty and Equality as the great aim
"of

---

* Happy France! Cradle of Illumination, where the morning of Reason has dawned, dispelling the clouds of Monarchy and Christianity, where the babe has sucked the blood of the unenlightened, and Murder! Fire! Help! has been the lullaby to sing it to sleep.

" of his doctrines, and Morality as the way to attain it,
" and every thing in the New Testament will be com-
" prehensible; and Jesus will appear as the Redeemer
" of slaves. Man is fallen from the condition of Li-
" berty and Equality, the STATE OF PURE NATURE.
" He is under subordination and civil bondage, arising
" from the vices of man. This is the FALL, and
" ORIGINAL SIN. The KINGDOM OF GRACE is that
" restoration which may be brought about by Illumi-
" nation and a just Morality. This is the NEW BIRTH.
" When man lives under government, he is fallen, his
" worth is gone, and his nature tarnished. By subdu-
" ing our passions, or limiting their cravings, we may
" recover a great deal of our original worth, and live
" in a state of grace. This is the redemption of men
" —this is accomplished by Morality; and when this
" is spread over the world, we have THE KINGDOM
" OF THE JUST.

" But, alas! the task of self-formation was too hard
" for the subjects of the Roman empire, corrupted by
" every species of profligacy. A chosen few received
" the doctrines in secret, and they have been handed
" down to us (but frequently almost buried under rub-
" bish of man's invention) by the Free Masons. These
" three conditions of human society are expressed by
" the rough, the split, and the polished stone. The
" rough stone, and the one that is split, express our
" condition under civil government; rough by every
" fretting inequality of condition; and split, since we
" are no longer one family; and are farther divided
" by differences of government, rank property, and
" religion; but when reunited in one family, we are
" represented by the polished stone. G. is Grace;
" the Flaming Star is the Torch of Reason. Those
" who possess this knowledge are indeed ILLUMINATI.
" Hiram is our fictitious Grand Master, slain for the

" REDEMP-

CHAP. II. THE ILLUMINATI.

" REDEMPTION OF SLAVES; the Nine Masters are
" the Founders of the Order. Free Masonry is a
" Royal Art, inasmuch as it teaches us to walk with-
" out trammels, and to govern ourselves."

Reader, are you not curious to learn something of this all-powerful morality, so operative on the heart of the truly illuminated—of this *disciplina arcani*, entrusted only to the chosen few, and handed down to Professor Weishaupt, to Spartacus, and his associates, who have cleared it of the rubbish heaped on it by the dim-sighted Masons, and now beaming in its native lustre on the minds of the *Areopagitæ*? The teachers of ordinary Christianity have been labouring for almost 2000 years, with the New Testament in their hands; many of them with great address, and many, I believe, with honest zeal. But alas! they cannot produce such wonderful and certain effects, (for observe, that Weishaupt repeatedly assures us that his means are certain,) probably for want of this *disciplina arcani*, of whose efficacy so much is said. Most fortunately, Spartacus has given us a brilliant specimen of the ethics which illuminated himself on a trying occasion, where an ordinary Christian would have been much perplexed, or would have taken a road widely different from that of this illustrious apostle of light. And seeing that several of the *Areopagitae* co-operated in the transaction, and that it was carefully concealed from the profane and dim-sighted world, we can have no doubt but that it was conducted according to the *disciplina arcani* of Illumination. I shall give it in his own words.

Spartacus to Marius, September 1783.

" I am now in the most embarrassing situation; it
" robs me of all rest, and makes me unfit for every
" thing.

" thing. I am in danger of losing at once my honour
" and my reputation, by which I have long had such
" influence. What think you?—my sister-in-law is
" with child. I have sent her to Euriphon, and am
" endeavouring to procure a marriage-licence from
" Rome. How much depends on this uncertainty—
" and there is not a moment to lose. Should I fail,
" what is to be done? What a return do I make by
" this to a person to whom I am so much obliged!"
(We shall see the probable meaning of this exclamation by and by). " We have tried every method in
" our power to destroy the child; and I hope she is
" determined on every thing—even d——." (Can this
mean death?) " But alas! Euriphon is, I fear, too ti-
" mid," (alas! poor woman, thou art now under
the *disciplina arcani*,) " and I see no other expedient.
" Could I be but assured of the silence of Celsus, (a
" physician at Ingolstadt,) he *can* relieve me, and he
" *promised me as much* three years ago. Do speak to
" him, if you think he will be staunch. I would not let
" Cato" (his dearest friend, and his chief or only confident in the scheme of Illumination) " know it yet,
" because the affair in other respects requires his whole
" friendship." (Cato had all the pretty receipts.)
" Could you but help me out of this distress, you
" would give me life, honour, and peace, *and strength
" to work again in the great cause*. If you cannot, be
" assured I will venture on the most desperate stroke,"
(poor sister!) " for it is fixed.—I will not lose my ho-
" nour. I cannot conceive what devil has made me go
" astray—*me who have always been so careful on such oc-
" casions*. As yet all is quiet, and none know of it but
" you and Euriphon. Were it but time to undertake
" any thing—but alas! it is the fourth month. Those
" damned priests too—for the action is so criminally
" accounted by them, and scandalises the blood. This
" makes

" makes the utmost efforts and the most desperate
" measures absolutely necessary."

It will throw some light on this transaction if we read a letter from Spartacus to Cato about this time.

" One thing more, my dearest friend—Would it be
" agreeable to you to have me for a brother-in-law?
" If this should be agreeable, and if it can be brought
" about without prejudice to my honour, as I hope it
" may, I am not without hopes that the connection
" may take place. But in the mean time keep it a
" secret, and only give me permission to enter into
" correspondence on the subject with the good lady,
" to whom I beg you will offer my respectful compli-
" ments, and I will explain myself more fully to you
" by word of mouth, and tell you my whole situation.
" But I repeat it—the thing must be gone about with
" address and caution. I would not for all the world
" deceive a person who certainly has not deserved so
" of me."

What interpretation can be put on this? Cato seems to be brother to the poor woman—he was unwittingly to furnish the drugs, and he was to be dealt with about consenting to a marriage, which could not be altogether agreeable to him, since it required a dispensation, she being already the sister-in-law of Weishaupt, either the sister of his former wife, or the widow of a deceased brother. Or perhaps Spartacus really wishes to marry Cato's sister, a different person from the poor woman in the straw; and he conceals this adventure from his trusty friend Cato, till he sees what becomes of it. The child may perhaps be got rid of, and then Spartacus is a free man. There is a letter to Cato, thanking him for his friendship in the affair of the child—but it gives no light. I meet with another account, that the sister of Zwack threw herself from the top of a tower, and beat out her brains. But it is not said that

that it was an only fifter; if it was, the probability is, that Spartacus had paid his addreffes to her, and fucceeded, and that the fubfequent affair of his marriage with his fifter-in-law, or fomething worfe, broke her heart. This feems the beft account of the matter. For Hertel (Marius) writes to Zwack in November 1782: " Spartacus is this day gone home, but has left " his fifter-in-law pregnant behind (this is from Baffus " Hoff). About the new year he hopes to be made " merry by a ———, who will be before all kings and " princes—a young Spartacus. The Pope alfo will " refpect him, and legitimate him before the time."

Now, vulgar Chriftian, compare this with the former declaration of Weifhaupt, where he appeals to the tenor of his former life, which had been fo feverely fcrutinifed, without diminifhing his high reputation and great influence, and his ignorance and abhorrence of all thofe things found in Cato's repofitories. You fee this was a furprife—he had formerly proceeded cautioufly—" He is the beft man," fays Spartacus, " who beft conceals his faults."—He was difappointed by Celfus, *who had promifed him his affiftance on fuch occafions* three years ago, during all which time he had been bufy in " forming himfelf." How far he has advanced, the reader may judge.

One is curious to know what became of the poor woman: fhe was afterwards taken to the houfe of Baron Baffus; but here the foolifh woman, for want of that courage which Illumination and the bright profpect of eternal fleep fhould have produced, took fright at the *difciplini arcani*, left the houfe, and in the hidden fociety of a midwife and nurfe brought forth a young Spartacus, who now lives to thank his father for his endeavours to murder him. A " *damned prieft*," the good Bifhop of Freyfingen, knowing the cogent reafons, procured the difpenfation, and Spartacus was
obliged,

obliged, like another dim-fighted mortal, to marry her. The fcandal was hufhed, and would not have been difcovered had it not been for thefe private writings.

But Spartacus fays " that when you think
" him funk to the bottom, he will fpring up with
" double vigour." In a fubfequent work, called *Short Amendment of my Plan*, he fays, " If men were
" not habituated to wicked manners, his letters would
" be their own juftification." He does not fay that he is without fault; " but they are faults of the under-
" ftanding—not of the heart. He had, firft of all, to
" form himfelf; and this is a work of time." In the affair of his fifter-in-law he admits the facts, and the attempts to deftroy the child; " but this is far from
" proving any depravity of heart. In his condition,
" his honour at ftake, what elfe was left him to do?
" His greateft enemies, the Jefuits, have taught that
" in fuch a cafe it is lawful to make away with the
" child," and he quotes authorities from their books.*
" In the introductory fault he has the example of the
" beft of men. The fecond was its natural confe-
" quence, it was altogether involuntary, and, in the
" eye of a philofophical judge" (I prefume of the Gallic School) " who does not fquare himfelf by the harfh
" letters of *a blood-thirfty lawgiver*, he has but a very
" trifling account to fettle. He had become a public
" teacher, and was greatly followed; this example
" *might have ruined many young men*. The eyes of the
" Order alfo were fixed on him. The edifice refted
" on his credit; had he fallen, *he could no longer have*
    R   " been

---

* This is flatly contradicted in a pamphlet by F. Stuttler, a Catholic clergyman of moft refpectable character, who here expofes, in the moft incontrovertible manner, the impious plots of Weifhaupt, his total difregard to truth, his counterfeit antiques, and all his lies againft the Jefuits.

" been in a condition to treat the matters of virtue so as to
" make a lasting impression. It was chiefly his anxiety
" to support the credit of the Order which determined
" him to take this step. It makes *for* him, but by no
" means *against* him; and the persons who are most
" in fault are the slavish inquisitors, who have pub-
" lished the transaction, in order to make his charac-
" ter more remarkable, and to hurt the Order through
" his person; and they have not scrupled, for this hel-
" lish purpose, to stir up a child against his father!!!"

I make no reflections on this very remarkable, and highly useful story, but content myself with saying, that this justification by Weishaupt (which I have been careful to give in his own words) is the greatest instance of effrontery and insult on the sentiments of mankind that I have ever met with. We are all supposed as completely corrupted as if we had lived under the full blaze of Illumination.

In other places of this curious correspondence we learn that Minos, and others of the *Areopagitæ*, wanted to introduce Atheism at once, and not go hedging in the manner they did; affirming it was easier to shew at once that Atheism was friendly to society, than to explain all their Masonic Christianity, which they were afterwards to shew to be a bundle of lies. Indeed this purpose, of not only abolishing Christianity, but all positive religion whatever, was Weishaupt's favourite scheme from the beginning. Before he canvassed for his Order, in 1774, he published a fictitious antique, which he called *Sidonii Apollinarus Fragmenta*, to prepare (as he expressly says in another place) mens minds for the doctrines of Reason, which contains all the detestable doctrines of Robinet's book *De la Nature*. The publication of the second part was stopped. Weishaupt says in his APOLOGY FOR THE ILLUMINATI, that before 1780 he had retracted his opinions about Materialism.

alifm, and about the inexpediency of Princes. But this is falfe: Philo fays exprefsly, that every thing remained on its original footing in the whole practice and dogmas of the Order when he quitted it in July 1784. All this was concealed, and even the abominable Mafonry, in the account of the Order which Weifhaupt publifhed at Regenfburg; and it required the conftant efforts of Philo to prevent bare or flat Atheifm from being uniformly taught in their degrees. He had told the council that Zeno would not be under a roof with a man who denied the immortality of the foul. He complains of Minos's cramming irreligion down their throats in every meeting, and fays, that he frightened many from entering the Order. " Truth," fays Philo, " is a clever, but a modeft girl, who muft " be led by the hand like a gentlewoman, but not " kicked about like a whore." Spartacus complains much of the fqueamifhnefs of Philo; yet Philo is not a great deal behind him in irreligion. When defcribing to Cato the Chriftianity of the Prieft-degree, as he had manufactured it, he fays, " It is all one whe-
" ther it be true or falfe, we muft have it, that we
" may tickle thofe who have a hankering for religion."
All the odds feems to be, that he was of a gentler difpofition, and had more deference even for the abfurd prejudices of others. In one of his angry letters to Cato he fays: " The vanity and felf-conceit of Spar-
" tacus would have got the better of all prudence, had
" I not checked him, and prevailed on the *Areopagitæ*
" but to defer the developement of the bold principles
" till we had firmly fecured the man. I even wifhed
" to entice the candidate the more by giving him back
" all his former bonds of fecrecy, and leaving him at
" liberty to walk out without fear; and I am certain
" that they were, by this time, fo engaged that we
" fhould not have loft one man. But Spartacus had
" compofed an exhibition of his laft principles, for a
" difcourfe

discourse of reception, in which he painted his three
"favourite mysterious degrees, which were to be con-
"ferred by him alone, in colours which had fascina-
"ted his own fancy. But they were the colours of
"hell, and would have scared the most intrepid; and
"because I represented the danger of this, and by
"force obtained the omission of this picture, he be-
"came my implacable enemy. I abhor treachery
"and profligacy, and leave him to blow himself and
"his Order into the air."

Accordingly this happened. It was this which terrified one of the four professors, and made him impart his doubts to the rest. Yet Spartacus seems to have profited by the apprehensions of Philo; for in the last reception, he, for the first time, exacts a bond from the intrant, engaging himself for ever to the Order, and swearing that he will never draw back. Thus admitted, he becomes a sure card. The course of his life is in the hands of the Order, and his thoughts on a thousand dangerous points; his reports concerning his neighbours and friends; in short, his honour and his neck. The Deist, thus led on, has not far to go before he becomes a Naturalist or Atheist; and then the eternal sleep of death crowns all his humble hopes.

Before giving an account of the higher degrees, I shall just extract from one letter more on a singular subject.

Minos to Sebastian, 1782.

"The proposal of Hercules to establish a Minerval
"school for girls is excellent, but requires much cir-
"cumspection. Philo and I have long conversed on
"this subject. We cannot improve the world with-
"out improving women, who have such a mighty in-
"fluence on the men. But how shall we get hold of
                                                "them?

" them ? How will their relations, particularly their
" mothers, immerfed in prejudices, confent that others
" fhall influence their education ? We muft begin with
" grown girls. Hercules propofes the wife of Ptole-
" my Magus. I have no objection ; and I have four
" ftep-daughters, fine girls. The oldeft in particular
" is excellent. She is twenty-four, has read much, is
" above all prejudices, and in religion fhe thinks as I do.
" They have much acquaintance among the young la-
" dies their relations. (N. B. We don't know the rank
" of Minos, but as he does not ufe the word *Damen,*
" but *Frauenzimmer,* it is probable that it is not high.)
" It may immediately be a very pretty Society, under
" the management of Ptolemy's wife, but really un-
" der *his* management. You muft contrive pretty de-
" grees, and dreffes, and ornaments, and elegant and
" decent rituals. No man muft be admitted. This
" will make them become more keen, and they will
" go much farther than if we were prefent, or than if
" they thought that we knew of their proceedings.
" Leave them to the fcope of their own fancies, and
" they will foon invent myfteries which will put us to
" the blufh, and create an enthufiafm which we can
" never equal. They will be our great apoftles. Re-
" flect on the refpect, nay the awe and terror infpired
" by the female myftics of antiquity. (Think of the
" Daniads—think of the Theban *Bacchantes.*) Ptole-
" my's wife mutt direct them, and fhe will be inftruct-
" ed by Ptomlemy, and my ftep-daughters will con-
" fult with me. We muft always be at hand to pre-
" vent the introduction of any improper queftion. We
" muft prepare themes for their difcuffion—thus we
" fhall confefs them, and infpire them with our fenti-
" ments. No man however muft come near them.
" This will fire their roving fancies, and we may ex-
" pect rare myfteries. But I am doubtful whether
" this

"this Affociation will be durable. Women are fickle
"and impatient. Nothing will pleafe them but hur-
",ying from degree to degree, through a heap of in-
"fignificant ceremonies, which will foon lofe their
"novelty and influence. To reft ferioufly in one
"rank, and to be ftill and filent when they have found
"out that the whole is a cheat, (hear the words of an
"experienced Mafon,) is a talk of which they are in-
"capable. They have not our motives to perfevere
"for years, allowing themfelves to be led about, and
"even then to hold their tongues when they find that
"they have been deceived. Nay there is a rifk that
"they may take it into their heads to give things an
"oppofite turn, and then, by voluptuous allurements,
"heightened by affected modefty and decency, which
"give them an irrefiftible empire over the beft men,
"they may turn our Order upfide down, and in their
"turn will lead the new one."

Such is the information which may be got from the private correfpondence. It is needlefs to make more extracts of every kind of vice and trick. I have taken fuch as fhew a little of the plan of the Order, as far as the degree of *Illuminatus Minor*, and the vile purpofes which are concealed under all their fpecious declamation. A very minute account is given of the plan, the ritual, ceremonies, &c. and even the inftructions and difcourfes, in a book called the *Achte Illuminat*, publifhed at *Edeffa* (Frankfurt) in 1787. Philo fays, "that this is quite accurate, but that he does "not know the author." I proceed to give an account of their higher degrees, as they are to be feen in the book called *Neuefte Arbeitung des Spartacus und Philo*. And the authenticity of the accounts is attefted by Grollman, a private gentleman of independent fortune, who read them, figned and fealed by Spartacus and the *Areopagitæ*.

The

CHAP. II.   THE ILLUMINATI.   135

The series of ranks and progress of the pupil were arranged as follows:

- **Nursery**
  - Preparation,
  - Novice,
  - Minerval,
  - Illumin. Minor.
- **Masonry**
  - *Symbolic*
    - Apprentice,
    - Fellow Craft,
    - Master,
  - *Scotch*
    - Illum. Major, Scotch Novice
    - Illum. dirigens, Scotch Knight.
- **Mysteries**
  - Lesser
    - Presbyter, Priest,
    - Prince, Regent,
  - Greater
    - Magus,
    - Rex.

The reader must be almost sick of so much villany, and would be disgusted with the minute detail, in which the cant of the Order is ringing continually in his ears. I shall therefore only give such a short extract as may fix our notions of the object of the Order, and the morality of the means employed for attaining it. We need not go back to the lower degrees, and shall begin with the ILLUMINATUS DIRIGENS, or SCOTCH KNIGHT.

After a short introduction, teaching us how the holy secret Chapter of Scotch Knights is assembled, we have, I. Fuller accounts and instructions relating to the whole. II. Instructions for the lower classes of Masonry. III. Instructions relating to Mason Lodges in general. IV. Account of a reception into this degree, with the bond which each subscribes before he can be admitted. V. Concerning the Solemn Chapter for reception. VI. Opening of the Chapter. VII. Ritual of Reception, and the Oath. VIII. Shutting of the Chapter. IX. *Agapé*,

Agapé, or Love-Feaft. X. Ceremonies of the confecration of the Chapter. Appendix A, Explanation of the Symbols of Free Mafonry. B, Catechifm for the Scotch Knight. C, Secret Cypher.

In N° I. it is faid that the " chief ftudy of the " Scotch Knight is to work on all men in fuch a way " as is moft infinuating. II. He muft endeavour to " acquire the poffeffion of confiderable property. III. " In all Mafon Lodges we muft try fecretly to get the " upper hand. The Mafons do not know what Free-" Mafonry is, their high objects, nor their higheft " Superiors, and fhould be directed by thofe who will " lead them along the right road. In preparing a can-" didate for the degree of Scotch Knighthood, we " muft bring him into dilemmas by enfnaring queftions. " —We muft endeavour to get the difpofal of the mo-" ney of the Lodges of the Free Mafons, or at leaft " take care that it be applied to purpofes favourable " to our Order—but this muft be done in a way that " fhall not be remarked. Above all, we muft pufh " forward with all our fkill, the plan of Eclectic Ma-" fonry, and for this purpofe follow up the circular " letter already fent to all the Lodges with every " thing that can increafe their prefent embarraffment." In the bond of N° IV. the candidate binds himfelf to " confider and treat the Illuminati as the Superiors of " Free Mafonry, and endeavour in all the Mafon " Lodges which he frequents, to have the Mafonry of " the Illuminated, and particularly the Scotch Novi-" tiate, introduced into the Lodge." (This is not very different from the Mafonry of the *Chevalier de l'Aigle* of the Rofaic Mafonry, making the Mafter's degree a fort of commemoration of the paffion, but without giving that character to Chriftianity which is peculiar to Illuminatifm.) Jefus Chrift is reprefented as the enemy of fuperftitious obfervances, and the af-

fertor

fertor of the Empire of Reason and of Brotherly love, and his death and memory as dear to mankind. This evidently paves the way for Weishaupt's Christianity. The Scotch Knight also engages " to consider the
" Superiors of the Order as the unknown Superiors of
" Free Masonry, and to contribute all he can to their
" gradual union." In the Oath, N° VII. the candidate says, " I will never more be a flatterer of the great,
" I will never be a lowly servant of princes ; but I will
" strive with spirit, and with address, for virtue, wis-
" dom, and liberty. I will powerfully oppose super-
" stition, slander, and despotism ; so that, like a true
" son of the Order, I may serve the world. I will
" never sacrifice the general good, and the happiness
" of the world, to my private interest. I will boldly
" defend my brother against slander, will follow out
" the traces of the pure and true Religion pointed out
" to me in my instructions, and in the doctrines of
" Masonry ; and will faithfully report to my Su-
" periors the progress I make therein."

When he gets the stroke which dubs him a Knight, the Preses says to him, " Now prove thyself, by thy
" ability, equal to Kings, and never from this time
" forward bow thy knee to one who is, like thyself but
" a man."

N° IX. is an account of the Love-Feast.

1*st*, There is a Table Lodge, opened as usual, but in virtue of the ancient Master-word. Then it is said, " Let moderation, fortitude, morality, and genuine
" love of the Brethren, with the overflowing of inno-
" cent and careless mirth reign here." (This is almost verbatim from Toland.)

2*d*, In the middle of a bye-table is a chalice, a pot of wine, an empty plate, and a plate of unleavened bread—All is covered with a green cloth.

3*d*, When

3d, When the Table Lodge is ended, and the Prefect sees no obstacle, he strikes on this bye-table the stroke of Scotch Master, and his signal is repeated by the Senior Warden. All are still and silent. The Prefect lifts off the cloth.

4th, The Prefect asks, whether the Knights are in the disposition to partake of the Love-Feast in earnest, peace, and contentment. If none hesitates or offers to retire, he takes the plate with the bread and says,

" J. of N. our Grand-Master, in the night in which
" he was betrayed by his friends, persecuted for his
" love for truth, imprisoned, and condemned to die,
" assembled his trusty Brethren, to celebrate his last
" Love-Feast—which is signified to us in many ways.
" He took bread (taking it) and broke it (breaking
" it) and blessed it, and gave it to his disciples, &c.
" —This shall be the mark of our Holy Union, &c.
" Let each of you examine his heart, whether love
" reigns in it, and whether he, in full imitation of our
" Grand-Master, is ready to lay down his life for his
" Brethren.

" Thanks be to our Grand-Master, who has ap-
" pointed this feast as a memorial of his kindness, for
" the uniting of the hearts of those who love him.—
" Go in peace, and blessed be this new Association
" which we have formed.—Blessed be ye who remain
" loyal and strive for the good cause."

5th, The Prefect immediately closes the Chapter with the usual ceremonies of the *Loge de Table.*

6th, It is to be observed, that no priest of the Order must be present at this Love-Feast, and that even the Brother Servitor quits the Lodge.

I must observe here, that Philo, the manufacturer of this ritual, has done it very injudiciously; it has no resemblance whatever to the Love-Feast of the primitive Christians, and is merely a copy of a similar thing in one of the steps of French Masonry. Philo's reading in church-history was probably very scanty, or he trusted that the candidates would not be very nice in their examination of it, and he imagined that it would do well enough, and "tickle such as had a religious "hankering." Spartacus disliked it exceedingly—it did not accord with his serious conceptions, and he justly calls it *Jouer la Religion.*

The discourse of reception is to be found also in the secret correspondence (*Nachtrag* II. *Abtheilung*, p. 44.). But it is needless to insert it here. I have given the substance of this and of all the Cosmo-political declamations already in the panegeric introduction to the account of the process of education. And in Spartacus's letter, and in Philo's, I have given an abstract of the introduction to the explanation given in this degree of the symbols of Free Masonry. With respect to the explanation itself, it is as slovenly and wretched as can be imagined, and shews that Spartacus trusted to much more operative principles in the human heart for the reception of his nonsense than the dictates of unbiassed reason. None but promising subjects were admitted thus far—such as would not boggle; and their principles were already sufficiently apparent to assure him that they would be contented with any thing that made game of religion, and would be diverted by the seriousness which a chance devotee might exhibit during these silly caricatures of Christianity and Free Masonry. But there is considerable address in the way that Spartacus prepares his pupils for having all this mummery shewn in its true colours, and overturned.

"Examine, read, think on these symbols. There "are many things which one cannot find out without "a guide, nor even learn without instruction. They "require study and zeal. Should you in any future "period think that you have conceived a clearer no-
"tion

"tion of them, that you have found a paved road,
"declare your difcoveries to your Superiors; it is
"thus that you improve your mind; they expect this
"of you; *they* know the true path—but will not point
"it out—enough if they affift you in every approach
"to it, and warn you when you recede from it. They
"have even put things in your way to try your powers
"of leading yourfelf through the difficult track of dif-
"covery. In this procefs the weak head finds only
"child's play—the initiated finds objects of thought
"which language cannot exprefs, and the thinking
"mind finds food for his faculties." By fuch fore-
warnings as thefe Weifhaupt leaves room for any de-
viation, for any fentiment or opinion of the individual
that he may afterwards choofe to encourage, and "to
"whifper in their ear (as he expreffes it) many things
"which he did not find it prudent to infert in a print-
"ed compend."

But all the principles and aim of Spartacus and of his Order are moft diftinctly feen in the third or Myftery Clafs. I proceed therefore to give fome account of it. By the Table it appears to have two degrees, the Leffer and the Greater Myfteries, each of which have two departments, one relating chiefly to Religion and the other to Politics.

The Prieft's degree contains, 1. an Introduction, 2. Further Accounts of the Reception into this degree, 3. What is called Inftruction in the Third Chamber, which the candidate muft read over. 4. The Ritual of Reception. 5. Inftruction for the Firft Degree of the Prieft's Clafs, called *Inftructio in Scientificis*. 6. Account of the Confecration of a Dean, the Superior of this Lower Order of Priefts.

The Regent degree contains, 1. Directions to the Provincial concerning the difpenfation of this degree. 2. Ritual of Reception. 3. Syftem of Direction for the whole Order. 4. Inſtruction for the whole Regent degree. 5. Inſtruction for the Prefects or Local Superiors. 6. Inſtruction for the Provincials.

The moſt remarkable thing in the Prieſt's degree is the Inſtruction in the Third Chamber. It is to be found in the private correſpondence (*Nachtrage Original Schriften* 1787, 2d. *Abtheilung*, page 44.). There it has the title *Diſcourſe to the Illuminati Dirigentes*, or Scotch Knights. In the critical hiſtory, which is annexed to the *Neueſte Arbeitung*, there is an account given of the reaſon for this denomination; and notice is taken of ſome differences between the inſtructions here contained and that diſcourſe.

This inſtruction begins with ſore complaints of the low condition of the human race; and the cauſes are deduced from religion and ſtate-government. " Men
" originally led a patriarchal life, in which every fa-
" ther of a family was the ſole lord of his houſe and
" his property, while he himſelf poſſeſſed general free-
" dom and equality. But they ſuffered themſelves to
" be oppreſſed—gave themſelves up to civil ſocieties,
" and formed ſtates. Even by this they fell; and this
" is the fall of man, by which they were thruſt into
" unſpeakable miſery. To get out of this ſtate, to
" be freed and born again, there is no other mean
" than the uſe of pure Reaſon, by which a general
" morality may be eſtabliſhed, which will put man in
" a condition to govern himſelf, regain his original
" worth, and diſpenſe with all political ſupports, and
" and particularly with rulers. This can be done in
" no other way but by ſecret aſſociations, which will
" by degrees, and in ſilence, poſſeſs themſelves of the
" government of the States, and make uſe of thoſe
" means for this purpoſe, which the wicked uſe for at-
" attaining their baſe ends. Princes and Prieſts are
" in particular, and *kat' exochen* the wicked, whoſe
" hands

" hands we must tie up by means of these associations, if we cannot root them out altogether.

" Kings are parents. The paternal power ceases with the incapacity of the child; and the father injures his child, if he pretends to retain his right beyond this period. When a nation comes of age, their state of wardship is at an end."

Here follows a long declamation against patriotism, as a narrow-minded principle when compared with true Cosmo-politism. Nobles are represented as " a race of men that serve not the nation but the Prince, whom a hint from the Sovereign stirs up against the nation, who are retained servants and ministers of despotism, and the mean for oppressing national liberty. Kings are accused of a tacit convention, under the flattering appellation of the balance of power, to keep nations in subjection.

" The means to regain Reason her rights—to raise liberty from its ashes—to restore to man his original rights—to produce the previous revolution in the mind of man—to obtain an eternal victory over oppressors—and to work the redemption of mankind, are secret schools of wisdom. When the worthy have strengthened their association by numbers, they are secure, and then they begin to become powerful, and terrible to the wicked, of whom many will, for safety, amend themselves—many will come over to our party, and we shall bind the hands of the rest, and finally conquer them. Whoever spreads general Illumination, augments mutual security; Illumination and security make princes unnecessary; Illumination performs this by creating an effective Morality, and Morality makes a nation of full age fit to govern itself; and since it is not impossible to produce a just Morality, it is possible to regain freedom for the world."

" We

"We muſt therefore ſtrengthen our band, and eſta-bliſh a legion, which ſhall reſtore the rights of man, original liberty and independence.

"Jeſus Chriſt"—but I am ſick of all this. The following queſtions are put to the candidate:

1. "Are our civil conditions in the world the deſtinations that ſeem to be the end of our nature, or the purpoſes for which man was placed on this earth, or are they not? Do ſtates, civil obligations, popular religion, fulfil the intentions of men who eſtabliſhed them? Do ſecret aſſociations promote inſtruction and true human happineſs, or are they the children of neceſſity, of the multifarious wants, of unnatural conditions, or the inventions of vain and cunning men?"

2. "What civil aſſociation, what ſcience do you think to the purpoſe, and what are not?"

3. "Has there ever been any other in the world, is there no other more ſimple condition, and what do you think of it?"

4. "Does it appear poſſible, after having gone through all the nonentities of our civil conſtitutions, to recover for once our firſt ſimplicity, and get back to this honourable uniformity?"

5. "How can one begin this noble attempt; by means of open ſupport, by forcible revolution, or by what other way?"

6. "Does Chriſtianity give us any hint to this purpoſe? Does it not recogniſe ſuch a bleſſed condition as once the lot of man, and as ſtill recoverable?"

7. "But is this holy religion the religion that is now profeſſed by any ſect on earth, or is it a better?"

8. "Can we learn this religion—can the world, as it is, bear the light? Do you think that it would be of ſervice, before numerous obſtacles are removed,

"if

" if we taught men this purified religion, sublime phi-
" losophy, and the art of governing themselves? Or
" would not this hurt, by rousing the interested passi-
" ons of men habituated to prejudices, who would op-
" pose this as wicked?"

9. " May it not be more advisable to do away these
" corruptions by little and little, in silence, and for
" this purpose to propagate these salutary and heart-
" consoling doctrines in secret?"

10. " Do we not perceive traces of such a secret
" doctrine in the ancient schools of philosophy, in the
" doctrines and instructions of the Bible, which Christ,
" the Redeemer and Deliverer of the human race,
" gave to his trusty disciples?—Do you not observe
" an education, proceeding by steps of this kind, hand-
" ed down to us from his time till the present?"

In the ceremonial of Reception, crowns and sceptres are represented as tokens of human degradation. "The
" plan of operation, by which our higher degrees act,
" must work powerfully on the world, and must give
" another turn to all our present constitutions."

Many other questions are put to the pupil during his preparation, and his answers are given in writing. Some of these rescripts are to be found in the secret correspondence. Thus, "How far is the position true,
" that all those means may be used for a good purpose
" which the wicked have employed for a bad?" And along with this question there is an injunction to take counsel from the opinions and conduct of the learned and worthy out of the society. In one of the answers, the example of a great philosopher and Cosmopolite is adduced, who betrayed a private correspondence entrusted to him, for the service of freedom: the case was Doctor Franklin's. In another, the power of the Order was extended to the putting the individual to death; and the reason given was, that " this power was allowed
" to

" to all Sovereignties, for the good of the State, and
" therefore belonged to the Order, which was to go-
" vern the world."———" N. B. We muſt acquire the
" direction of education—of church-management—of
" the profeſſorial chair, and of the pulpit. We muſt
" bring our opinions into faſhion by every art—ſpread
" them among the people by the help of young wri-
" ters. We muſt preach the warmeſt concern for hu-
" manity, and *make people indifferent to all other relations*.
" We muſt take care that our writers be well puffed,
" and that the Reviewers do not depreciate them;
" therefore we muſt endeavour by every mean to gain
" over the Reviewers and Journaliſts; and we muſt
" alſo try to gain the bookſellers, who in time will ſee
" that it is their intereſt to ſide with us."

I conclude this account of the degree of Preſbyter with remarking, that there were two copies of it employed occaſionally. In one of them all the moſt offenſive things in reſpect of church and ſtate were left out. The ſame thing was done in the degree of *Chevalier du Soleil* of the French Maſonry. I have ſeen three different forms.

In the Regent degree, the proceedings and inſtructions are conducted in the ſame manner. Here, it is ſaid, " We muſt as much as poſſible ſelect for this de-
" gree perſons who are free, independent of all princes;
" particularly ſuch as have frequently declared them-
" ſelves diſcontented with the uſual inſtitutions, and
" their wiſhes to ſee a better government eſtabliſhed."

Catching queſtions are put to the candidate for this degree; ſuch as,

1. " Would the ſociety be objectionable which
" ſhould (till the greater revolution of nature ſhould
" be ripe) put monarchs and rulers out of the condi-
" tion to do harm; which ſhould in ſilence prevent
" the abuſe of power, by ſurrounding the great with

T " its

" its members, and thus not only prevent their doing
" mischief, but even make them do good?"

2. " Is not the objection unjust, That such a Soci-
" ciety may abuse its power? Do not our rulers fre-
" quently abuse their power, though we are silent?
" This power is not so secure as in the hands of our
" Members, whom we train up with so much care,
" and place about princes after mature deliberation
" and choice. If any government can be harmless
" which is erected by man, surely it must be ours,
" which is founded on morality, foresight, talents, li-
" berty, and virtue," &c.

The candidate is presented for reception in the character of a slave; and it is demanded of him what has brought him into this most miserable of all conditions. He answers—Society—the State—Submissiveness—False Religion. A skeleton is pointed out to him, at the feet of which are laid a Crown and a Sword. He is asked, whether that is the skeleton of a King, a Nobleman, or a Beggar? As he cannot decide, the President of the meeting says to him, " the character of " being a Man is the only one that is of importance."

In a long declamation on the hackneyed topics, we have here and there some thoughts which have not yet come before us.

" We must allow the underlings to imagine, (but
" without telling them the truth,) that we direct all
" the Free Mason Lodges, and even all other Orders,
" and that the greatest monarchs are under our guid-
" ance, which indeed is here and there the case.

" There is no way of influencing men so powerful-
" ly as by means of the women. These should there-
" fore be our chief study; we should insinuate our-
" selves into their good opinion, give them hints of
" emancipation from the tyranny of public opinion,
" and of standing up for themselves; it will be an im-
" mense

" menfe relief to their enflaved minds to be freed from
" any one bond of reftraint, and it will fire them the
" more, and caufe them to work for us with zeal,
" without knowing that they do fo; for they will only
" be indulging their own defire of perfonal admira-
" tion.

" We muft win the common people in every cor-
" ner. This will be obtained chiefly by means of the
" fchools, and by open, hearty behaviour, fhow, con-
" defcenfion, popularity, and toleration of their pre-
" judices, which we fhall at leifure root out and difpel.

" If a writer publifhes any thing that attracts notice,
" and is in itfelf juft, but does not accord with our
" plan, we muft endeavour to win him over, or decry
" him.

" A chief object of our care muft be to keep down
" that flavifh veneration for princes which fo much
" difgraces all nations. Even in the *foi-difant* free En-
" gland, the filly Monarch fays, We are gracioufly
" pleafed, and the more fimple people fay, Amen. Thefe
" men, commonly very weak heads, are only the far-
" ther corrupted by this fervile flattery. But let us at
" once give an example of our fpirit by our behaviour
" with Princes; we muft avoid all familiarity—never
" entruft ourfelves to them—behave with precifion,
" but with civility, as to other men—fpeak of them
" on an equal footing—this will in time teach them
" that they are by nature men, if they have fenfe and
" fpirit, and that only by convention they are Lords.
" We muft affiduoufly collect anecdotes, and the ho-
" nourable and mean actions, both of the leaft and
" the greateft; and when their names occur in any re-
" cords which are read in our meetings, let them
" ever be accompanied by thefe marks of their real
" worth.

" The

" The great strength of our Order lies in its conceal-
" ment; let it never appear in any place in its own
" name, but always covered by another name, and
" another occupation. *None is fitter than the three lower
" degrees of Free Masonry; the public is accustomed to it;
" expects little from it, and therefore takes little notice of it.*
" Next to this the form of a learned or literary society
" is best suited to our purpose, and had Free Masonry
" not existed, this cover would have been employed;
" and it may be much more than a cover, *it may be a
" powerful engine in our hands. By establishing reading
" societies, and subscription libraries, and taking these under
" our direction, and supplying them through our labours, we
" may turn the public mind which way we will.*

" In like manner we must try to obtain an influence
" in the military academies, (this may be of mighty
" consequence,) the printing-houses, booksellers shops,
" chapters, and in short in all offices which have any
" effect, either in forming, or in managing, or even
" in directing the mind of man: painting and engrav-
" ing are highly worth our care*."

" Could our Prefect" (observe it is to the *Illuminati
Regentes* he is speaking, whose officers are *Prefecti*)
" fill the judicatories of a state with our worthy mem-
" bers, he does all that man can do for the Order. It
" is better than to gain the Prince himself. Princes
" should never get beyond the Scotch knighthood.
" They either never prosecute any thing, or they twist
" every thing to their own advantage.

" A Literary Society is the most proper form for
" the introduction of our Order into any state where
" we are yet strangers."   (Mark this!)
" The

---

* (They were strongly suspected of having published some scandalous caricatures, and some very immoral prints.) They scrupled at no mean, however base, for corrupting the nation. Mirabeau had done the same thing at Berlin. By political caricatures
and filthy prints, they corrupt even such as cannot read.

"The power of the Order muſt ſurely be turned to the advantage of its Members. All muſt be aſſiſted. They muſt be preferred to all perſons otherwiſe of equal merit. Money, ſervices, honour, goods, and blood, muſt be expended for the fully proved Brethren, and the unfortunate muſt be relieved by the funds of the Society."

As evidence that this was not only their inſtructions, but alſo their aſſiduous practice, take the following report from the overſeer of Greece (Bavaria).

In Cato's hand-writing.

" The number (about 600) of Members relates to Bavaria alone.

" In Munich there is a well-conſtituted meeting of *Illuminati Majores*, a meeting of excellent *Illuminati Minores*, a reſpectable Grand Lodge, and two Minerval Aſſemblies. There is a Minerval Aſſembly at Freyſſing, at Landſberg, at Burghauſen, at Straſburg, at Ingolſtadt, and at laſt at Regenſburg*.

" At Munich we have bought a houſe, and by clever meaſures have brought things ſo far, that the citizens take no notice of it, and even ſpeak of us with eſteem. We can openly go to the houſe every day, and carry on the buſineſs of the Lodge. This is a great deal for this city. In the houſe is a good muſeum of natural hiſtory, and apparatus for experiments: alſo a library which daily increaſes. The garden is well occupied by botanic ſpecimens, and the whole has the appearance of a ſociety of zealous naturaliſts.

" We get all the literary journals. We take care, by well-timed pieces, to make the citizens and the Princes

* In this ſmall *turbulent* city there were eleven ſecret ſocieties of Maſons, Roſycrucians, Clair-voyants, &c.

" Princes a little more noticed for certain little flips.
" We oppose the monks with all our might, and with
" great success.

" The Lodge is constituted entirely according to our
" system, and has broken off entirely from Berlin, and
" we have nearly finished our transactions with the
" Lodges of Poland, and shall have them under our
" direction.

" By the activity of our Brethren, the Jesuits have
" been kept out of all the professorial chairs at Ingol-
" stadt, and our friends prevail."

" The widow Duchess has set up her academy en-
" tirely according to our plan, and we have all the
" Professors in the Order. Five of them are excellent,
" and the pupils will be prepared for us.

" We have got Pylades put at the head of the Fisc,
" and he has the church-money at his disposal. By
" properly using this money, we have been enabled
" to put our brother ——'s household in good order;
" which he had destroyed by going to the Jews. We
" have supported more Brethren under similar misfor-
" tunes.

" Our Ghostly Brethren have been very fortunate
" this last year, for we have procured for them several
" good benefices, parishes, tutorships, &c.

" Through our means Arminius and Cortes have
" gotten Professorships, and many of our younger
" Brethren have obtained Bursaries by our help.

" We have been very successful against the Jesuits,
" and brought things to such a bearing, that their re-
" venues, such as the Mission, the Golden Alms, the
" Exercises, and the Conversion Box, are now under
" the management of our friends. So are also their con-
" cerns in the university and the German school founda-
" tions. The application of all will be determined
" presently, and we have six members and four friends
" in

" in the Court. This has coft our fenate fome nights
" want of fleep.

" Two of our beft youths have got journies from the
" Court, and they will go to Vienna, where they will
" do us great fervice.

" All the German Schools, and the Benevolent So-
" ciety, are at laft under our direction.

" We have got feveral zealous members in the courts
" of juftice, and we are able to afford them pay, and
" other good additions.

" Lately, we have got poffeffion of the Bartholomew
" Inftitution for young clergymen, having fecured all
" its fupporters. Through this we fhall be able to
" fupply Bavaria with fit priefts.

" By a letter from Philo we learn, that one of the
" higheft dignities in the church was obtained for a
" zealous Illuminatus, in oppofition even to the au-
" thority and right of the Bifhop of Spire, who is re-
" prefented as a bigoted and tyrannical prieft."

Such were the leffer myfteries of the Illuminati. But there remain the higher myfteries. The fyftem of thefe has not been printed, and the degrees were conferred only by Spartacus himfelf, from papers which he never entrufted to any perfon. They were only read to the candidate, but no copy was taken. The publifher of the *Neuefte Arbeitung* fays that he has read them (fo fays Grollman). He fays, " that in the firft degree of
" MAGUS or PHILOSOPHUS, the doctrines are the
" fame with thofe of Spinoza, where all is material,
" God and the world are the fame thing, and all re-
" ligion whatever is without foundation, and, the con-
" trivance of ambitious men." The fecond degree,
or REX, teaches, " that every peafant, citizen, and
" houfeholder is a fovereign, as in the Patriarchal
" ftate, and that nations muft be brought back to that
" ftate, by whatever means are conducible—peaceably,

" ably, if it can be done; but, if not, then by force
" —for all fubordination muſt vaniſh from the face of
" the earth."

The author ſays further, that the German Union was, to his certain knowledge, the work of the Illuminati.

The private correſpondence that has been publiſhed is by no means the whole of what was diſcovered at Landſhut and Baſſus Hoff, and government got a great deal of uſeful information, which was concealed, both out of regard to the families of the perſons concerned, and alſo that the reſt might not know the utmoſt extent of the diſcovery, and be leſs on their guard. A third collection was found under the foundation of the houſe in which the Lodge *Theodor vom guten Rath* had been held. But none of this has appeared. Enough ſurely has been diſcovered to give the public a very juſt idea of the deſigns of the Society and its connections.

Lodges were diſcovered, and are mentioned in the private papers already publiſhed, in the following places.

Munich	Weſtphalia (ſeveral)
Ingolſtadt	Heidelberg
Frankfort	Manheim
Echſtadt	Straſburgh (5)
Hanover	Spire
Brunſwick	Worms
Calbe	Duſſeldorff
Magdeburgh	Cologne
Caſſel	Bonn (4)
Ofnabruck	Livonia (many)
Weimar	Courland (many)
Upper Saxony (ſeveral)	Frankendahl
Auſtria (14)	Alſace (many)
	Vienna

CHAP. II. THE ILLUMINATI. 153

Vienna (4)   Deuxponts
Hesse (many)   Cousel
Buchenwerter   Treves (2)
Mompeliard   Aix-la-Chapelle (2)
Stutgard (3)   Bartschied
Carlsruhe   Hahrenberg
Anspach   Switzerland (many)
Neuwied (2)   Rome
Mentz (2)   Naples
Poland (many)   Ancona
Turin   Florence
England (8)   France
Scotland (2)   Holland (many)
Warsaw (2)   Dresden (4)
America (several.) N. B. This was before 1786.

I have picked up the names of the following members.

Spartacus,   Weishaupt, Professor.
Philo,   Knigge, Freyherr, i. e.
                          Gentleman.
Amelius,   Bode, F. H.
Bayard,   Busche, F. H.
Diomedes,   Constanza, Marq.
Cato,   Zwack, Lawyer.
                        Torring, Count.
                        Khreitmaier, Prince.
                        Utschneider, Professor.
                        Cossandey, Professor.
                        Renner, Professor.
                        Grunberger, Professor.
                        Balderbusch, F. H.
                        Lippert, Counsellor.
                        Kundl, ditto.
                        Bart, ditto.
                                    Leiberhauer,

	Leiberhauer, Prieſt.
	Kundler, Profeſſor.
	Lowling, Profeſſor.
	Vachency, Counſellor.
	Morauſky, Count.
	Hoffſtetter, Surveyor of Roads.
	Strobl, Bookſeller.
Pythagoras,	Weſtenrieder, Profeſſor.
	Babo, Profeſſor.
	Baader, Profeſſor.
	Burzes, Prieſt.
	Pfruntz, Prieſt.
Hannibal,	Baſſus, Baron.
Brutus,	Savioli, Count.
Lucian,	Nicholai, Bookſeller.
	Bahrdt, Clergyman.
Zoroaſter, Confucius,	Baierhamer.
Hermes Triſmegiſtus,	Socher, School Inſpector.
	Dillis, Abbé.
Sulla,	Meggenhoff, Paymaſter.
	Danzer, Canon.
	Braun, ditto.
	Fiſcher, Magiſtrate.
	Frauenberger, Baron.
	Kaltner, Lieutenant.
Pythagoras, (2d,)	Drexl, Librarian.
Marius,	Hertel, Canon.
	Dachſel.
	Dilling, Counſellor.
	Seefeld, Count.
	Gunſheim, ditto.
	Morgellan, ditto.
Saladin,	Ecker, ditto.
	Ow, Major.
	Werner, Counſellor.

Cornelius,

Cornelius Scipio,	Berger, Counsellor.
	Wortz, Apothecary.
	Mauvillon, Colonel.
	Mirabeau, Count.
	Orleans, Duke.
	Hochinaer.
Tycho Brahe,	Gaspar, Merchant.
Thales,	Kapfinger.
Attila,	Sauer.
Ludovicus Bavarus,	Losi.
Shaftesbury,	Steger.
Coriolanus,	Tropponero, Zuschwartz.
Timon,	Michel.
Tamerlane,	Lange.
Livius,	Badorffer.
Cicero,	Pfest.
Ajax,	Massenhausen, Count.

I have not been able to find who personated Minos, Euriphon, Celsius, Mahomet, Hercules, Socrates, Philippo Strozzi, Euclides, and some others who have been uncommonly active in carrying forward the great cause.

The chief publications for giving us regular accounts of the whole, (besides the original writings,) are,
1. *Grosse Absicht des Illuminaten Ordens.*
2. ——— *Nachtrages (3.) an denselben.*
3. *Weishaupt's improved System.*
4. *System des Illum. Ordens aus dem Original-schriften gezogen.*

I may now be permitted to make a few reflections on the accounts already given of this Order, which has so distinctly concentrated the casual and scattered efforts of its prompters, the *Chevaliers Bienfaisants,* the *Philalethes,* and *Amis Reunis* of France, and carried on the system of enlightening and reforming the world.

The

The great aim profeſſed by the Order is to *make men happy;* and the means profeſſed to be employed, as the only and ſurely effective, is *making them good;* and this is to be brought about by *enlightening the mind,* and *freeing it from the dominion of ſuperſtition and prejudices.* This purpoſe is effected by its *producing a juſt and ſteady morality.* This done, and becoming univerſal, there can be little doubt but that the peace of ſociety will be the conſequence,—that government, ſubordination, and all the diſagreeable coercions of civil governments will be unneceſſary,—and that ſociety may go on peaceably in a ſtate of perfect liberty and equality.

But ſurely it requires no angel from heaven to tell us that if every man is virtuous, there will be no vice; and that there will be peace on earth, and good-will between man and man, whatever be the differences of rank and fortune; ſo that Liberty and Equality ſeem not to be the neceſſary conſequences of this juſt Morality, nor neceſſary requiſites for this national happineſs. We may queſtion, therefore, whether the Illumination which makes this a neceſſary condition is a clear and a pure light. It may be a falſe glare ſhowing the object only on one ſide, tinged with partial colours thrown on it by neighbouring objects. We ſee ſo much wiſdom in the general plans of nature, that we are apt to think that there is the ſame in what relates to the human mind, and that the God of nature accompliſhes his plans in this as well as in other inſtances. We are even diſpoſed to think that human nature would ſuffer by it. The rational nature of man is not contented with meat and drink, and raiment, and ſhelter, but is alſo pleaſed with exerting many powers and faculties, and with gratifying many taſtes, which could hardly have exiſtence in a ſociety where all are equal. We ſay that there can be no doubt but that the pleaſure ariſing from the contemplation of the works of art—
the

the pleasure of intellectual cultivation, the pleasure of mere ornament, are rational, distinguish man from a brute, and are so general, that there is hardly a mind so rude as not to feel them. Of all these, and of all the difficult sciences, all most rational, and in themselves most innocent, and most delightful to a cultivated mind, we should be deprived in a society where all are equal. No individual could give employment to the talents necessary for creating and improving these ornamental comforts of life. We are absolutely certain that, even in the most favourable situations on the face of the earth, the most untainted virtue in every breast could not raise man to that degree of cultivation that is possessed by citizens very low in any of the states of Europe; and in the situation of most countries we are acquainted with, the state of man would be much lower: for, at our very setting out, we must grant that the liberty and equality here spoken of must be complete; for there must not be such a thing as a farmer and his cottager. This would be as unjust, as much the cause of discontent, as the gentleman and the farmer.

This scheme therefore seems contrary to the designs of our Creator, who has every where placed us in those situations of inequality that are here so much reprobated, and has given us strong propensities by which we relish those enjoyments. We also find that they may be enjoyed in peace and innocence. And lastly, we imagine that the villain, who, in the station of a professor, would plunder a prince, would also plunder the farmer if he were his cottager. The Illumination therefore that appears to have the best chance of making mankind happy is that which will teach us the Morality which will respect the comforts of cultivated Society, and teach us to protect the possessors in the innocent enjoyment of them; that will enable us to perceive and admire the taste and
elegance

elegance of Architecture and Gardening, without any wish to sweep the palaces, the gardens, and their owner, from off the earth, merely because he is their owner.

We are therefore suspicious of this Illumination, and apt to ascribe this violent antipathy to Princes and subordination to the very cause that makes true Illumination, and just Morality proceeding from it, so necessary to public happiness, namely, the vice and injustice of those who cannot innocently have the command of those offensive elegancies of human life. Luxurious taste, keen desires, and unbridled passions, would prompt to all this; and this Illumination is, as we see, equivalent to them in effect. The aim of the Order is not to enlighten the mind of man, and shew him his moral obligations, and by the practice of his duties to make society peaceable, possession secure, and coercion unnecessary, so that all may be at rest and happy, even though all *were* equal; but to get rid of the coercion which must be employed in the place of Morality, that the innocent rich may be robbed with impunity by the idle and profligate poor. But to do this, an unjust casuistry must be employed instead of a just Morality; and this must be defended or suggested, by misrepresenting the true state of man, and of his relation to the universe, and by removing the restrictions of religion, and giving a superlative value to all those constituents of human enjoyment, which true Illumination shews us to be but very small concerns of a rational and virtuous mind. The more closely we examine the principles and practice of the Illuminati, the more clearly do we perceive that this is the case. Their first and immediate aim is to get the possession of riches, power, and influence, without industry; and to accomplish this, they want to abolish Christianity; and then dissolute manners and universal profligacy will procure them the adherence of all the wicked, and enable them

to

CHAP. II.   THE ILLUMINATI.   159

to overturn all the civil governments of Europe; after which they will think of farther conquests, and extend their operations to the other quarters of the globe, till they have reduced mankind to the state of one undistinguishable chaotic mass.

But this is too chimerical to be thought their real aim. Their Founder, I dare say, never entertained such hopes, nor troubled himself with the fate of distant lands. But it comes in his way when he puts on the mask of humanity and benevolence: it must embrace all mankind, only because it must be stronger than patriotism and loyalty, which stand in his way. Observe that Weishaupt took a name expressive of his principles. Spartacus was a gladiator, who headed an insurrection of Roman slaves, and for three years kept the city in terror. Weishaupt says in one of his letters, " I never was fond of empty titles; but surely " that man has a childish soul who would not as rea- " dily chuse the name of Spartacus as that of Octa- " vius Augustus." The names which he gives to several of his gang express their differences of sentiments. Philo, Lucian, and others, are very significantly given to Knigge, Nicholai, &c. He was vain of the name Spartacus, because he confidered himself as employed somewhat in the same way, leading slaves to freedom. Princes and Priests are mentioned by him on all occasions in terms of abhorrence.

Spartacus employs powerful means. The style of the Jesuits, (as he says,) he considers every mean as consecrated by the end for which it is employed, and he says with great truth,

" *Flectere si nequeo superos, Acheronta movelo.*"

To save his reputation, he scruples not to murder his innocent child, and the woman whom he had held in his arms with emotions of fondness and affection.

But

But left this should appear too selfish a motive, he says, " Had I fallen, my precious Order would have fallen " with me; the Order which is to blefs mankind. I " should not again have been able to speak of virtue so " as to make any lasting impression. My example " might have ruined many young men." This he thinks will excuse, nay sanctify any thing. " My " letters are my greatest vindication." He employs the Christian Religion, which he thinks a fallehood, and which he is afterwards to explode, as the mean for inviting Christians of every denomination, and gradually cajoling them, by clearing up their Christian doubts in succession, till he lands them in Deism; or if he finds them unfit, and too religious, he gives them a *Sta bene*, and then laughs at the fears, or perhaps madness, in which he leaves them. Having got them the length of Deism, they are declared to be fit, and he receives them into the higher mysteries. But left they should still shrink back, dazzled by the Pandemonian glare of Illumination which will now burst upon them, he exacts from them, for the first time, a bond of perseverance. But, as Philo says, there is little chance of tergiversation. The life and honour of most of the candidates are by this time in his hand. They have been long occupied in the vile and corrupting office of spies on all around them, and they are found fit for their present honours, because they have discharged this office to his satisfaction, by the reports which they have given in, containing stories of their neighbours, nay even of their own gang. They may be ruined in the world by disclosing these, either privately or publicly. A man who had once brought himself into this perilous situation durst not go back. He might have been left indeed in any degree of Illumination; and, if Religion has not been quite eradicated from his mind, he must be in that condition of painful anxiety and
doubt

doubt that makes him desperate, fit for the full operation of fanaticism, and he may be engaged, *in the cause of God,* " to commit all kind of wickedness and greedi-
" ness." In this state of mind, a man shuts his eyes, and rushes on. Had Spartacus supposed that he was dealing with good men, his conduct would have been the reverse of all this. There is no occasion for this bond from a person convinced of the excellency of the Order. But he knew them to be unprincipled, and that the higher mysteries were so daring, that even some of such men would start at them. But they must not blab.

Having thus got rid of Religion, Spartacus could with more safety bring into view the great aim of all his efforts—to rule the world by means of his Order. As the immediate mean for attaining this, he holds out the prospect of freedom from civil subordination. Perfect Liberty and Equality are interwoven with every thing; and the flattering thought is continually kept up, that "by the wise contrivance of this Order, the
" most complete knowledge is obtained of the real
" worth of every person; the Order will, *for its own*
" *sake,* and therefore *certainly,* place every man in
" that situation in which he can be most effective. The
" pupils are convinced that the Order *will* rule the
" world. Every member therefore becomes a ruler."
We all think ourselves qualified to rule. The difficult task is to obey with propriety; but we are honestly generous in our prospects of future command. It is therefore an alluring thought, both to good and bad men. By this lure the Order will spread. If they are active in insinuating their members into offices, and in keeping out others, (which the private correspondence shews to have been the case,) they may have had frequent experience of their success in gaining an influence on the world. This must whet their zeal. If

X   Weishaupt

Weishaupt was a sincere Cosmo-polite, he had the pleasure of seeing "his work prospering in his hands."

It surely needs little argument now to prove, that the Order of Illuminati had for its immediate object the abolishing of Christianity, (at least this was the intention of the Founder,) with the sole view of overturning the civil government, by introducing universal dissoluteness and profligacy of manners, and then getting the assistance of the corrupted subjects to overset the throne. The whole conduct in the preparation and instruction of the Presbyter and *Regens* is directed to this point. Philo says, "I have been at unwearied
" pains to remove the fears of some who imagine that
" our Superiors want to abolish Christianity; but by
" and by their prejudices will wear off, and they will
" be more at their ease. Were I to let them know
" that our General holds all Religion to be a lie, and
" uses even Deism, only to lead men by the nose—
" Were I to connect myself again with the Free Ma-
" sons, and tell them our designs to ruin their Fra-
" ternity by this circular letter (a letter to the Lodge
" in Courland)—Were I but to give the least hint to
" any of the Princes of Greece (Bavaria)—No, my
" anger shall not carry me so far.—An Order, forsooth,
" which in this manner abuses human nature—which
" will subject men to a bondage more intolerable than
" Jesuitism—I could put it on a respectable footing,
" and the world would be ours. Should I mention
" our fundamental principles, (even after all the pains
" I have been at to mitigate them,) so unquestionably
" dangerous to the world, who would remain? What
" signifies the innocent ceremonies of the Priest's de-
" gree, as I have composed it, in comparison with
" your maxim, that we may use for a good end those
" means which the wicked employ for a base purpose?"
Brutus

Brutus writes, "Numenius now acquiesces in the "mortality of the soul; but, I fear we shall lose Lu- "dovicus Bavarus. He told Spartacus, that he was "mistaken when he thought that he had swallowed "his stupid Masonry. No, he saw the trick, and did "not admire the end that required it. I don't know "what to do; a *Sta bene* would make him mad, and "he will blow us all up.

"The Order must possess the power of life and "death in consequence of our Oath; and with pro- "priety, for the same reason, and by the same right, "that any government in the world possesses it: for "the Order comes in their place, making them un- "necessary. When things cannot be otherwise, and "ruin would ensue if the Association did not employ "this mean, the Order must, as well as public rulers, "employ it for the good of mankind; therefore for "its own preservation." (N. B. Observe here the casuistry.) "Nor will the political constitutions suf- "fer by this, for there are always thousands equally "ready and able to supply the place."

We need not wonder that Diomedes told the Pro- fessors, "that death, inevitable death, from which no "potentate could protect them, awaited every traitor "of the Order;" nor that the French Convention proposed to take off the German Princes and Generals by sword or poison, &c.

Spartacus might tickle the fancy of his Order with the notion of ruling the world; but I imagine that his own immediate object was ruling the Order. The happiness of mankind was, like Weishaupt's Christi- anity, a mere tool, a tool which the *Regentes* made a joke of. But Spartacus would rule the *Regentes;* this he could not so easily accomplish. His despotism was insupportable to most of them, and finally brought all to light. When he could not persuade them by his

own

own firmness, and indeed by his superior talents and disinterestedness in other respects, and his unwearied activity, he employed jesuitical tricks, causing them to fall out with each other, setting them as spies on each other, and separating any two that he saw attached to each other, by making the one a Master of the other; and, in short, he left nothing undone that could secure his uncontrolled command. This caused Philo to quit the Order, and made *Bassus, Ton Torring, Kreitmaier*, and several other gentlemen, cease attending the meetings; and it was their mutual dissensions which made them speak too freely in public, and call on themselves so much notice. At the time of the discovery, the party of Weishaupt consisted chiefly of very mean people, devoted to him, and willing to execute his orders, that by being his servants, they might have the pleasure of commanding others.

The objects, the undoubted objects of this Association, are surely dangerous and detestable; namely, to overturn the present constitutions of the European States, in order to introduce a chimera which the history of mankind shews to be contrary to the nature of man.

Naturam expellas furcâ, tamen usque recurret.

Suppose it possible, and done in peace, the new system could not stand unless every principle of activity in the human mind be enthralled, all incitement to exertion and industry removed, and man brought into a condition incapable of improvement; and this at the expence of every thing that is valued by the best of men —by misery and devastation—by loosening all the bands of society. To talk of morality and virtue in conjunction with such schemes is an insult to common sense; dissoluteness of manners alone can bring men to think of it.

Is

Is it not aftonifhing, therefore, to hear people in this country exprefs any regard for this inftitution? Is it not moft mortifying to think that there are Lodges of Illuminated among us? I think that nothing bids fairer for weaning our inconfiderate countrymen from having any connection with them, than the faithful account here given. I hope that there are few, very few of our countrymen, and none whom we call friend, who can think that an Order which held fuch doctrines, and which practifed fuch things, can be any thing elfe than a ruinous Affociation, a gang of profligates. All their profeffions of the love of mankind are vain; their Illumination muft be a bewildering blaze, and totally ineffectual for its purpofe, for it has had no fuch influence on the leaders of the band; yet it feems quite adequate to the effects it has produced; for fuch are the characters of thofe who forget God.

If we in the next place attend to their mode of education, and examine it by thofe rules of common fenfe that we apply in other cafes of conduct, we fhall find it equally unpromifing. The fyftem of Illuminatifm is one of the explanations of Free Mafonry; and it has gained many partifans. Thefe explanations reft their credit and their preference on their own merits. There is fomething in themfelves, or in one of them as diftinguifhed from another, which procures it the preference for its own fake. Therefore, to give this Order any dependence on Free Mafonry is to degrade the Order. To introduce a Mafonic Ritual into a manly inftitution, is to degrade it to a frivolous amufement for great children. Men really exerting themfelves to reform the world, and qualified for the tafk, muft have been difgufted with fuch occupations. They betray a frivolous conception of the tafk in which they are really engaged. To imagine that men engaged in the ftruggle and rivalfhip of life, under the influence of

felfifh,

selfish, or mean, or impetuous paffions, are to be wheedled into candid fentiments, or a generous conduct, as a froward child may fometimes be made gentle and tractable by a rattle or humming-top, betrays a great ignorance of human nature, and an arrogant felf-conceit in thofe who can imagine that all but themfelves are babies. The further we proceed, the more do we fee of this *want of wifdom*. The whole procedure of their inftruction fuppofes fuch a complete furrender of freedom of thought, of common fenfe, and of common caution, that it feems impoffible that it fhould not have alarmed every fenfible mind. This indeed happened before the Order was feven years old. It was wife indeed to keep their *Areopagitæ* out of fight; but who can be fo filly as to believe that their unknown Superiors were all and always faultlefs men? But had they been the men they were reprefented to be,—If I have any knowledge of my own heart, or any capacity of drawing juft inferences from the conduct of others, I am perfuaded that the knowing his Superiors would have animated the pupil to exertion, that he might exhibit a pleafing fpectacle to fuch intelligent and worthy judges. Did not the Stoics profefs themfelves to be encouraged in the fcheme of life, by the thought that the immortal Gods were looking on and paffing their judgments on their manner of acting the part affigned them? But what abject fpirit will be contented with working, zealoufly working, for years, after a plan of which he is *never* to learn the full meaning? In fhort, the only knowledge that he can perceive is knowledge in its worft form, *Cunning*. This muft appear in the contrivances by which he will foon find that he is kept in complete fubjection. If he is a true and zealous Brother, he has put himfelf in the power of his Superiors by his refcripts, which they required of him on pretence of their learning his own

character,

character, and of his learning how to know the characters of other men. In these rescripts they have got his thoughts on many delicate points, and on the conduct of others. His Directors may ruin him by betraying him; and this without being seen in it. I should think that wise men would know that none but weak or bad men would subject themselves to such a task. They exclude the good, the manly, the only fit persons for assisting them in their endeavours to inform and to rule the world. Indeed I may say that this exclusion is almost made already by connecting the Order with Free Masonry. Lodges are not the resorts of such men. They may sometimes be found there for an hour's relaxation. But these places are the haunts of the young, the thoughtless, the idle, the weak, the vain, or of designing Literati; and accordingly this is the condition of three-fourths of the Illuminati whose names are known to the public. I own that the reasons given to the pupil for prescribing these tasks are artful, and well adapted to produce their effect. During the flurry of reception, and the glow of expectation, the danger may not be suspected; but I hardly imagine that it will remain unperceived when the pupil sits down to write his first lesson. Mason Lodges, however, were the most likely places for finding and enlisting members. Young men, warmed by declamations teeming with the flimsy moral cant of Cosmo-politism, are in the proper frame of mind for this Illumination. It now appears also, that the dissensions in Free Masonry must have had great influence in promoting this scheme of Weishaupt's, which was, in many particulars, so unpromising, because it presupposes such a degradation of the mind. But when the schismatics in Masonry disputed with warmth, trifles came to acquire unspeakable importance. The hankering after wonder was not in the least abated by

all

all the tricks which had been detected, and the impossibility of the wished-for discovery had never been demonstrated to persons prepossessed in its favour. They still *chose* to believe that the symbols contained some important secret; and happy will be the man who finds it out. The more frivolous the symbols, the more does the heart cling to the mystery; and, to a mind in this anxious state, Weishaupt's proffer was enticing. He laid before them a scheme which was somewhat feasible, was magnificent, surpassing our conceptions, but at the same time such as permitted us to expatiate on the subject, and even to amplify it at pleasure in our imaginations without absurdity. It does not appear to me wonderful, therefore, that so many were fascinated till they became at last regardless of the absurdity and inconsistency of the means by which this splendid object was to be attained. Hear what Spartacus himself says of hidden mysteries. " Of
" all the means I know to lead men, the most effec-
" tual is a concealed mystery. The hankering of the
" mind is irresistible; and if once a man has taken it
" into his head that there is a mystery in a thing, it
" is impossible to get it out, either by argument or
" experience. And then, we can so change notions
" by merely changing a word. What more contempti-
" ble than *fanaticism*; but call it *enthusiasm*; then add
" the little word *noble*, and you may lead him over
" the world. Nor are we, in these bright days, a bit
" better than our fathers, who found the pardon of
" their sins mysteriously contained in a much greater
" sin, viz. leaving their family, and going barefooted
" to Rome."

Such being the employment, and such the disciples, should we expect the fruits to be very precious? No. The doctrines which were gradually unfolded were such as suited those who continued in the *Cursus Aca-*
demicus.

demicus. Thofe who did not, becaufe they did not like them, got a *Sta bene;* they were not fit for advancement. The numbers however were great; Spartacus boafted of 600 in Bavaria alone in 1783. We don't know many of them; few of thofe we know were in the upper ranks of life; and I can fee that it required much wheedling, and many letters of long worded German compliments from the proud Spartacus, to win even a young Baron or a Graf juft come of age. Men in an eafy fituation in life could not brook the employment of a fpy, which is bafe, cowardly, and corrupting, and has in all ages and countries degraded the perfon who engages in it. Can the perfon be called wife who thus enflaves himfelf? Such perfons give up the right of private judgment, and rely on their unknown Superiors with the blindeft and moft abject confidence. For their fakes, and to rivet ftill fafter their own fetters, they engage in the moft corrupting of all employments—and for what?—To learn fomething more of an Order, of which every degree explodes the doctrine of a former one. Would it have hurt the young *Illuminatus* to have it explained to him all at once? Would not this fire his mind—when he fees with the fame glance the great object, and the fitnefs of the means for attaining it? Would not the exalted characters of the Superiors, fo much excelling himfelf in talents, and virtue, and happinefs, (otherwife the Order is good for nothing,) warm his heart, and fill him with emulation, fince he fees in them, that what is fo ftrongly preached to him is an attainable thing? No, no—it is all a trick; he muft be kept like a child, amufed with rattles, and ftars, and ribands—and all the fatisfaction he obtains is, like the Mafons, the diverfion of feeing others running the fame gauntlet.

Weifhaupt acknowledges that the great influence of the Order may be abufed. Surely, in no way fo eafily or so fatally as by corrupting or seductive lessons in the beginning. The mistake or error of the pupil is undiscoverable by himself, (according to the genuine principles of Illumination,) for the pupil must believe his Mentor to be infallible—with him alone he is connected—his lessons only must he learn. Who can tell him that he has gone wrong—or who can set him right?

Here, therefore, there is confusion and deficiency. There must be some standard to which appeal can be made; but this is inaccessible to all within the pale of the Order; it is therefore without this pale, and independent of the Order—and it is attainable only by abandoning the Order. The Quibus Licet, the Primo, the Soli, can procure no light to the person who does not know that he has been led out of the right road to virtue and happiness. The Superiors indeed draw much useful information from these reports, though they affect to stand in no need of it, and they make a cruel return.

All this is so much out of the natural road of instruction, that, on this account alone, we may presume that it is wrong. We are generally safe when we follow nature's plans. A child learns in his father's house, by seeing, and by imitating, and in common domestic education, he gets much useful knowledge, and the chief habits which are afterwards to regulate his conduct. Example does almost every thing; and, with respect to what may be called living, as distinguishable from profession, speculation and argumentative instruction are seldom employed, or of any use. The indispensableness of mutual forbearance and obedience, for domestic peace and happiness, forms most of these habits; and the child, under good parents, is kept in a situation that makes virtue easier than vice,

and

and he becomes wife and good without any express study about the matter.

But this Illumination plan is darkness over all—it is too artificial—and the topics, from which counsel is to be drawn, cannot be taken from the peculiar views of the Order—for these are yet a secret for the pupil—and must ever be a secret for him while under tuition. They must therefore be drawn from common sources, and the Order is of no use; all that can naturally be effectuated by this Affociation is the forming, and affiduoufly fostering a narrow, Jewifh, corporation spirit, totally opposite to the benevolent pretensions of the Order. The pupil can see nothing but this, that there is a set of men, whom he does not know, who may acquire incontroulable power, and may perhaps make use of him, but for what purpose, and in what way, he does not know; how can he know that his endeavours are to make man happier, any other way than as he might have known it without having put this collar round his own neck?

These reflections address themselves to all men who profess to conduct themselves by the principles and dictates of common sense and prudence, and who have the ordinary share of candour and good-will to others. It requires no singular sensibility of heart, nor great generosity, to make such people think the doctrines and views of the Illuminati false, absurd, foolish, and ruinous. But I hope that I address them to thousands of my countrymen and friends, who have much higher notions of human nature, and who cherish with care the affections and the hopes that are suited to a rational, a benevolent, and a high-minded being, capable of endless improvement.

To those who enjoy the cheering confidence in the superintendance and providence of God, who consider themselves as creatures whom he has made, and whom
he

he cares for, as the subjects of his moral government, this Order must appear with every character of falsehood and absurdity on its countenance. What CAN BE MORE IMPROBABLE than this, that He, whom we look up to as the contriver, the maker, and director of this goodly frame of things, should have so far mistaken his own plans, that this world of rational creatures should have subsisted for thousands of years, before a way could be found out, by which his intention of making men good and happy could be accomplished; and that this method did not occur to the great Artist himself, nor even to the wisest, and happiest, and best men upon earth; but to a few insignificant persons at Munich in Bavaria, who had been trying to raise ghosts, to change lead into gold, to tell fortunes, or discover treasures, but had failed in all their attempts; men who had been engaged for years in every whim which characterises a weak, a greedy, or a gloomy mind? Finding all these beyond their reach, they combined their powers, and, at once, found out this infinitely more important SECRET—for secret it must still be, otherwise not only the Deity, but even these philosophers, will still be disappointed.

Yet this is the doctrine that must be swallowed by the Minervals and the *Illuminati Minores*, to whom it is not yet safe to disclose the grand secret, *that there is no such superintendance of Deity.* At last, however, when the pupil has conceived such exalted notions of the knowledge of his teachers, and such low notions of the blundering projector of this world, it may be no difficult matter to persuade him that all his former notions were only old wives tales. By this time he must have heard much about superstition, and how men's minds have been dazzled by this splendid picture of a Providence and a moral government of the universe. It now appears incompatible with the great object of

the

the Order, the principles of univerſal liberty and equality—it is therefore rejected without farther examination, for this reaſon alone. This was preciſely the argument uſed in France for rejecting revealed religion. It was incompatible with their Rights of Man.

It is richly worth obſerving how this principle can warp the judgment, and give quite another appearance to the ſame object. The reader will not be difpleaſed with a moſt remarkable inſtance of it, which I beg leave to give at length.

Our immortal Newton, whom the philoſophers of Europe look up to as the honour of our ſpecies, whom even Mr. Bailly, the Preſident of the National Aſſembly of France, and Mayor of Paris, cannot find words ſufficiently energetic to praiſe; this patient, ſagacious, and ſuccefsful obſerver of nature, after having exhibited to the wondering world the characteriſtic property of that principle of material nature by which all the bodies of the ſolar ſyſtem are made to form a connected and permanent univerſe; and after having ſhown that this law of action alone was adapted to this end, and that if gravity had deviated but one thouſandth part from the inverſe duplicate ratio of the diſtances, the ſyſtem muſt, in the courſe of a very few revolutions, have gone into confuſion and ruin—he ſits down, and views the goodly ſcene,—and then cloſes his Principles of Natural Philoſophy with this reflection (his *Scholium generale*):

" This moſt elegant frame of things could not have
" ariſen, unleſs by the contrivance and the direction of
" a wiſe and powerful Being; and if the fixed ſtars are
" the centres of ſyſtems, theſe ſyſtems muſt be ſimilar;
" and all theſe, conſtructed according to the ſame
" plan, are ſubject to the government of *one* Being.
" All theſe he governs, not as the ſoul of the world,
" but as the Lord of all; therefore, on account of his
government,

" government, he is called the Lord God—*Pantokra-*
" *tor;* for God is a relative term, and refers to subjects.
" Deity is God's government, not of his own body, as
" those think who consider him as the soul of the
" world, but of his servants. The supreme God is a
" Being eternal, infinite, absolutely perfect. But a be-
" ing, however perfect, without government, is not
" God; for we say, *my* God, your God, the God of
" Israel. We cannot say *my* eternal, *my* infinite. We
" may have some notions indeed of his attributes, but
" can have none of his nature. With respect to bodies,
" we see only shapes and colour—hear only sounds—
" touch only surfaces. These are attributes of bodies;
" but of their essence we know nothing. As a blind
" man can form no notion of colours, we can form
" none of the manner in which God perceives, and
" understands, and influences every thing.

" Therefore we know God only by his attributes.
" What are these? The wise and excellent contri-
" vance,, structure, and final aim of all things. In
" these his perfections we admire him, and we wonder.
" In his direction or government, we venerate and
" worship him—we worship him as his servants; and
" God, without dominion, without providence, and
" final aims, is Fate—not the object either of reve-
" rence, of hope, of love, or of fear.

But mark the emotions which affected the mind of another excellent observer of Nature, the admirer of Newton, and the person who has put the finishing stroke to the Newtonian philosophy, by showing that the acceleration of the moon's mean motion, is the genuine result of a gravitation decreasing in the precise duplicate ratio of the distance inversely; I mean Mr. Delaplace, one of the most brilliant ornaments of the French academy of sciences. He has lately published the *Systeme du Monde,* a most beautiful compend of

astromony

astronomy and of the Newtonian philosophy. Having finished his work with the same observation, "That a gravitation inversely proportional to the squares of the distances was the only principle which could unite material Nature into a permanent system;" *he* also sits down—surveys the scene—points out the parts which he had brought within our ken—and then makes this reflection: "Beheld in its totality, astro-
"nomy is the noblest monument of the human mind,
"its chief title to intelligence. But, seduced by the
"illusions of sense, and by self-conceit, we have long
"considered ourselves as the centre of these motions;
"and our pride has been punished by the groundless
"fears which we have created to ourselves. We
"imagine, forsooth, that all this is for us, and that
"the stars influence our destinies! But the labours of
"ages have convinced us of our error, and we find
"ourselves on an insignificant planet, almost imper-
"ceptible in the immensity of space. But the sub-
"lime discoveries we have made richly repay this
"humble situation. Let us cherish these with care, as
"the delight of thinking beings—they have destroyed
"our mistakes as to our relation to the rest of the uni-
"verse; errors which were the more fatal, because
"the social Order depends on justice and truth alone.
"Far be from us the dangerous maxim, that it is some-
"times useful to depart from these, and to deceive
"men, in order to insure their happiness; but cruel
"experience has shewn us that these laws are never to-
"tally extinct."

There can be no doubt as to the meaning of these last words—they cannot relate to astrology—this was entirely out of date. The "attempts to deceive men, "in order to insure their happiness," can only be those by which we are made to think too highly of ourselves. "Inhabitants of this pepper-corn, we think
"ourselves

" ourselves the peculiar favourites of Heaven, nay the
" chief objects of care to a Being, the Maker of all ;
" and then we imagine that, after this life, we are to
" be happy or miserable, according as we accede or
" not to this subjugation to opinions which enslave us.
" But truth and justice have broken these bonds."—
But where is the force of the argument which entitles
this perfecter of the Newtonian philosophy to exult so
much? It all rests on this, That this earth is but as a
grain of mustard-seed. Man would be more worth attention had he inhabited Jupiter or the Sun. Thus
may a Frenchman look down on the noble creatures
who inhabit Orolong or Pelew. But whence arises the
absurdity of the intellectual inhabitants of this peppercorn being a proper object of attention? it is because
our shallow comprehensions cannot, at the same glance,
see an extensive scene, and perceive its most minute
detail.

David, a King, and a soldier, had some notions of
this kind. The heavens, it is true, pointed out to
him a Maker and Ruler, which is more than they seem
to have done to the Gallic philosopher; but David was
afraid that he would be forgotten in the crowd, and
cries out, " Lord what is man that thou art mindful of
" *him?*" But David gets rid of his fears, not by becoming a philosopher, and discovering all this to be
absurd,—he would still be forgotten,—he at once thinks
of what he is—a noble creature—high in the scale of
nature. " But," says he, " I had forgotten myself.
" Thou hast made man but a little lower than the an-
" gels—thou hast crowned him with glory and honour
" —thou hast put all things under his feet." Here
are exalted sentiments, fit for the creature whose ken
pierces through the immensity of the visible universe,
and who sees his relation to the universe, being nearly
allied to its Sovereign, and capable of rising continually

tinually in his rank, by cultivating thofe talents which diftinguifh and adorn it.

Thoufands, I truft, there are, who think that this life is but a preparation for another, in which the mind of man will have the whole wonders of creation and of providence laid open to its enraptured view—where it will fee and comprehend with one glance what Newton, the moft patient and fuccefsful of all the obfervers of nature, took years of meditation to find out—where it will attain that pitch of wifdom, goodnefs, and enjoyment, of which our confciences tell us we are capable, though it far furpaffes that of the wifeft, the beft, and the happieft of men. Such perfons will confider this Order as degrading and deteftable, and as in direct oppofition to their moft confident expectations: For it pretends to what is impoffible, to perfect peace and happinefs in this life. They believe, and they feel, that man muft be made perfect through fufferings, which fhall call into action powers of mind that otherwife would never have unfolded themfelves—powers which are frequently fources of the pureft and moft foothing pleafures, and naturally make us reft our eyes and hopes on that ftate where every tear fhall be wiped away, and where the kind affections fhall become the never-failing fources of pure and unfading delight. Such perfons fee the palpable abfurdity of a preparation which is equally neceffary for all, and yet muft be confined to the minds of a few, who have the low and indelicate appetite for frivolous play-things, and for grofs fenfual pleafures. Such minds will turn away from this boafted treat with loathing and abhorrence.

I am well aware that fome of my readers may fmile at this, and think it an enthufiaftical working up of the imagination, fimilar to what I reprobate in the cafe of Utopian happinefs in a ftate of univerfal Liberty and Equality. It is like, they will fay, to the declamation

mation in a fermon by perfons of the trade, who are trained up to fineffe, by which they allure and tickle weak minds.

I acknowledge that in the prefent cafe I do not addrefs myfelf to the cold hearts, who contentedly

"*Sink and flumber in their cells of clay;*

——Peace to all fuch;——but to the "*felices animæ,* "*quibus hæc cognofcere cura;*"—to thofe who *have enjoyed* the pleafures of fcience, who have been fuccefsful—who have made difcoveries—who have really illuminated the world—to the Bacons, the Newtons, the Lockes.—Allow me to mention one, Daniel Bernoulli, the moſt elegant mathematician, the only philofopher, and the moſt worthy man, of that celebrated family. He faid to a gentleman, (Dr. Staehling,) who repeated it to me, that " when reading fome of " thofe wonderful gueffes of Sir Ifaac Newton, the " fubfequent demonſtration of which has been the " chief fource of fame to his moſt celebrated commen-" tators—his mind has fometimes been fo overpower-" ed by thrilling emotions, that he has wifhed that " moment to be his laſt; and that it was this which " gave him the cleareſt conception of the happinefs " of heaven." If fuch delightful emotions could be excited by the perception of mere truth, what muſt they be when each of thefe truths is an inſtance of wifdom, and when we recollect, that what we call wifdom in the works of nature, is always the nice adaptation of means for producing *beneficent* ends; and that each of thefe affecting qualities is fufceptible of degrees which are boundlefs, and exceed our higheſt conceptions? What can this complex emotion or feeling be but rapture? But Bernoulli is a Doctor of Theology—and therefore a fufpicious perfon, perhaps one of the

combination

combination hired by defpots to enflave us. I will take another man, a gentleman of rank and family, a foldier, who often fignalifed himfelf as a naval commander—who at one time forced his way through a powerful fleet of the Venetians with a fmall fquadron, and brought relief to a diftreffed garrifon. I would defire the reader to perufe the conclufion of Sir Kenhelm Digby's *Treatifes on Body and Mind*; and after having reflected on the ftate of fcience at the time this author wrote, let him coolly weigh the incitements to manly conduct which this foldier finds in the differences obferved between body and mind; and then let him fay, on his confcience, whether they are more feeble than thofe which he can draw from the eternal fleep of death. If he thinks that they are—he is in the proper frame for initiation into Spartacus's higher myfteries. He may be either MAGUS or REX.

Were this a proper place for confidering the queftion as a queftion of fcience or truth, I would fay, that every man who has been a *fuccefsful* ftudent of nature, and who will reft his conclufions on the fame maxims of probable reafoning that have procured him fuccefs in his paft refearches, will confider it as next to certain that there is another ftate of exiftence for rational man. For he muft own, that if this be not the cafe, there is a moft fingular exception to a propofition which the whole courfe of his experience has made him confider as a truth founded on univerfal induction, viz. that *nature accomplifhes all her plans*, and that every clafs of beings attains all the improvement of which it is capable. Let him but turn his thoughts inward, he will feel that his intellect is capable of improvement, in comparifon with which Newton is but a child. I could purfue this argument very far, and (I think) warm the heart of every man whom I fhould wifh to call my friend.

What

What opinion will be formed of this Affociation by the modeft, the lowly-minded, the candid, who acknowledge that they too often feel the fuperior force of prefent and fenfible pleafures, by which their minds are drawn off from the contemplation of what their confciences tell them to be right,—to be their dutiful and filial fentiments and emotions refpecting their great and good Parent—to be their dutiful and neighbourly affections, and their proper conduct to all around them —and which diminifh their veneration for that purity of thought and moderation of appetite which becomes their noble natures? What muft *they* think of this Order? Confcious of frequent faults, which would offend themfelves if committed by their deareft children, they look up to their Maker with anxiety—are grieved to have fo far forgotten their duty, and fearful that they may again forget it. Their painful experience tells them that their reafon is often too weak, their information too fcanty, or its light is obftructed by paffion and prejudices, which diftort and difcolour every thing; or it is unheeded during their attention to prefent objects. Happy fhould they be, if it fhould pleafe their kind Parent to remind them of their duty from time to time, or to influence their mind in any way that would compenfate for their own ignorance, their own weaknefs, or even their indolence and neglect. They dare not expect fuch a favour, which their modefty tells them they do not deferve, and which they fear may be unfit to be granted; but when fuch a comfort is held out to them, with eager hearts they receive it—they blefs the kindnefs that granted it, and the hand that brings it.——Such amiable characters have appeared in all ages, and in all fituations of mankind. They have not in all inftances been wife—often have they been precipitate, and have too readily caught at any thing which pretended to give them the fo much

wifhed-wished-for assistances; and, unfortunately, there have been enthusiasts, or villains, who have taken advantage of this universal wish of anxious man; and the world has been darkened by cheats, who have misrepresented God to mankind, have filled us with vain terrors, and have then quieted our fears by fines, and sacrifices, and mortifications, and services, which they said were more than sufficient to expiate all our faults. Thus was our duty to our neighbour, to our own dignity, and to our Maker and Parent, kept out of sight, and religion no longer came in aid to our sense of right and wrong; but, on the contrary, by these superstitions it opened the doors of heaven to the worthless and the wicked.—But I wish not to speak of these men, but of the good, the candid, the MODEST, the HUMBLE, who know their failings, who love their duties, but wish to know, to perceive, and to love them still more. These are they who think and believe that " the Gospel has brought life and immortality to " light," that is, within their reach. They think it worthy of the Father of mankind, and they receive it with thankful hearts, admiring above all things the simplicity of its morality, comprehended in one sentence, " Do to another what you can reasonably wish " that another should do to you," and THAT PURITY OF THOUGHT AND MANNERS WHICH DISTINGUISHES IT FROM ALL THE SYSTEMS OF MORAL INSTRUCTION THAT HAVE EVER BEEN OFFERED TO MEN. Here they find a ground of resignation under the troubles of life, and a support in the hour of death, quite suited to the diffidence of their own character. Such men are ready to grant that the Stoics were persons of noble and exalted minds, and that they had worthy conceptions of the rank of man in the scale of God's works; but they confess that they themselves do not feel all that support from Stoical principles which man

too

too frequently needs; and they say that they are not singular in their opinions, but that the bulk of mankind are prevented, by their want of heroic fortitude, by their situation, or their want of the opportunities of cultivating their native strength of mind, from ever attaining this hearty submission to the will of the Deity. They maintain, that the Stoics were but a few, a very few, from among many millions—and therefore *their* being satisfied was but a trifle amidst the general discontent, and anxiety, and despair.—Such men will most certainly start back from this Illumination with horror and fright—from a Society which gives the lie to their fondest expectations, makes a sport of their grounds of hope, and of their deliverer; and which, after laughing at their credulity, bids them shake off all religion whatever, and denies the existence of that Supreme Mind, the pattern of all excellence, who till now had filled their thoughts with admiration and love —from an Order which pretends to free them from spiritual bondage, and then lays on their necks a load ten times more oppressive and intolerable, from which they have no power of ever escaping. Men of sense and virtue will spurn at such a proposal; and even the profligate, who trade with Deity, must be sensible that they will be better off with their priests, whom they know, and among whom they may make a selection of such as will with patience and gentleness clear up their doubts, calm their fears, and encourage their hopes.

And all good men, all lovers of peace and of justice, will abhor and reject the thought of overturning the present constitution of things, faulty as it may be, merely in the endeavour to establish another, which the vices of mankind may subvert again in a twelvemonth. They must see, that in order to gain their point, the proposers have found it necessary to destroy the grounds of morality, by permitting the most wicked

ed means for accomplishing any end that our fancy, warped by passion or interest, may represent to us as of great importance. They see, that instead of morality, vice must prevail, and that therefore there is no security for the continuance of this Utopian felicity; and, in the mean time, desolation and misery must lay the world waste during the struggle, and half of those for whom we are striving will be swept from the face of the earth. We have but to look to France, where in eight years there have been more executions and spoliations and distresses of every kind by the *pouvoir revolutionnaire*, than can be found in the long records of that despotic monarchy.

There is nothing in the whole constitution of the Illuminati that strikes me with more horror than the proposals of Hercules and Minos to enlist the women in this shocking warfare with all that " is good, and " pure, and lovely, and of good report." They could not have fallen on any expedient that will be more effectual and fatal. If any of my countrywomen shall honour these pages with a reading, I would call on them, in the most earnest manner, to consider this as an affair of the utmost importance to themselves. I would conjure them by the regard they have for their own dignity, and for their rank in society, to join against these enemies of human nature and profligate degraders of the sex; and I would assure them that the present state of things almost puts it in their power to be the saviours of the world. But if they are remiss, and yield to the seduction, they will fall from that high state to which they have arisen in Christian Europe, and again sink into that insignificancy or slavery in which the sex is found in all ages and countries out of the hearing of Christianity.

I hope that my countrywomen will consider this solemn address to them as a proof of the high esteem in
which

which I hold them. They will not be offended then if, in this season of alarm and anxiety, when I wish to impress their minds with a serious truth, I shall wave ceremony, which is always designing, and speak of them in honest but decent plainness.

Man is immersed in luxury. Our accommodations are now so numerous that every thing is pleasure. Even in very sober situations in this highly-cultivated Society, there is hardly a thing that remains in the form of a necessary of life, or even of a mere conveniency—every thing is ornamented—it must not appear of use—it must appear as giving some sensible pleasure. I do not say this by way of blaming—it is nature—man is a refining creature, and our most boasted acquirements are but refinements on our necessary wants. Our hut becomes a palace, our blanket a fine dress, and our arts become sciences. This discontent with the natural condition of things, and this disposition to refinement, is a characteristic of our species, and is the great employment of our lives. The direction which this propensity chances to take in any age or nation, marks its character in the most conspicuous and interesting manner. All have it in some degree, and it is very conceivable that, in some, it may constitute the chief object of attention. If this be the case in any nations, it is surely most likely to be so in those where the accommodations of life are the most numerous—therefore in a rich and luxurious nation. I may surely, without exaggeration or reproach, give that appellation to our own nation at this moment. If you do not go to the very lowest class of people, who must labour all day, is it not the chief object of all to procure *perceptible pleasure* in one way or another? The sober and busy struggle in the thoughts and hopes of getting the means of enjoying the *comforts* of life without farther labour—and many have no other object than pleasure.

Then

Then let us reflect that it is woman that is to *grace* the whole—It is in nature, it is the very conftitution of man, that woman, and every thing connected with woman, muft appear as the ornament of life. That this mixes with every other focial fentiment, appears from the conduct of our fpecies in all ages and in every fituation. This I prefume would be the cafe even though there were no qualities in the fex to juftify it. This fentiment refpecting the fex is neceffary, in order to rear fo helplefs, fo nice, and fo improveable a creature as man; without it, the long abiding tafk could not be performed:—and I think that I may venture to fay that it is performed in the different ftates of fociety nearly in proportion as this preparatory and indifpenfable fentiment is in force.

On the other hand, I think it no lefs evident that it is the defire of the women to be agreeable to the men, and that they will model themfelves according to what they think will pleafe. Without this adjuftment of fentiments by nature, nothing would go on. We never obferve any fuch want of fymmetry in the works of God. If, therefore, thofe who take the lead, and give the fafhion in fociety, were wife and virtuous, I have no doubt but that the women would fet the brighteft pattern of every thing that is excellent. But if the men are nice and faftidious fenfualifts, the women will be refined and elegant voluptuaries.

There is no deficiency in the female mind, either in talents or in difpofitions; nor can we fay with certainty that there is any fubject of intellectual or moral difcuffion in which women have not excelled. If the delicacy of their conftitution, and other phyfical caufes, allow the female fex a fmaller fhare of fome mental powers, they poffefs others in a fuperior degree, which are no lefs refpectable in their own nature, and of as great importance to fociety. Inftead of defcanting at large on their powers of mind, and supporting my assertions by the instances of a Hypatia, a Schurman, a Zenobia, an Elizabeth, &c. I may repeat the account given of the sex by a person of uncommon experience, who saw them without disguise, or any motive that could lead them to play a feigned part—Mr. Ledyard, who traversed the greatest part of the world, for the mere indulgence of his taste for observation of human nature; generally in want, and often in extreme misery.

"I have (says he) always remarked that women,
" in all countries, are civil, obliging, tender, and hu-
" mane: that they are ever inclined to be gay and
" cheerful, timorous and modest; and that they do
" not hesitate, like men, to perform a kind or gene-
" rous action.—Not haughty, not arrogant, not su-
" percilious, they are full of courtesy, and fond of so-
" ciety—more liable in general to err than man, but
" in general, also, more virtuous, and performing
" more good actions than he. To a woman, whether
" civilized or savage, I never addressed myself in the
" language of decency and friendship—without receiv-
" ing a decent and friendly answer—with man it has
" often been otherwise.

" In wandering over the barren plains of in-
" hospitable Denmark, through honest Sweden, and
" frozen Lapland, rude and churlish Finland, unprin-
" cipled Russia, and the wide spread regions of the wan-
" dering Tartar,—if hungry, dry, cold, wet, or sick,
" the women have ever been friendly to me, and uni-
" formly so; and to add to this virtue, (so worthy of
" the appellation of benevolence,) these actions have
" been performed in so free and so kind a manner, that
" if I was thirsty, I drank the sweetest draught, and
" if hungry, I ate the coarse meal with a double
" relish."

And

And thefe are they whom Weifhaupt would corrupt! One of thefe, whom he had embraced with fondnefs, would he have murdered, to fave his honour, and qualify himfelf to preach virtue! But let us not be too fevere on Weifhaupt—let us wafh ourfelves clear of all ftain before we think of reprobating him. Are we not guilty in fome degree, when we do not cultivate in the women thofe powers of mind, and thofe difpofitions of heart, which would equally dignify them in every ftation as in thofe humble ranks in which Mr. Ledyard moft frequently faw them? I cannot think that we do this. They are not only to *grace* the whole of cultivated fociety, but it is in their faithful and affectionate perfonal attachment that we are to find the fweeteft pleafures that life can give. Yet in all thefe fituations where the manner in which they are treated is not dictated by the ftern laws of neceffity, are they not trained up for mere amufement—are not ferious occupations confidered as a tafk which hurts their lovelinefs? What is this but felfifhnefs, or as if they had no virtues worth cultivating? Their *bufinefs* is fuppofed to be the ornamenting themfelves, as if nature did not dictate this to them already, with at leaft as much force as is neceffary. Every thing is prefcribed to them *becaufe it makes them more lovely*—even their moral leffons are enforced by this argument, and Mifs Woolftoncraft is perfectly right when fhe fays that the fine leffons given to young women by Fordyce or Rouffeau are nothing but felfifh and refined voluptuoufnefs. This advocate of her fex puts her fifters in the proper point of view, when fhe tells them that they are, like man, the fubjects of God's moral government,—like man, preparing themfelves for boundlefs improvement in a better ftate of exiftence. Had fhe adhered to this view of the matter, and kept it conftantly in fight, her book (which doubtlefs contains many excellent things, highly
deferving

deserving of their serious consideration) would have been a most valuable work. She justly observes, that the virtues of the sex are great and respectable, but that in our mad chace of pleasure, only pleasure, they are little thought of or attended to. Man trusts to his own uncontroulable power, or to the general goodness of the sex, that their virtues will appear when we have occasion for them ;—" but we will send for these some " other time :"—Many noble displays do they make of the most difficult attainments. Such is the patient bearing up under misfortunes, which has no brilliancy to support it in the effort. This is more difficult than braving danger in an active and conspicuous situation. How often is a woman left with a family, and the shattered remains of a fortune, lost perhaps by dissipation or by indolence—and how seldom, how very seldom, do we see woman shrink from the task, or discharge it with negligence? Is it not therefore folly next to madness, not to be careful of this our greatest blessing—of things which so nearly concern our peace—nor guard ourselves, and these our best companions and friends, from the effects of this fatal Illumination? It has indeed brought to light what dreadful lengths men will go, when under the fanatical and dazzling glare of happiness in a state of liberty and equality, and spurred on by insatiable luxury, and not held in check by moral feelings and the restraints of religion—and mark, reader, that the women have here also taken the complexion of the men, and have even gone beyond them. If we have seen a son present himself to the National Assembly of France, professing his satisfaction with the execution of his father three days before, and declaring himself a true citizen, who prefers the nation to all other considerations; we have also seen, on the same day, wives denouncing their husbands, and (O shocking to human nature!) mothers denouncing their sons, as bad ci-

tizens

tizens and traitors. Mark too what return the women have met with for all their horrid services, where, to exprefs their fentiments of civifm and abhorrence of royalty, they threw away the character of their fex, and bit the amputated limbs of their murdered countrymen*. Surely thefe patriotic women merited that the rights of their fex fhould be confidered in full council, and they were well entitled to a feat ; but there is not a fingle act of their government in which the fex is confidered as having any rights whatever, or that they are things to be cared for.

Are not the accurfed fruits of Illumination to be feen in the prefent humiliating condition of woman in France? pampered in every thing that can reduce them to the mere inftruments of animal pleafure. In their prefent ftate of national moderation (as they call it) and fecurity, fee Madame Tallien come into the public theatre, accompanied by other *beautiful* women, (I was about to have mifnamed them Ladies,) laying afide all modefty, and prefenting themfelves to the public view, with bared limbs, *à la Sauvage*, as the alluring objects of defire. I make no doubt but that this is a ferious matter, encouraged, nay, prompted by government. To keep the minds of the Parifians in the prefent fever of diffolute gaiety, they are at more expence from the national treafury for the fupport of the fixty theatres, than all the penfions and honorary offices in Britain, three times told, amount to. Was not their abominable farce in the church of Notre Dame a bate of the fame kind in the true fpirit of Weifhaupt's *Eroterion*?

" We

---

* I fay this on the authority of a young gentleman, an emigrant, who faw it, and who faid, that they were women, not of the dregs of the Palais Royal, nor of infamous character, but well dreffed.—I am forry to add, that the relation, accompanied with looks of horror and difguft, only provoked a contemptuous fmile from an illuminated British Fair-one.

"We do not," said the high priest, "call you to the worship of inanimate idols. Behold a master-piece of nature, (lifting up the veil which concealed the naked charms of the beautiful Madmf. Barbier) : This sacred image should inflame all hearts." And it did so ; the people shouted out, " No more altars, no more priests, no God but the God of Nature."

Orleans, the first prince of the blood, did not scruple to prostitute his daughter, if not to the embraces, yet to the wanton view of the public, with the precise intention of inflaming their desires. (See the account given of the dinners at Sillery's, by Camille Desmoulines, in his speech against the Brissotins.) But what will be the end of all this ? The fondlings of the wealthy will be pampered in all the indulgences which fastidious voluptuousness finds necessary for varying or enhancing its pleasures; but they will either be slighted as toys, or they will be immured ; and the companions of the poor will be drudges and slaves.

I am fully persuaded that it was the enthusiastic admiration of Grecian democracy that recommended to the French nation the dress *à la Grecque*, which exhibits not the elegant, ornamented beauty, but the alluring female, fully as well as Madame Tallien's dress *à la Sauvage*. It was no doubt with the same adherence to *serious principle*, that Mademoiselle Therouanne was most beautifully dressed *à l'Amazonne* on the 5th of October 1789, when she turned the heads of so many young officers of the regiments at Versailles. The Cythera, the *hominum divumque voluptas*, at the cathedral of Notre Dame, was also dressed *à la Grecque:* There is a most evident and characteristic change in the whole system of female dress in France. The *Filles de l'Opera* always gave the *ton*, and were surely withheld by no rigid principle. They sometimes produced very extravagant and fantastic forms, but these were

almost

almost always in the style of the highest ornament, and they trusted, for the rest of the impression which they wished to make, to the fascinating expression of elegant movements. This indeed was wonderful, and hardly conceivable by any who have not seen a grand ballet performed by good actors. I have shed tears of the most sincere and tender sorrow during the exhibition of Antigone, set to music by Traëtta, and performed by Madame Meilcour and S^re Torelli, and Zantini. I can easily conceive the impression to be still stronger, though perhaps of another kind, when the former superb dresses are changed for the expressive simplicity of the Grecian. I cannot help thinking that the female ornaments in the rest of Europe, and even among ourselves, have less elegance since we lost the sanction of the French court. But see how all this will terminate, when we shall have brought the sex so low, and will not even wait for a Mahometan paradise. What can we expect but such a dissoluteness of manners, that the endearing ties of relation and family, and mutual confidence within doors, will be slighted, and will cease; and every man must stand up for himself, single and alone?

> *Fœcunda culpæ sæcula nuptias*
> *Primum inquinavére, et genus, et domos.*
> *Hoc fonte derivata clades*
> *In patriam populumque fluxit.* HOR. iii. 6. 17.

This is not the suggestion of prudish fear, I think it is the natural course of things, and that France is at this moment giving to the world the fullest proof of Weishaupt's sagacity, and the judgment with which he has formed his plans. Can it tend to the improvement of our morals or manners to have our ladies frequent the gymnastic theatres, and see them decide, like the

Roman

Roman matrons, on the merits of a naked gladiator or wrestler? Have we not enough of this already with our vaulters and posture-masters, and should we admire any lady who had a rage for such spectacles? Will it improve our taste to have our rooms ornamented with such paintings and sculptures as filled the cenaculum, and the study of the refined and elegant moralist Horace, who had the art—*ridendo dicere verum?* Shall we be improved when such indulgences are thought compatible with such lessons as he generally gives for the conduct of life? The pure Morality of Illuminatism is now employed in stripping Italy of all those precious remains of ancient art and voluptuousness; and Paris will ere long be the deposit and the resort of artists from all nations, there to study the works of ancient masters, and to return from thence panders of public corruption. The plan is masterly, and the low-born Statesmen and Generals of France may in this respect be set on a level with a Colbert or a Condé. But the consequences of this Gallic dominion over the minds of fallen man will be as dreadful as their dominion over their lives and fortunes.

Recollect in what manner Spartacus proposed to corrupt his sisters (for we need not speak of the manner in which he expected that this would promote his plan—this is abundantly plain). It was by destroying their moral sentiments, and their sentiments of religion. Recollect what is the recommendation that the Atheist Minos gives of his step-daughters, when he speaks of them, as proper persons for the Lodge of Sisters. " They have got over all prejudices, and, in matters " of religion they think as I do." These profligates judged rightly that this affair required much caution, and that the utmost attention to decency, and even delicacy, must be observed in their rituals and ceremonies, otherwise the women would be *disgusted*. This was

was judging fairly of the feelings of a female mind. But they judged falsely, and only according to their own coarse experience, when they attributed their disgust and their fears to coyness. Coyness is indeed the instinctive attribute of the female. In woman it is very great, and it is perhaps the genuine source of the *disgust* of which the Illuminati were suspicious. But they have been dim-sighted indeed, or very unfortunate in their acquaintance, if they never observed any other source of repugnance in the mind of woman to what is immoral or immodest—if they did not see dislike—moral disapprobation. Do they mean to insinuate, that in that regard which modest women express in all their words and actions, for what every one understands by the terms decency, modesty, and the disapprobation of every.thing that violates those feelings, the women only show female coyness? Then are they very blind instructors. But they are not so blind. The account given of the initiation of a young Sister at Frankfort, under the feigned name *Psycharion*, shows the most scrupulous attention to the moral feelings of the sex; and the confusion and disturbance which, after all their care, it occasioned among the ladies, shows, that when they thought all right and delicate, they had been but coarse judges. Minos damns the ladies there, because they are too free, too rich, too republican, and too wise, for being led about by the nose (this is his own expression). But Philo certainly thought more correctly of the sex in general, when he says, Truth is a modest girl: She may be handed about like a lady, by good sense and good manners, but must not be bullied and driven about like a strumpet. I would here insert the discourses or addresses which were made on that occasion to the different classes of the assembly, girls, young ladies, wives, young men, and strangers, which

are

are really ingenious and well composed, were they not such as would offend my fair countrywomen.

The religious sentiments by which mortals are to be assisted, even in the discharge of their moral duties, and still more, the sentiments which are purely religious, and have no reference to any thing here, are precisely those which are most easily excited in the mind of woman. Affection, admiration, filial reverence, are, if I mistake not exceedingly, those in which the women far surpass the men; and it is on this account that we generally find them so much disposed to devotion, which is nothing but a sort of fond indulgence of those affections without limit to the imagination. The enraptured devotee pours out her soul in expressions of these feelings, just as a fond mother mixes the caresses given to her child with the most extravagant expressions of love. The devotee even endeavours to excite higher degrees of these affections, by expatiating on such circumstances in the divine conduct with respect to man as naturally awaken them; and he does this without any fear of exceeding; because Infinite Wisdom and Goodness will always justify the sentiment, and free the expression of it from all charge of hyperbole or extravagance.

I am convinced, therefore, that the female mind is well adapted to cultivation by means of religion, and that their native softness and kindness of heart will always be sufficient for procuring it a favourable reception from them. It is therefore with double regret that I see any of them join in the arrogant pretensions of our Illuminated philosophers, who see no need of such assistances for the knowledge and discharge of their duties. There is nothing so unlike that general modesty of thought, and that diffidence, which we are disposed to think the character of the female mind. I

am

am inclined to think, that such deviations from the general conduct of the sex are marks of a harsher character, of a heart that has less sensibility, and is on the whole less amiable than that of others. Yet it must be owned that there are some such among us. Much, if not the whole of this perversion, has, I am persuaded, been owing to the contagion of bad example in the men. They are made familiar with such expressions—their first horror is gone, and (would to heaven that I were mistaken!) some of them have already wounded their consciences to such a degree, that they have some reason to wish that religion may be without foundation.

But I would call upon all, and *these* women in particular, to consider this matter in another light—as it may affect themselves in this life; as it may affect their rank and treatment in ordinary society. I would say to them, that if the world shall once adopt the belief that this life is our all, then the true maxim of rational conduct will be, to " eat and to drink, since to-morrow we are to die;" and that when they have nothing to trust to but the fondness of the men, they will soon find themselves reduced to slavery. The crown which they now wear will fall from their heads, and they will no longer be the arbiters of what is lovely in human life. The empire of beauty is but short; and even in republican France, it will not be many years that Madame Tallien can fascinate the Parisian Theatre by the exhibition of her charms. Man is fastidious and changeable, he is the stronger animal, and can always take his own will with respect to woman. At present he is with-held by respect for her moral worth—and many are with-held by religion—and many more are with-held by public laws, which laws were framed at a time when religious truths influenced the minds and the conduct of men. When the sentiments of men change, they will not be so foolish as to keep in force laws which cramp their strongest desires. Then will the rich have their Harems, and the poor their drudges.

Nay, it is not merely the circumstance of woman's being considered as the moral companion of man that gives the sex its empire among us. There is something of this to be observed in all nations. Of all the distinctions which set our species above the other sentient inhabitants of this globe, making us as unlike to the best of them as they are to a piece of inanimate matter, there is none more remarkable than the differences observable in the appearances of those desires by which the race is continued. As I observed already, such a distinction is indispensably necessary. There must be a *moral* connection, in order that the human species may be a race of rational creatures, improveable, not only by the increasing experience of the individual, but also by the heritable experience of the successive generations. It may be observed between the solitary pairs in Labrador, where human nature starves, like the stunted oak in the crevice of a baron rock; and it is seen in the cultivated societies of Europe, where our nature in a series of ages becomes a majestic tree. Whatever may be the native powers of mind in the poor but gentle Esquimaux, she can do nothing for the species but nurse a young one, who cannot run his race of life without incessant and hard labour to keep soul and body together—here therefore her station in society can hardly have a name, because there can hardly be said to be any association, except what is necessary for repelling the hostile attacks of Indians, who seem to hunt them without provocation as the dog does the hare. In other parts of the world,
we

we see that the consideration in which the sex is held, nearly follows the proportions of that aggregate of many different particulars, which we consider as constituting the cultivation of a society. We may perhaps err, and we probably do err, in our estimation of those degrees, because we are not perfectly acquainted with what is the real excellence of man. But as far as we *can* judge of it, I believe that my assertion is acknowledged. On this authority, I might presume to say, that it is in Christian Europe that man *has* attained his highest degree of cultivation—and it is undoubtedly here that the women have attained the highest rank. I may even add, that it is in that part of Europe where the essential and distinguishing doctrines of Christian morality are most generally acknowledged and attended to by the laws of the country, that woman acts the highest part in general society. But here we must be very careful how we form our notion, either of the society, or of the female rank—it is surely not from the two or three dozens who fill the highest ranks in the state. Their number is too small, and their situation is too particular, to afford the proper average. Besides, the situation of the individuals of this class in all countries is very much the same—and in all it is very artificial—accordingly their character is fantastical. Nor are we to take it from that class that is the most numerous of all, the lowest class of society, for these are the labouring poor, whose conduct and occupations are so much dictated to them by the hard circumstances of their situation, that scarcely any thing is left to their choice. The situation of women of this class must be nearly the same in all nations. But this class is still susceptible of some variety—and we see it—and I think that even here there is a perceptible superiority of the female rank in those countries where

the

the pureſt Chriſtianity prevails. We muſt however take our meaſures or proportions from a numerous claſs, but alſo a claſs in ſomewhat of eaſy circumſtances, where moral ſentiments call ſome attention, and perſons have ſome choice in their conduct. And here, although I cannot pretend to have had many opportunities of obſervation, yet I have had ſome. I can venture to ſay that it is not in Ruſſia, nor in Spain, that woman is, on the whole, the moſt important as a member of the community. I would ſay, that in Britain her important rights are more generally reſpected than any where elſe. No where is a man's character ſo much hurt by conjugal infidelity—no where is it ſo difficult to rub off the ſtigma of baſtardy, or to procure a decent reception or ſociciety for an improper connection; and I believe it will readily be granted, that the ſhare of the women in ſucceſſions, their authority in all matters of domeſtic truſt, and even their opinions in what concerns life and manners, are fully more reſpected here than in any country.

I have long been of the opinion, (and every obſervation that I have been able to make ſince I firſt formed it confirms me in it,) that woman is indebted to Chriſtianity alone for the high rank ſhe holds in ſociety. Look into the writings of antiquity—into the works of the Greek and Latin poets—into the numberleſs panegyrics of the ſex, to be found both in proſe and verſe—I can find little, very little indeed, where woman is treated with reſpect—there is no want of love, that is, of fondneſs, of beauty, of charms, of graces. But of woman as the equal of man, as a moral companion, travelling with him the road to felicity—as his adviſer—his ſolace in misfortune—as a pattern from which he may ſometimes

copy

copy with advantage;—of all this there is hardly a trace. Woman is always mentioned as an object of paffion. Chaftity, modefty, fober-mindednefs, are all confidered in relation to this fingle point; or fometimes as of importance in refpect of economy or domeftic quiet. Recollect the famous fpeech of Meteltellus Numidicus to the Roman people, when, as, Cenfor, he was recommending marriage.

" Si fine uxore poffemus Quirites effe, omnes eâ
" moleftiâ careremus. Sed quoniam ita natura tradi-
" dit, ut nec cum illis commodè, nec fine illis ullo
" modo vivi poffet, faluti perpetuæ potius quam brevi
" voluptati confulendum."

Aul. Gell. Noct. Att. I. 6.

What does Ovid, the great panegyrift of the fex, fay for his beloved daughter, whom he had praifed for her attractions in various places of his Triftia and other compofitions? He is writing her Epitaph—and the only thing he can fay of her as a rational creature is, that fhe was—*Domifida*—not a Gadabout.—Search Apuleius, where you will find many female characters *in abstracto*—You will find that his little Photis (a cook-maid and ftrumpet) was neareft to his heart, after all his philofophy. Nay, in his pretty ftory of Cupid and Pfyche, which the very wife will tell you is a fine leffon of moral philofophy, and a reprefentation of the operations of the intellectual and moral faculties of the human foul, a ftory which gave him the fineft opportunity, nay, almoft made it neceffary for him to infert whatever can ornament the female character; what is his Pfyche but a beautiful, fond, and filly girl; and what are the whole fruits of any acquaintance with the fex?—Pleafure. But why take more pains in the fearch?—Look at their immortal
goddefies—

goddesses—is there one among them whom a wise man would select for a wife or a friend?—I grant that a Lucretia is praised—a Portia, an Arria, a Zenobia—but these are individual characters—not representatives of the sex. The only Grecian ladies who made a figure by intellectual talents, were your Aspasias, Sapphos, Phrynes, and other nymphs of this cast, who had emerged from the general insignificance of the sex, by throwing away what we are accustomed to call its greatest ornament.

I think that the first piece in which woman is pictured as a respectable character, is the oldest novel that I am acquainted with, written by a Christian Bishop, Heliodorus—I mean the Adventures of Theagenes and Chariclea. I think that the Heroine is a greater character than you will meet with in all the annals of antiquity. And it is worth while to observe what was the effect of this painting. The poor Bishop had been deposed, and even excommunicated, for doctrinal errors, and for drawing such a picture of a heathen. The magistrates of Antioch, the most voluptuous and corrupted city of the East, wrote to the Emperor, telling him that this book had reformed the ladies of their city, where Julian the Emperor and his Sophists had formerly preached in vain, and they therefore prayed that the good Bishop might not be deprived of his mitre.—It is true, we read of Hypatia, daughter of Theon, the mathematician at Alexandria, who was a prodigy of excellence, and taught philosophy, *i. e.* the art of leading a good and happy life, with great applause in the famous Alexandrian school.—But she also was in the times of Christianity, and was the intimate friend of Syncellus and other Christian Bishops.

It

It is undoubtedly Christianity that has set woman on her throne, making her in every respect the equal of man, bound to the same duties, and candidate for the same happiness. Mark how woman is described by a Christian poet,

> ———" Yet when I approach
> Her loveliness, so absolute she seems,
> And in herself complete, so well to know
> Her own, that what she wills to do or say
> Seems *wisest, virtuousest, discreetest, best.*
>
> Neither her outside, form'd so fair,———
> So much delights me, as *those graceful acts,*
> *Those thousand decencies* that daily flow
> From all her words and actions, mix'd with love
> And sweet compliance, which declare unfeign'd
> *Union of mind, or in us both one soul.*
>
> ———And, to consummate all,
> *Greatness of mind,* and *nobleness,* their seat
> Build in her loveliest, *and create an awe*
> *About her, as a guard angelic plac'd.*"
>   MILTON.

This is really moral painting, without any abatement of female charms.

This is the natural consequence of that purity of heart, which is so much insisted on in the Christian morality. In the instructions of the heathen philosophers, it is either not mentioned at all, or at most, it is recommended coldly, as a thing proper, and worthy of a mind attentive to great things.—But, in Christianity, it is insisted on as an indispensable duty, and enforced by many arguments peculiar to itself.

It is worthy of observation, that the most prominent superstitions which have dishonoured the Christian churches, have been the excessive refinements which the enthusiastic admiration of heroic purity has allowed the holy trade to introduce into the manufacture of our spiritual fetters. Without this enthusiasm, cold expediency would not have been able to make the Monastic vow so general, nor have given us such numbers of convents. These were generally founded by such enthusiasts—the rulers indeed of the church *encouraged* this to the utmost, as the best levy for the spiritual power—but they could not *enjoin* such foundations. From the same source we may derive the chief influence of auricular confession. When these were firmly established, and were venerated, almost all the other corruptions of Christianity followed of course. I may almost add, that though it is here that Christianity has suffered the most violent attacks, it is here that the place is most tenable.—Nothing tends so much to knit all the ties of society as the endearing connections of family, and whatever tends to lessen our veneration for the marriage-contract, weakens them in the most effectual manner. Purity of manners is the most effectual support, and pure thoughts are the only sources from which pure manners can flow. I readily grant that in former times this veneration for personal purity was carried to an extravagant height, and that several very ridiculous fancies and customs arose from this. Romantic love and chivalry are strong instances of the strange vagaries of our imagination, when carried along by this enthusiastic admiration of female purity; and so unnatural and forced, that they could only be temporary fashions. But I believe that, with all their ridicule, it would be a happy nation where this was the general creed and practice. Nor can I help thinking a nation on its decline, when the domestic connections cease to be venerated, and the illegitimate offspring of a nabob or a nobleman are received with ease into good company.

Nothing

Nothing is more clear than that the design of the Illuminati was to abolish Christianity—and we now see how effectual this would be for the corruption of the fair sex, a purpose which they eagerly wished to gain, that they might corrupt the men. But if the women would retain the rank they now hold, they will be careful to preserve in full force on their minds this religion, so congenial to their dispositions, which nature has made affectionate and kind.

And with respect to the men, is it not egregious folly to encourage any thing that can tend to blast our sweetest enjoyments? Shall we not do this most effectually if we attempt to corrupt what nature will always make us consider as the highest elegance of life? The divinity of the Stoics was, "*Mens sana in corpore sano*," —but it is equally true,

"*Gratior est pulchro veniens e corpore virtus.*"

If, therefore, instead of professedly tainting what is of itself beautiful, we could really work it up to

"That fair form, which, wove in fancy's loom,
"Floats in light visions round the poet's head,"

and make woman a pattern of perfection, we should undoubtedly add more to the heartfelt happiness of life than by all the discoveries of the Illuminati. See what was the effect of Theagenes and Chariclea.

And we should remember that with the fate of woman that of man is indissolubly knit. The voice of nature spoke through our immortal bard, when he made Adam say,

———"From thy state
"Mine never shall be parted, bliss or woe."

Should

Should we suffer the contagion to touch our fair partner, all is gone, and too late shall we say,

" O faireſt of creation ! laſt and beſt·
" Of all God's works, creature in whom excell'd
" Whatever can to fight or thought be form'd,
" *Holy*, *divine*, *good*, *amiable*, *or ſweet !*
" How art thou loſt,—and now to death devote?
" And *me* with *thee* haſt ruin'd; for with thee
" Certain my reſolution is to die."

CHAP. III.

The German Union.

WHEN such a fermentation had been excited in the public mind, it cannot be supposed that the formal suppression of the Order of the Illuminati in Bavaria, and in the Duchy of Wirtemberg, by the reigning princes, would bring all to rest again. By no means. The minds of men were predisposed for a change by the restless spirit of speculation in every kind of enquiry, and the leaven had been carefully and skilfully disseminated in every quarter of the empire, and even in foreign countries. Weishaupt said, on good grounds, that " if the Order should be discovered and suppressed, he would restore it with tenfold energy in a twelvemonth." Even in those states where it was formally abolished, nothing could hinder the enlisting new members, and carrying on all the purposes of the Order. The Areopagitæ might indeed be changed, and the seat of the direction transferred to some other place, but the Minerval and his Mentor could meet as formerly, and a ride of a few miles into another State, would bring him to a Lodge, where the young would be amused, and the more advanced would be engaged in serious mischief. Weishaupt never liked children's play. He indulged Philo in it, because he saw him taken with such rattles: but his own projects were dark and solemn, and it was a relief to him now to be freed from that mummery. He soon found the bent of the person's mind on whom he had set his talons, and, he says, that " no man ever escaped him whom he thought it worth while to secure." He had already filled the lists with enough of the young and gay, and when the prefent condition of the Order required fly and experienced heads, he no longer courted them by play-things. He communicated the ranks and the inftructions by a letter, without any ceremony. The correspondence with Philo at the time of the breach with him, fhews the fuperiority of Spartacus. Philo is in a rage, provoked to find a pitiful profeffor difcontented with the immenfe fervices which he had received from a gentleman of his rank, and treating him with authority, and with difingenuity.—He tells Spartacus what ftill greater fervices he can do the Order, and that he can alfo ruin it with a breath.—But in the midft of this rage, he propofes a thoufand modes of reconcilement. The fmalleft conceffion would make him hug Spartacus in his arms. But Spartacus is deaf to all his threats, and firm as a rock. Though he is confcious of his own vile conduct, he abates not in the fmalleft point, his abfolute authority—requires the moft implicit fubmiffion, which he fays " is due not to him, but to the Order, and without which the Order muft immediately go to ruin."—He does not even deign to challenge Philo to do his worft, but allows him to go out of the Order without one angry word. This fhows his confidence in the energy of that fpirit of reftlefs difcontent, and that hankering after reform which he had fo fuccefsfully fpread abroad.

This had indeed arifen to an unparalleled height, unexpected even by the feditious themfelves. This appeared in a remarkable manner by the reception given to the infamous letters on the conftitution of the Pruffian States.

The general opinion was, that Mirabeau was the author of the letters themfelves, and it was perfectly underftood by every perfon, that the tranflation into French was a joint contrivance of Mirabeau and Nicholai.

cholai. I was affured of this by the Britifh Minifter at that Court. There are fome blunders in refpect of names, which an inhabitant of the country could hardly be guilty of, but are very confiftent with the felf-conceit and precipitancy of this Frenchman.— There are feveral inftances of the fame kind in two pieces, which are known for certain to be his, viz. the *Chronique fcandaleufe* and the *Hiftoire fecrette de la Cour de Berlin*. Thefe letters were in every hand, and were mentioned in every converfation, even in the Pruffian dominions—and in other places of the empire they were quoted, and praifed, and commented on, although fome of their contents were nothing fhort of rebellion.

Mirabeau had a large portion of that felf-conceit which diftinguifhes his countrymen. He thought himfelf qualified not only for any high office in adminiftration, but even for managing the whole affairs of the new King. He therefore endeavoured to obtain fome poft of honour. But he was difappointed, and, in revenge, did every thing in his power to make thofe in adminiftration the objects of public ridicule and reproach. His licentious and profligate manners were fuch as excluded him from the fociety of the people of the firft claffes, whom it behoved to pay fome attention to perfonal dignity. His opinions were in the higheft degree corrupted, and he openly profeffed Atheifm. This made him peculiarly obnoxious to the King, who was determined to correct the difturbances and difquiets which had arifen in the Pruffian ftates from the indifference of his predeceffor in thofe matters. Mirabeau therefore attached himfelf to a junto of writers and fcribblers, who had united in order to diffeminate licentious principles, both in refpect of religion and of government. His wit and fancy were great, and he had not perhaps his equal for eloquent

and

and biting fatire. He was therefore careffed by thofe writers as a moft valuable acquifition to their Society. He took all this deference as his juft due; and was fo confident in his powers, and fo foolifh, as to advife, and even to admonifh, the King. Highly obnoxious by fuch conduct, he was excluded from any chance of preferment, and was exceedingly out of humour. In this ftate of mind he was in a fit frame for Illumination. Spartacus had been eyeing him for fome time, and at laft communicated this honour to him through the intermedium of Mauvillon, another Frenchman, Lieutenant-Colonel in the fervice of the Duke of Brunfwick. This perfon had been moft active during the formal exiftence of the Order, and had contributed much to its reception in the Proteftant ftates—he remained long concealed. Indeed his Illumination was not known till the invafion of Holland by the French. Mauvillon then ftepped forth, avowed his principles, and recommended the example of the French to the Germans. This encouragement brought even Philo again on the ftage, notwithftanding his refentment againft Spartacus, and his folemn declaration of having abjured all fuch focieties.—Thefe, and a thoufand fuch facts, fhow that the feeds of licentious Cofmopolitifm had taken deep root, and that cutting down the crop had by no means deftroyed the baneful plant.—But this is not all—a new method of cultivation had been invented, and immediately adopted, and it was now growing over all Europe in another form.

I have already taken notice of the general perverfion of the public mind which co-operated with the fchifms of Free Mafonry in procuring a liftening ear to Spartacus and his affociates. It will not be doubted but that the machinations of the Illuminati increafed this, even among thofe who did not enter

into

into the Order. It was eafier to diminſh the refpect for civil eſtabliſhments in Germany than in almoſt any other country. The frivolity of the ranks and court-offices in the different confederated petty ſtates made it impoſſible to combine dignity with the habits of a ſcanty income.—It was ſtill eafier to expofe to ridicule and reproach thofe numberlefs abufes which the folly and the vices of men had introduced into religion. The influence on the public mind which naturally attaches to the venerable office of a moral inſtructor, was prodigiouſly diminiſhed by the continual difputes of the Catholics and Proteſtants, which were carried on with great heat in every little principality. The freedom of enquiry, which was fupported by the ſtate in Proteſtant Germany, was terribly abufed, (for what will the folly of man not abufe?) and degenerated into a wanton licentiouſnefs of thought, and a rage for ſpeculation and ſcepticifm on every fubject whatever. The ſtruggle, which was originally between the Catholics and the Proteſtants, had changed, during the gradual progrefs of luxury and immorality, into a conteſt between reafon and fuperſtition. And in this conteſt the denomination of fuperſtition had been gradually extended to every doctrine which profeſſed to be of divine revelation, and reafon was declared to be, for certain, the only way in which the Deity can inform the human mind.

Some refpectable Catholics had publiſhed works filled with liberal fentiments. Thefe were reprefented as villainous machinations to inveigle Proteſtants. On the other hand, fome Proteſtant divines had propofed to imitate this liberality by making conceſſions which might enable a good Catholic to live more at eafe among the Proteſtants, and might even accelerate an union of faiths. This was hooted beyond meafure, as Jefuitical, and big with danger.

While

While the fceptical junto, headed by the editors of the *Deutfche Bibliothek* and the *Berlin Monatfchrift,* were recommending every performance that was hoftile to the eftablifhed faith of the country, Leuchtfenring was equally bufy, finding Jefuits in every corner, and went about with all the inquietude of a madman, picking up anecdotes. Zimmerman, the refpectable phyfician of Frederick King of Pruffia, gives a diverting account of a vifit which he had from Leuchtfenring at Hanover, all trembling with fears of Jefuits, and wifhing to perfuade him that his life was in danger from them. Nicholai was now on the hunt, and during this crufade Philo laid hands on him, being introduced to his acquaintance by Leuchtfenring, who was, by this time, cured of his zeal for Proteftanifm, and had become a difciple of Illuminatifm. Philo had gained his good opinion by the violent attack which he had publifhed on the Jefuits and Rofycrucians by the orders of Spartacus.—He had not far to go in gaining over Nicholai, who was at this time making a tour through the Lodges. The fparks of Illumination which he perceived in many of them pleafed him exceedingly, and he very cheerfully received the precious fecret from Philo.

This acquifition to the Order was made in January 1782. Spartacus was delighted with it, confidered Nicholai as a moft excellent champion, and gave him the name of *Lucian,* the great fcoffer at all religion, as aptly expreffing his character.

Nicholai, on his return to Berlin, publifhed many volumes of his difcoveries. One would imagine that not a Jefuit had efcaped him. He mentions many ftrange fchifmatics, both in religion and in Mafonry—But he never once mentions an *Illuminatus.*—When they were firft checked, and before the difcovery of the fecret correfpondence, he defended them, and ftrongly reprobated the proceedings of the
Elector

Elector of Bavaria, calling it vile perfecution.—
Nay, after the difcovery of the letters found in
Zwack's houfe, he perfifted in his defence, vindicated the poffeffion of the abominable receipts, and
highly extolled the character of Weifhaupt.—But
when the difcovery of papers in the houfe of Batz
informed the public that he himfelf had long been
an *Illuminatus*, he was fadly put to it to reconcile his
defence with any pretenfions to religion*.——
Weifhaupt faved him from difgrace, as he thought,
by his publication of the fyftem of Illuminatifm—
Nicholai then boldly faid that he knew no more of
the Order than was contained in that book, that is,
only the two firft degrees.

But before this, Nicholai had made to himfelf a
moft formidable enemy. The hiftory of this conteft is curious in itfelf, and gives us a very inftructive
picture of the machinations of that *conjuration des
philofophes*, or gang of fcribblers who were leagued
againft the peace of the world. The reader will
therefore find it to our purpofe. On the authority
of a lady in Courland, a Countefs von der Recke,
Nicholai had accufed Dr. Stark of Darmftadt (who
made fuch a figure in Free Mafonry) of Jefuitifm,
and of having even fubmitted to the *tonfure*. Stark
was a moft reftlefs fpirit—had gone through every
myftery in Germany, Illuminatifm excepted, and
had ferreted out many of Nicholai's hidden tranfac-

---

* He impudently pretended that the papers containing the
fyftem and doctrines of Illuminatifm, came to him at Berlin, from
an unknown hand. But no one believed him.—it was inconfiftent
with what is faid of him in the fecret correfpondence. He had
faid the fame thing concerning the French tranflation of the Letters on the Conftitution of the Pruffian States. Fifty copies were
found in his ware-houfe. He faid that they had been fent from Strafburg, and that he had never fold one of them.—Suppofing both
thefe affertions to be true, it appears that Nicholai was confidered
as a very proper hand for difperfing fuch poifon.

tions.

tions. He was alſo an unwearied book-maker, and dealt out theſe diſcoveries by degrees, keeping the eye of the public continually upon Nicholai. He had ſuſpected his Illumination for ſome time paſt, and when the ſecret came out, by Spartacus' letter, where he boaſts of his acquiſition, calling Nicholai a moſt ſturdy combatant, and ſaying that he was *contentiſſimus*, Stark left no ſtone unturned till he diſcovered that Nicholai had been initiated in all the horrid and moſt profligate myſteries of Illuminatiſm, and that Spartacus had at the very firſt entruſted him with his moſt darling ſecrets, and adviſed with him on many occaſions*.

This complete blaſting of his moral character could not be patiently borne, and Nicholai was in his turn the bitter enemy of Stark, and, in the pa-

* Of this we have complete proof in the private correſpondence. Philo, ſpeaking in one of his letters of the gradual change which was to be produced in the minds of their pupils from Chriſtianity to Deiſm, ſays, " Nicholai informs me, that even the pious " Zollikofer has now been convinced that it would be proper to ſet " up a deiſtical church in Berlin." It is in vain that Nicholai ſays that his knowledge of the Order was only of what Weiſhaupt had publiſhed; for Philo ſays that that corrected ſyſtem had not been introduced into it when he quitted it in 1784. But Nicholai deſerves no credit—he is one of the moſt ſcandalous examples of the operation of the principles of Weiſhaupt. He procured admiſſion into the Lodges of Free Maſons and Roſycrucians, merely to act the diſhonourable part of a ſpy, and he betrayed their ſecrets as far as he could. In the appendix to the 7th volume of his journey, he declaims againſt the Templar Maſons, Roſycrucians, and Jeſuits, for their blind ſubmiſſion to unknown ſuperiors, for their ſuperſtitions, their prieſthoods, and their baſe principles—and yet had been five years in a ſociety in which all theſe were carried to the greateſt height. He remains true to the Illuminati alone, becauſe they had the ſame object in view with himſelf and his atheiſtical aſſociates, His defence of Proteſtantiſm is all a cheat; and perhaps he may be conſidered as an enemy equally formidable with Weiſhaupt himſelf. This is the reaſon why he occupies ſo many of theſe pages.

roxyſms

roxyſms of his anger, publiſhed every idle tale, although he was often obliged to contradict them in the next Review. In the courſe of this attack and defence, Dr. Stark diſcovered the revival of the Illuminati, or at leaſt a ſociety which carried on the ſame great work in a ſomewhat different way.

Dr. Stark had written a defence againſt one of Nicholai's accuſations, and wiſhed to have it printed at Leipzig. He therefore ſent the manuſcript to a friend, who reſided there. This friend immediately propoſed it to a moſt improper perſon, Mr. Pott, who had written an anonymous commentary on the King of Pruſſia's edict for the uniformity of religious worſhip in his dominions. This is one of the moſt ſhameleſs attacks on the eſtabliſhed faith of the nation, and the authority and conduct of the Prince, that can be imagined. Stark's friend was ignorant of this, and ſpoke to Pott, as the partner of the great publiſher Walther. They, without heſitation, undertook the publiſhing; but when ſix weeks had paſſed over, Stark's friend found that it was not begun. Some exceptionable paſſages, which treated with diſreſpect the religion of Reaſon, were given as the cauſe of delay; and he was told that the author had been written to about them, but had not yet returned an anſwer. This was afterwards found to be falſe. Then a paſſage in the preface was objected to, as treating roughly a lady in Courland, which Walther could not print, becauſe he had connections with that court. The author muſt be entreated to change his expreſſions. After another delay, paper was wanting. The MS. was withdrawn. Walther now ſaid that he would print it immediately, and again got it into his hands, promiſing to ſend the ſheets as they came from the preſs. Theſe not appearing for a long time, the agent made enquiry, and found that it was ſent to Michaelis at Halle, to be printed there. The agent immediately went thither, and found that it was printing with great alterations, another title, and a guide or key, in which the work was perverted and turned into ridicule by a Dr. Bahrdt, who refided in that neighbourhood. An action of recovery and damages was immediately commenced at Leipzig, and after much conteft, an interdict was put on Michaelis's edition, and a proper edition was ordered immediately from Walther, with fecuritty that it fhould appear before Bahrdt's key. Yet when it was produced at the next fair, the bookfellers had been already fupplied with the fpurious edition ; and as this was accompanied by the key, it was much more faleable ware, and completely fupplanted the other.

This is furely a ftrong inftance of the machinations by which the Illuminati have attempted to deftroy the Liberty of the Prefs, and the power they have to difcourage or fupprefs any thing that is not agreeable to the tafte of the literary junto. It was in the courfe of this tranfaction that Dr. Stark's agent found people talking in the coffee-houfes of Leipzig and Halle of the advantages of public libraries, and of libraries by fubfcription, in every town, where perfons could, at a fmall expence, fee what was paffing in the learned world. As he could not but acquiefce in thefe points, they who held this language began to talk of a general Affociation, which fhould act in concert over all Germany, and make a full communication of its numerous literary productions by forming focieties for reading and inftruction, which fhould be regularly fupplied with every publication. Flying fheets and pamphlets were afterwards put into his hands, ftating the great ufe of fuch an Affociation, and the effect which it would fpeedily produce by enlightening the nation. By and by he

learned

learned that such an Association did really exist, and that it was called the GERMAN UNION, for ROOTING OUT SUPERSTITION AND PREJUDICES, AND ADVANCING TRUE CHRISTIANITY. On enquiry, however, he found that this was to be a Secret Society, because it had to combat prejudices which were supported by the great of this world, and because its aim was to promote that general information which priests and despots dreaded above all things. This Association was accessible only through the reading societies, and oaths of secrecy and fidelity were required. In short, it apppeared to be the old song of the Illuminati.

This discovery was immediately announced to the public, in an anonymous publication in defence of Dr. Stark. It is supposed to be his own performance. It discloses a scene of complicated villiany and folly, in which the Lady in Courland makes a very strange figure. She appears to be a wild fanatic, deeply engaged in magic and ghost-raising, and leagued with Nicholai, Gedicke, and Biester, against Dr. Stark. He is very completely cleared of the facts alledged against him; and his three male opponents appear void of all principle and enemies of all religion. Stark however would, in Britain, be a very singular character, considered as a clergyman. The frivolous secrets of Masonry have either engrossed his whole mind, or he has laboured in them as a lucrative trade, by which he took advantage of the folly of others. The contest between Stark and the Triumvirate at Berlin engaged the public attention much more than we should imagine that a thing of so private a nature would do. But the characters were very notorious; and it turned the attention of the public to those clandestine attacks which were made in every quarter on the civil and religious establishments. It was obvious to every person, that these reading societies had all on a sudden become very numerous; and the characters of those who patronised them only increased the suspicions which were now raised.

The first work that speaks expressly of the German Union, is a very sensible performance "*On the Right of Princes to direct the Religion of their Subjects.*" The next is a curious work, a sort of narrative *Dialogue on the Characters of Nicholai, Gedicke, and Biester*. It is chiefly occupied with the contest with Dr. Stark, but in the 5th part, it treats particularly of the German Union.

About the same time appeared some farther account, in a book called *Archives of Fanaticism and Illuminatism*. But all these accounts are very vague and unsatisfactory. The fullest account is to be had in a work published at Leipzig by Gotchen the bookseller. It is entitled, "*More Notes than Text, or the German Union of XXII, a new Secret Society for the Good of Mankind,*" Leipzig 1789. The publisher says that it was sent him by an unknown hand, and that he published it with all speed, on account of the many mischiefs which this Society, (of which he had before heard several reports,) might do to the world, and to the trade, if allowed to go on working in secret. From this work, therefore, we may form a notion of this redoubtable Society, and judge how far it is practicable to prevent such secret machinations against the peace and happiness of mankind.

There is another work, "*Further information concerning the German Union.* (Nahere Beleuchtung der Deutsche Union,) *also showing how, for a moderate price, one may become a Scotch Free*

" *Free Mason.*" *Frankford and Leipzig*, 1789. The author says that he had all the papers in his hands; whereas the author of *More Notes than Text* acknowledges the want of some. But very little additional light is thrown on the subject by this work, and the first is still the most instructive, and will chiefly be followed in the account which is now to be laid before the reader.

The book *More Notes than Text* contains plans and letters, which the Twenty-two United Brethren have allowed to be given out, and of which the greatest part were printed, but were entrusted only to assured members.

No. I. is the first plan, printed on a single quarto page, and is addressed, *To all the Friends of Reason, of Truth, and of Virtue.* It is pretty well written, and states among other things, that " be-
" cause a great number of persons are labouring,
" with united effort, to bring Reason under the
" yoke, and to prevent all instruction, it is there-
" fore necessary that there be a combination which
" shall work in opposition to them so that man-
" kind may not sink anew into irrecoverable bar-
" barism, when Reason and Virtue shall have been
" completely subdued, overpowered by the re-
" straints which are put on our opinions."——
" For this noble purpose a company of twenty-
" two persons, public instructors, and men in pri-
" vate stations, have united themselves, according
" to a plan which they have had under considera-
" tion for more than a year and a half, and which,
" in their opinion, contains a method that is fair
" and irresistible by any human power, for pro-
" moting the enlightening and forming of man-
" kind, and that will gradually remove all the ob-
" stacles which superstition supported by force
" has hitherto put in the way."

This

This addreſs is intended for an enliſting advertiſement, and, after a few inſignificant remarks on the Aſſociation, a rix-dahler is required along with the ſubſcription of acquieſcence in the plan, as a compenſation for the expences attending this mode of intimation and conſent.

Whoever pays the rix-dahler, and declares his wiſh to join the Aſſociation, receives in a few days, No. II. which is a form of the Oath of ſecrecy, alſo printed on a ſingle 4to page. Having ſubſcribed this, and given a full deſignation of himſelf, he returns it agreeably to a certain addreſs; and ſoon after, he gets No. III. printed on a 4to ſheet. This number contains what is called the Second Plan, to which all the ſubſequent plans and circular letters refer. A copy therefore of this will give us a pretty full and juſt notion of the Order, and its mode of declaration. It is intitled,

The Plan of the Twenty-Two,

and begins with this declaration : " We have unit-
" ed, in order to accompliſh the aim of the ex-
" alted Founder of Chriſtianity, viz. the enlighten-
" ing of mankind, and the dethronement of ſu-
" perſtition and fanaticiſm, by means of a ſecret
" fraternization of all who love the work of God.

" Our firſt exertion, which has already been
" very extenſive, conſiſts in this, that, by means
" of confidential perſons, we allow ourſelves to
" be announced every where as a Society united
" for the above-mentioned purpoſe; and we in-
" vite and admit into brotherhood with ourſelves
" every perſon who has a ſenſe of the importance
" of this matter, and wiſhes to apply to us and
" ſee our plans.

" We

"We labour first of all to draw into our Asso-
"ciation all good and learned writers. This we
"imagine will be the easier obtained, as they
"must derive an evident advantage from it.
"Next to such men, we seek to gain the masters
"and secretaries of the Post-offices, in order to
"facilitate our correspondence.

"Besides these, we receive persons of every
"condition and station, excepting princes and
"their ministers. Their favourites, however,
"may be admitted, and may be useful by their
"influence in behalf of Truth and Virtue.

"When any person writes to us, we send him
"an oath, by which he must abjure all treachery
"or discovery of the Association, till circum-
"stances shall make it proper for us to come for-
"ward and show ourselves to the world. When
"he subscribes the oath, he receives the plan, and
"if he finds this to be what satisfies his mind as
"a thing good and honourable, he becomes our
"friend only in so far as he endeavours to gain
"over his friends and acquaintances. Thus
"we learn who are really our zealous friends,
"and our numbers increase in a double pro-
"portion.

"This procedure is to continue till Provi-
"dence shall so far bless our endeavours, that
"we acquire an active Brother and coadjutor in
"every place of note, where there is any lite-
"rary profession; and for this purpose we have
"a secretary and proper office in the center of
"the Association, where every thing is expedit-
"ed, and all reports received. When this happy
"epoch arrives, we begin our second operation."
That is to say,

"We intimate to all the Brotherhood in every
"quarter, on a certain day, *that* THE GERMAN
"UNION

"UNION *has now acquired a consistence*, and we
"now divide the fraternised part of the nation
"into ten or twelve *Provinces* or *Dioceses*, each
"directed by its *Diocesan* at his office; and these
"are so arranged in due subordination, that all
"business comes into the UNION-HOUSE as into
"the center of the whole.

"Agreeably to this manner of proceeding there
"are two classes of the Brotherhood, the *Ordi-*
"*nary* and the *Managing* Brethren. The latter
"alone know the aim of the association, and all
"the means for attaining it; and they alone
"constitute the UNION, the name, and the con-
"nection of which is not intended to be at all
"conspicuous in the world.

"To this end the business takes a new exter-
"nal form. The Brethren, to wit, speak not of
"the Union in the places where they reside, nor
"of a Society, nor of enlightening the people;
"but they assemble, and act together in every
"quarter, merely as a LITERARY SOCIETY,
"bring into it all the lovers of reading and of
"useful knowledge; and such in fact are the
"*Ordinary Brethren*, who only know that an
"Association exists in their place of residence
"for the encouragement of literary men, but
"by no means that it has any connection with
"any other similar Society, and that they all
"constitute one whole. But these Societies will
"naturally point out to the intelligent Brethren
"such persons as are proper to be selected for
"carrying forward the great work. For per-
"sons of a serious turn of mind are not mere
"loungers in such company, but show in their
"conversation the interest they take in real in-
"struction. And the cast of their reading, which
"must not be checked in the beginning in the
"smallest

" smallest degree, although it may be gradually
" directed to proper subjects of information, will
" point out in the most unequivocal manner their
" peculiar ways of thinking on the important
" subjects connected with our great object. Here,
" therefore, the active Brethren will observe in
" secret, and will select those whom they think
" valuable acquisitions to the sacred Union. They
" will invite such persons to unite with them-
" selves in their endeavours to enlighten the
" rest of mankind, by calling their attention to
" profitable subjects of reading, and to proper
" books. Reading Societies, therefore, are to be
" formed in every quarter, and to be furnished
" with proper books. In this provision attention
" must be paid to two things. The taste of the
" public must be complied with, that the So-
" ciety may have any effect at all in bringing
" men together who are born for somewhat more
" than just to look about them. But the general
" taste may, and must also be carefully and skil-
" fully directed to subjects that will enlarge the
" comprehension, will fortify the heart, and, by
" habituating the mind to novelty, and to suc-
" cessful discovery, both in physics and in morals,
" will hinder the timid from being startled at
" doctrines and maxims which are singular, or
" perhaps opposite to those which are current
" in ordinary society. Commonly a man speaks
" as if he thought he was uttering his own sen-
" timents, while he is only echoing the general
" sound. Our minds are dressed in a prevailing
" fashion as much as our bodies, and with stuff
" as little congenial to sentiment, as a piece
" of woollen cloth is to the human skin. So care-
" less and indolent are men, even in what they
" call serious conversation. Till reflection be-

" comes

" comes a habit, what is really a thought startles,
" however simple, and, if really uncommon, it
" astonishes and confounds. Nothing, therefore,
" can so powerfully tend to the improvement of
" the human character, as well-managed Read-
" ing Societies.

" When these have been established in different
" places, we must endeavour to accomplish the
" following intermediate plans: 1. To introduce
" a general literary Gazette or Review, which,
" by uniting all the learned Brethren, and com-
" bining with judgment and address all their
" talents, and steadily proceeding according to
" a distinct and precise plan, may in time sup-
" plant every other Gazette, a thing which its
" intrinsic merit and comprehensive plan will
" easily accomplish. 2. To select a secretary for
" our Society, who shall have it in charge to
" commission the books which they shall select
" in conformity to the great aim of the Associa-
" tion, and who shall undertake to commission
" all other books for the curious in his neigh-
" bourhood. If there be a bookseller in the place,
" who can be gained over and sworn into the
" Society, it will be proper to choose him for
" this office, since, as will be made more
" plain afterwards, the trade will gradually
" come into the plan, and fall into the hands
" of the Union.

" And now, every eye can perceive the pro-
" gressive moral influence which the Union will
" acquire on the nation. Let us only conceive
" what superstition will lose, and what instruc-
" tion must gain by this; when, 1. In every
" Reading Society the books are selected by our
" Fraternity. 2. When we have confidential
" persons in every quarter, who will make it
                                    " their

" their ferious concern to fpread fuch perform-
" ances as promote the enlightening of mankind,
" and to introduce them even into every cot-
" tage. 3. When we have the loud voice of the
" public on our fide, and fince we are able,
" either to banifh into the fhade all the fanatical
" writings which appear in the reviews that are
" commonly read, or to warn the public againft
" them; and, on the other hand, to bring into
" notice and recommend thofe performances
" alone which give light to the human mind.
" 4. When we by degrees bring the whole trade
" of bookfelling into our hands, (as the good
" writers will fend all their performances into
" the market through our means) we fhall bring
" it about, that at laft the writers who labour in
" the caufe of fuperftition and reftraint, will
" have neither a publifher nor readers. 5. When,
" laftly, by the fpreading of our Fraternity, all
" good hearts and fenfible men will adhere to
" us, and by our means will be put in a con-
" dition that enables them to work in filence
" upon all courts, families, and individuals in
" every quarter, and acquire an influence in the
" appointment of court-officers, ftewards, fecre-
" taries, parifh-priefts, public teachers, and pri-
" vate tutors.

" Remark, That we fhall fpeedily get the trade
" into our hands, (which was formerly the aim
" of the Affociation called the *Gelehrtenbuch-*
" *handlung*) is conceivable by this, that every
" writer who unites with us immediately acquires
" a triple number of readers, and finds friends
" in every place who promote the fale of his
" performance; fo that his gain is increafed ma-
" nifold, and confequently all will quit the book-
" fellers, and accede to us by degrees. Had the
" above

" above named Affociation been conftructed in
" this manner, it would, long ere now, have
" been the only fhop in Germany."

The book called *Fuller Information*, &c. gives a more particular account of the advantages held forth to the literary manufacturers of Germany by this Union *for God's work*. The clafs of literary Brothers, or writers by trade, was divided into *Mefopolites*, *Aldermen*, *Men*, and *Cadets*.

The MESOPOLITES, or Metropolitans, are to be attached to the archive-office, and to be taken care of in the Union-houfe, when in ftraits through age or misfortune. They will be occupied in the department of the fciences or arts, which this Affociation profefs principally to cherifh. They are alfo Brethren of the third degree of Scotch Free Mafonry, a qualification to be explained afterwards. The Union-houfe is a building which the oftenfible Founder of the Union profeffed to have acquired, or fpeedily to acquire at ———, through the favour and protection of a German Prince, who is not named.

ALDERMEN are perfons who hold public offices, and are engaged to exercife their genius and talents in the fciences. Thefe alfo are Brothers of the third rank of Scotch Free Mafonry, and out of their number are the Diocefans and the Directors of the Reading Societies felected.

The members who are defigned fimply MEN, are Brothers of the fecond rank of Mafonry, and have alfo a definite fcientific occupation affigned them.

The CADETS are writers who have not yet merited any particular honours, but have exhibited fufficient difpofitions and talents for different kinds of literary manufacture.

Every

Every member is bound to bring the productions of his genius to market through the Union. An Alderman receives for an original work 80 per cent. of the returns, and 70 for a tranflation. The member of the next clafs receives 60, and the Cadet 50. As to the expence of printing, the Alderman pays nothing, even though the work fhould lie on hand unfold; but the *Man* and the *Cadet* muft pay one-half. Three months after publication at the fairs an account is brought in, and after this, yearly, when and in what manner the author fhall defire.

In every Diocefe will be eftablifhed at leaft one Reading Society, of which near 800 are propofed. To each of thefe will a copy of an *Alderman's* work be fent. The fame favour will be fhown to a differtation by a *Man*, or by a *Cadet*, provided that the manufcript is documented by an Alderman, or formally approved by him upon ferious perufal. This *imprimatur*, which muft be confidered as a powerful recommendation of the work, is to be publifhed in the *General Review* or *Gazette*. This is to be a vehicle of political as well as of literary news; and it is hoped that, by its intrinfic worth, and the recommendation of the members, it will foon fupplant all others. (With refpect to affairs of the Union, a fort of cypher was to be employed in it. Each Diocefan was there defigned by a letter, of a fize that marked his rank, and each member by a number. It was to appear weekly, at the very fmall price of five-and-twenty fhillings.)—But let us return to the plan.

When every thing has been eftablifhed in the manner fet forth above, the Union will affume the following republican form, (the reader always recollecting that this is not to appear to the

the world, and to be known only to the *managing* Brethren.

Here, however, there is a great blank. The above-named sketch of this Constitution did not come to the hands of the person who furnished the bookseller with the rest of the information. But we have other documents which give sufficient information for our purpose. In the mean time, let us just take the papers as they stand.

No. IV. Contains a list of the German Union, which the sender received in manuscript. Here we find many names which we should not have expected, and miss many that were much more likely to have been partners in this patriotic scheme. There are several hundred names, but very few designations; so that it is difficult to point out the individuals to the public. Some however are designed, and the writer observes that names are found, which, when applied to some individuals whom he knows, accord surprisingly with the anecdotes that are to be seen in the private correspondence of the Illuminati, and in the romance called Materials for the History of Socratism (Illuminatism)*. It is but a disagreeable remark, that the list of the Union contains

---

* This, by the by, is a very curious and entertaining work, and, had the whole affair been better known in this country, would have been a much better antidote against the baneful effects of that Association than any thing that I can give to the public, being written with much accuteness and knowledge of the human mind, and agreeably diversified with anecdote and ironical exhibition of the affected wisdom and philanthropy of the knavish Founder and his coadjutors. If the present imperfect and desultory account shall be found to interest the public, I doubt not but that a translation of this novel, and some other fanciful performances on the subject, will be read with entertainment and profit.

the

the names of many public teachers, both from the pulpit, and from the accademic chair in all its degrees; and among thefe are feveral whofe cyphers fhow that they have been active hands. Some of thefe have in their writings given evident proofs of their mifconception of the fimple truths, whether dogmatical or hiftorical, of revealed religion, or of their inclination to twift and manufacture them fo as to chime in with the religion and morality of the Sages of France. But it is more diftreffing to meet with unequivocal names of fome who profefs in their writings to confider thefe fubjects as an honeft man fhould confider them, that is, according to the plain and common fenfe of the words; whereas we have demonftrative proofs that the German Union had the diametrically oppofite purpofe in view. The only female in the lift is the *Crafin von der Eecke*, the Lady who gave Dr. Stark of Darmftadt fo much trouble about his *Tonfure*. This Lady, as we have already feen, could not occupy herfelf with the frivolity of drefs, flirtation, or domeftic cares. " *Femina fonte patet, vir pectore.*" She was not pleafed however at finding her name in fuch a Plebeian lift, and gave oath, along with Biefter at the centre, that fhe was not of the Affociation. I fee that the public was not fatisfied with this denial. The Lady has publifhed fome more fcandal againft Stark fince that time, and takes no notice of it; and there have appeared many accounts of very ferious literary connections between thefe two perfons and the man who was afterwards difcovered to be the chief agent of the Union.

No. V. is an important document. It is a letter addreffed to the fworn members of the Union, reminding the beloved fellow-workers that " the by-
" gone

"gone management of the bufinefs has been ex-
"penfive, and that the XXII. do not mean to make
"any particular charge for their own compenfation.
"But that it was neceffary that all and each of the
"members fhould know precifely the object of the
"Affociation, and the way which mature confidera-
"tion had pointed out as the moft effectual method
"of attaining this object. Then, and not till then,
"could the worthy members act by one plan, and
"confequently with united force. To accomplifh
"this purpofe, one of their number had compofed
"a Treatife *on Inftruction, and the means of promot-
"ing it**" This work has been revifed by the whole
number, and may be confidered as the refult of their
deepeft reflection. They fay, that it would be a
fignal misfortune fhould this Affociation, this undertaking, fo important for the happinefs of mankind,
be cramped in the very beginning of its brilliant
progrefs. They therefore propofe to print this
work, this Holy Scripture of their faith and practice,
by fubfcription. (They here give a fhort account
of the work.) And they requeft the members to
encourage the work by fubfcribing, and by exerting
more than their ufual activity in procuring fubfcrip-
tions, and in recommending the performance in the
newfpapers. Four perfons are named as Diocefans,
who are to receive the money, which they beg may
be fpeedily advanced in order to purchafe paper,
that the work may be ready for the firft fair (Eafter
1788.)

No. VI. is a printed paper (as is No. V.) without
date, farther recommending the Effay on Inftruction.
No. VII. is in manufcript, without date. It is ad-

* Ueber AUFFKLARUNG und deren Beforderungs-Mittel. The only proper tranflation of this word would be, *clearing up* or *enlighten-ing.* *Inftruction* feems the fingle word that comes neareft to the precife meaning of *Auffklarung*, but is not fynonymous.

dreffed

dreſſed to " a worthy man," intimating that the like are ſent to others, to whom will alſo ſpeedily be forwarded an improved plan, with a requeſt to cancel or deſtroy the former contained in No. III. It is added, that the Union now contains, among many others, more than two hundred of the moſt reſpectable perſons in Germany, of every rank and condition, and that in the courſe of the year, (1788,) a general liſt will be ſent, with a requeſt that the receiver will point out ſuch as he does not think worthy of perfect confidence. It concludes with another recommendation of the book *on Inſtruction*, on the returns from which firſt work of the German Union the ſupport of the ſecretary's office is to depend.

Accordingly No. VIII. contains this plan, but it is not entitled *The Improved Plan*. Such a denomination would have called in doubt the infallibility of the XXII. It is therefore called the *Progreſſive* (vorlaufig) plan, a title which leaves room for every ſubſequent change. It differs from the former only in ſome unimportant circumſtances. Some expreſſions, which had given offence or raiſed ſuſpicions, are ſoftened or cancelled. Two copies of this, which we may call A and B, are given, differing alſo in ſome circumſtances.

" The great aim of the German Union is the good
" of mankind, which is to be attained only by means
" of mental illumination (*Aufklarung*) and the de-
" throning of fanaticiſm and moral deſpotiſm."
Neither paper has the expreſſion which immediately followed in the former plan, " that this had been
" the aim of the exalted founder of Chriſtianity."
The paper A refers, on the preſent ſubject, to a diſſertation printed in 1787, without a name, *On the freedom of the Preſs and its Limitation*. This is one of the moſt licentious pieces that has been publiſhed

on the subject, not only enforcing the most unqualified liberty of publishing every thing a man pleases, but exemplifying it in the most scandalous manner; libelling characters of every sort, and persons of every condition, and this frequently in the most abusive language, and expressions so coarse, as shewed the author to be either habituated to the coarsest company, or determined to try boldly once for all, what the public eye can bear. The piece goes on: "The
" Union considers it as a chief part of its secret plan
" of operation, to include the trade of bookselling
" in their circle. By getting hold of this, they
" have it in their power to increase the number of
" writings which promote instruction, and to lessen
" that of those which mar it, since the authors of
" the latter will by degrees lose both their publish-
" ers and their readers. That the present book-
" sellers may do them no harm, they will by degrees
" draw in the greater part of them to unite with
" them."—The literary newspaper is here strongly insisted on, and, in addition to what was said in the former plan, it is said, " that they will include po-
" litical news, as of mighty influence on the public
" mind, and as a subject that merits the closest at-
" tention of the moral instructor. For what illumi-
" nation is that mind susceptible of, that is so blind-
" ed by the prejudice created and nursed by the
" habits of civil subordination, that it worships stu-
" pidity or wickedness under a coronet, and neglects
" talents and virtue under the bearskin cap of the
" boor? We must therefore represent political
" transactions, and public occurrences, not as they
" affect that artificial and fantastical creature of ima-
" gination that we see every where around us wheel-
" ed about in a chariot, but as it affects a MAN, ra-
" tional, active, free born man. By thus stripping
" the transaction of all foreign circumstances, we
" see

" fee it as it affects, or ought to affect, ourfelves.
" Be affured that this new form of political intelli-
" gence will be highly interefting, and that the
" Gazette of the Union will foon fuperfede all others,
" and, of itfelf, will defray all our neceffary ex-
" pences."

This is followed by fome allufions to a fecret correfpondence that is quick, unfufceptible of all difcovery or treachery, and attended with no expence,
by which the bufinefs of the fecret plan (*different
from either of thofe communicated to the fworn Brethren at large*) is carried on, and which puts the
members in a condition to learn every thing that
goes on in the world, for or againft their caufe, and
alfo teaches them to know mankind, to gain an influence over all, and enables them effectually to promote their beft fubjects into all offices, &c. and finally,
from which every member, whether ftatefman, merchant, or writer, can draw his own advantages. Some
paffages here and in another place make me imagine
that the Union hoped to get the command of the
poft-offices, by having their Brethren in the direction.

It is then faid, that " it is fuppofed that the levy
" will be fufficiently numerous in the fpring of the
" enfuing year. When this takes place, a general
" fynod will be held, in which the *plan of fecret
" operations* will be finally adjufted, and accommo-
" dated to local circumftances, fo as to be digefted
" into a law that will need no farther alteration. A
" proper perfon will fet off from this fynod, with
" full powers to vifit every quarter where there are
" fworn Brethren, and he will there eftablifh a
" Lodge after the ancient fimple ritual, and will
" communicate verbally the *plan of fecret opera-
" ration*, and certain inftructions. Thefe Lodges
" will then eftablifh a managing fund or box. Each
" Lodge

" Lodge will also establish a Reading Society, under
" the management of a bookseller residing in the
" place, or of some person acquainted with the me-
" chanical conduct of things of this nature. There
" must also be a collector and agent, (*Expediteur,*)
" so that in a moment the Union will have its of-
" fices or *comptoirs* in every quarter, through which
" it carries on the trade of bookselling, and guides
" the ebb and flow of its correspondence. And thus
" the whole machine will be set in motion, and its
" activity is all directed from the centre."

I remark, that here we have not that exclusion of Princes and ministers that was in the former plan; they are not even mentioned. The exclusion in express terms could not but surprise people, and appear somewhat suspicious.

No. IX. is a printed circular letter to the sworn Brethren, and is subscribed " by their truly associat-
" ed Brother Barthels, *Oberamtsman* (first bailiff)
" for the King of Prussia, at Halle on the Saal."

In this letter the Brethren are informed that " the
" XXII. were wont to meet sometimes at Halle, and
" sometimes at Berlin. But unavoidable circum-
" stances oblige them not only to remain concealed
" for sometime, but even to give up their relation
" to the Union, and withdraw themselves from any
" share in its proceedings. These circumstances
" are but temporary, and will be completely ex-
" plained in due time. They trust, however, that
" this necessary step on their part will not abate the
" zeal and activity of men of noble minds, engag-
" ed in the cause by the conviction of their own
" hearts. They have therefore communicated to
" their worthy Brother Barthels all necessary in-
" formations, and have unanimously conferred on
" him the direction of the secretary's office, and
" have provided him with every document and
" mean

" mean of carrying on the correspondence. He has
" devoted himself to the honourable office, giving
" up all other employments. They observe that by
" this change in the manner of proceeding, the As-
" sociation is freed from an objection made with
" justice to all other secret societies, namely, that
" the members subject themselves to blind and un-
" qualified submission to unknown superiors."—
" The Society is now in the hands of its own avow-
" ed members. Every thing will soon be arranged
" according to a constitution purely republican; a
" Diocesan will be chosen, and will direct in every
" province, and report to the centre every second
" month, and instructions and other informations
" will issue in like manner from the centre.

" If this plan shall be approved of by the Asso-
" ciated, H. Barthels will transmit to all the Dio-
" ceses general lists of the Union, and the PLAN OF
" SECRET OPERATION, the result of deep medita-
" tion of the XXII. and admirably calculated for
" carrying on with irresistable effect their noble and
" patriotic plan. To stop all cabal, and put an end
" to all slander and suspicion, H. Barthels thinks it
" proper that the Union shall step forward, and de-
" clare itself to the world, and openly name some
" of its most respectable members. The public
" must however be informed only with respect to
" the *exterior* of the Society, for which purpose he
" had written a sheet to be annexed as an appendix
" to the work, *On Instruction*, declaring that to be
" the work of the Society, and a sufficient indica-
" tion of its most honourable aim. He desires
" such members as choose to share the honour
" with him, to send him their names and proper
" designations, that they may appear in that Ap-
" pendix. And, lastly, he requests them to in-
" struct him, and co-operate with him, according

" to

" to the concerted rules of the Union, in promot‑
" ing the caufe of God and the happinefs of man‑
" kind."

The appendix now alluded to makes No. X. of the packet fent to the Bookfeller Gofchen of Leipzig, and is dated December 1788. It is alfo found in the book *On Inftruction,* &c. printed at Leipzig in 1789, by Walther. Here, however, the Appendix is dated January 1789. This edition agrees in the main with that in the book from which I have made fuch copious extracts, but differs in fome particulars that are not unworthy of remark.

" In the packet it is written, " *The Under‑*
" *figned as Member and Agent of the German*
" *Union,* in order to rectify feveral miftakes and
" injurious flanders and accufations, thinks it ne‑
" ceffary that the public itfelf fhould judge of their
" object and conduct."—Towards the end it is faid, " and all who have any doubts may apply
" to thofe named below, and are invited to write
" to them." No names however are fubjoined. In the Appendix to the book it is only faid, " the
" agent of the German Union," &c. and " per‑
" fons who wifh to be better informed may write
" to the agent, under the addrefs, *To the German*
" *Union*—under cover to the fhop of Walther,
" bookfeller in Leipzig."—Here too there are no names, and it does not appear that any perfon has chofen to come from behind the curtain*.

---

* Walther is an eminent bookfeller, and carries on the bufinefs of publifhing to a great extent, both at Leipzig and other places. He was the publifher of the moft virulent attacks on the King of Pruffia's Edict on Religion, and was brought into much trouble about the Commentary by Pott which is mentioned above. He alfo publifhes many of the fceptical and licentious writings which have fo much difturbed the peace of Germany.

There

There has already been so much said about *Enlightening*, that the reader must be almost tired of it. He is assured in this performance that the Illumination proposed by the Union is not that of the *Wolfenbuttle Fragments*, nor that of HORUS, nor that of *Bahrdt*. The *Fragments* and *Horus* are books which aim directly, and without any concealment, to destroy the authority of our Scriptures, either as historical narrations or as revelations of the intentions of providence and of the future prospects of man. The Theological writings of *Bahrdt* are gross perversions, both of the sense of the text, and of the moral instructions contained in it, and are perhaps the most exceptionable performances on the subject. They are stigmatised as absurd, and coarse, and indecent, even by the writers on the same side; yet the work recommended so often as containing the elements of that Illumination which the world has to expect from the Union, not only coincides in its general principles with these performances, but is almost an abstract of some of them, particularly of his *Popular Religion*, his *Paraphrase on the Sermon on the Mount*, and his *Morality of Religion*. We have also seen that the book on the Liberty of the Press is quoted and recommended as an elementary book. Nay both the work on Instruction and that on the Liberty of the Press are now known to be Bahrdt's.

But these principles, exceptionable as they may be, are probably not the worst of the institution. We see that the *outside* alone of the Union is to be shewn to the public. Barthels felicitates the public that there is no subordination and blind obedience to unknown Superiors; yet, in the same paragraph, he tells us that there is a secret plan of operations, that is known only to the Centre and the Confidential Brethren. The author of *Fuller Information* says that he has this plan, and would print it, were

he

he not reſtrained by a promiſe*. He gives us enough however to ſhow us that the higher myſteries of the Union are preciſely the ſame with thoſe of the Illuminati. Chriſtianity is expreſsly ſaid to have been a Myſtical Aſſociation, and its founder the Grand Maſter of a Lodge. The Apoſtles, Peter, James, John, and Andrew, were the *Elect*, and Brethren of the Third Degree, and initiated into all the myſteries. The remaining Apoſtles were only of the Second Degree ; and the Seventy-two were of the Firſt degree. Into this degree ordinary Chriſtians may be admitted, and prepared for further advancement. The great miſtery is, that J——C——was a *Naturaliſt*, and taught the doctrine of a Supreme Mind, the Spectator, but not the Governer of the World, pretty nearly in the ſenſe of the Stoics. The Initiated Brethren were to be inſtructed by reading proper books. Thoſe particularly recommended are *Baſedow's Practical Knowledge, Eberhard's Apology for Socrates, Bahrdt's Apology for Reaſon, Steinbardt's Syſtem of Moral Education, Meiner's Ancient Myſteries, Bahrdt's Letters on the Bible,* and *Bahrdt's Completion of the Plan and Aim of J—— C——*. Theſe books are of the moſt Antichriſtian character, and ſome of them aim at ſhaking off all moral obligation whatever.

Along with theſe religious doctrines, are inculcated the moſt dangerous maxims of civil conduct. The deſpotiſm that is aimed at over the minds of men, and the machinations and intrigues for obtaining poſſeſſion of places of truſt and influence, are equally alarming; but being perfectly ſimilar to thoſe of the Illuminati, it is needleſs to mention them.

The chief intelligence that we get from this author is that the CENTRE of the Union is at a

---

* This I find to be falſe, and the book a common job.

houſe

house in the neighbourhood of Halle. It is a sort of tavern, in a vineyard immediately without the city. This was bought by Doctor KARL FRIEDERICH BAHRDT, and fitted up for the amusement of the University Students. He calls it BAHRDT'S RUHE (Bahrdt's Repose). The author thinks that this must have been the work of the Association, because Bahrdt had not a farthing, and was totally unable for such an undertaking. He may however have been the contriver of the institution. He has never affirmed or denied this in explicit terms; nor has he ever said who are the XXII coadjutors. Wucherer, an eminent bookseller at Vienna, seems to have been one of the most active hands, and in one year admitted near two hundred members, among whom is his own shoemaker. He has published some of the most profligate pamphlets which have yet appeared in Germany.

The publication of the list of members alarmed the nation; persons were astonished to find themselves in every quarter in the midst of villains who were plotting against the peace and happiness of the country, and destroying every sentiment of religion, morality, or loyalty. Many persons published in the newspapers and literary journals affirmations and proofs of the false insertion of their names. Some acknowledged that curiosity had made them enter the Association, and even continue their correspondence with the Centre, in order to learn something of what the Fraternity had in view, but declared that they had never taken any part in its proceedings. But, at the same time, it is certain that many Reading Societies had been set up during these transactions, in every quarter of Germany, and that the ostensible managers were in general of very suspicious characters, both as to morals and loyalty. The Union had actually fet up a prefs of their own at Calbe, in the neighbourhood of Halberftadt. Every day there appeared ftronger proofs of a combination of the Journalifts, Reviewers, and even of the publifhers and bookfellers, to fupprefs the writings which appeared in defence of the civil and ecclefiaftical conftitutions of the States of Germany. The extenfive literary manufacture of Germany is carried on in fuch a manner that it is impoffible for any thing lefs than the joint operation of the whole federated powers to prevent this. The fpirit of freethinking and innovating in religious matters had been remarkably prevalent in the dominions of the King of Pruffia, having been much encouraged by the indifference of the late King. One of the vileft things publifhed on this occafion was an abominable farce, called the Religion Edict. This was traced to Bahrdt's Ruhe, and the Doctor was arrefted, and all his papers feized and ranfacked. The civil Magiftrate was glad of an opportunity of expifcating the German Union, which common fame had alfo traced hither. The correfpondence was accordingly examined, and many difcoveries were made, which there was no occafion to communicate to the public, and the profecution of the bufinefs of the Union was by this means ftopped. But the perfons in high office at Berlin agree in faying that the Affociation of writers and other turbulent perfons in Germany has been but very faintly hit by this blow, and is almoft as active as ever.

The German Union appears a mean and precipitate Affociation. The Centre, the Archives, and the Secretary are contemptible. All the Archives that were found were the plans and lifts of the members and a parcel of letters of correfpondence. The correfpondence and other bufinefs was managed by
an

an old man in some very inferior office or judicatory, who lived at bed and board in Bahrdt's house for about six shillings a week, having a chest of papers and a writing-desk in the corner of the common room of the house.

Bahrdt gives a long narration of his concern in the affair, but we can put little confidence in what he says: yet as we have no better authority, I shall give a very short abstract of it, as follows:

He said, that he learned Cosmo-political Free Masonry in England, when he was there getting pupils for his academy---but neglected it on his return to Germany. Some time after his settlement he was roused by a visit from a stranger who passed for an Englishman, but whom he afterwards found to be a Dutch officer---(he gives a description which bears considerable resemblance to the Prince or General Salms who gave so much disturbance to the States General)---He was still more excited by an anonymous letter giving him an account of a Society which was employed in the instruction of mankind, and a plan of their mode of operations, nearly the same with that of No. III. He then set up a Lodge of Free Masonry on Cosmo-political principles, as a preparation for engaging in this great plan---he was stopped by the National Lodge, because he had no patent from it.---This obliged him to work in secret.---He met with a gentleman in a coffee-house, who entreated him to go on, and promised him great assistance---this he got from time to time, as he stood most in need of it, and he now found that he was working in concert with many powerful though unknown friends, each in his own circle. The plan of operation of the XXII. was gradually unfolded to him, and he got solemn promises of being made acquainted with his colleagues. But he now found, that after he had so essentially served their noble cause,

cause, he was dropped by them in the hour of danger, and thus was made the sacrifice for the public good. The last packet which he received was a request from a *Friend to the Union* to print two performances sent him, with a promise of 100 dahlers for his trouble. These were the abominable farce called the Religion Edict, and some Differtations on that Royal Proclamation.

He then gives an account of his system of Free Masonry, not very different from Weishaupt's Masonic Christianity—and concludes with the following abstract of the advantages of the Union—Advancement of Science—A general interest and concern for Arts and Learning—Excitement of Talents—Check of Scribbling—Good Education—Liberty—Equality—Hospitality—Delivery of many from Misfortunes—Union of the Learned—and at last—perhaps—Amen.

What the meaning of this enigmatical conclusion is we can only guess—and our conjectures cannot be very favourable.

The narration, of which this is a very short index, is abundantly entertaining; but the opinion of the most intelligent is, that it is in a great measure fictitious, and that the contrivance of the Union is mostly his own. Although it could not be legally proved that he was the author of the farce, every person in court was convinced that he was, and indeed it is perfectly in Bahrdt's very singular manner. This invalidates the whole of his story—and he afterwards acknowledges the farce (at least by implication) in several writings, and boasts of it.

For these reasons I have omitted the narration in detail. Some information, however, which I have received since, seems to confirm his account, while it diminishes its importance. I now find that the book called *Fuller Information* is the performance of
a clergyman

a clergyman called *Schutz*, of the lowest clafs, and by no means of an eminent character.—Another performance in the form of a dialogue between X, Y, and Z, giving nearly the fame account, is by Pott, the dear friend of Bradht and of his Union, and author of the Commentary on the Edict. Schutz got his materials from one Roper, an expelled ftudent of debauched morals, who fubfifted by copying and vending filthy manufcripts. Bahrdt fays, that he found him naked and ftarving, and, out of pity, took him into his houfe, and employed him as an amanuenfis. Roper ftole the papers at various times, taking them with him to Leipzig, whither he went on pretence of ficknefs. At laft Schutz and he went to Berlin together, and gave the information on which Bahrdt was put in prifon. In fhort they all appear to have been equally profligates and traitors to each other, and exhibit a dreadful, but I hope a ufeful picture of the influence of this Illumination which fo wonderfully fafcinates Germany.

This is all the direct information that I can pick up of the founder and the proceedings of the German Union. The project is coarfe, and palpably mean, aiming at the dahlers of entry-money and of annual contribution, and at the publication and profitable fale of Dr. Bahrdt's books. This circumftance gives it ftrong features of its parentage—Philo fpeaks of Bahrdt in his *Final Declaration* in terms of contempt and abhorence. There is nothing ingenious, nothing new, nothing enticing, in the plans; and the immediate purpofe of indulging the licentious tafte of the public comes fo frequently before the eye, that it bears all the marks of that groffnefs of mind, precipitancy, and impatient overfight that are to be found in all the voluminous writings of Dr. Bahrdt. Many in Germany, however, afcribe the Union to Weifhaupt, and fay that it is the Illuminati

minati working in another form. There is no denying that the principles, and even the manner of proceeding, are the fame in every effential circumſtance. Many paragraphs of the declamations circulated through Germany with the plans, are tranſcribed verbatim from Weiſhaupt's *Corrected ſyſtem of Illuminatiſm*. Much of the work *On Inſtruction, and the Means for promoting it*, is very nearly a copy of the fame work, blended with ſlovenly extracts from ſome of his own writings—There is the fame feries of deluſions from the beginning, as in Illuminatiſm—Free Maſonry and Chriſtianity are compounded—firſt with marks of reſpect—then Chriſtianity is twiſted to a purpoſe foreign from it, but the fame with that aimed at by Weiſhaupt—then it is thrown away altogether, and Natural Religion and Atheiſm ſubſtituted for it—For no perſon will have a moment's heſitation in ſaying, that this is the creed of the author of the books *On Inſtruction* and *On the Liberty of the Preſs*. Nor can he doubt that the political principles are equally anarchical with thoſe of the Illuminati.—The endeavours alſo to get poſſeſſion of public offices—of places of education—of the public mind, by the Reading Societies, and by publications—are ſo many tranſcripts from the Illuminati. Add to this, that Dr. Bahrdt was an *Illuminatus*—and wrote the *Better than Horus*, at the command of Weiſhaupt. Nay, it is well known that Weiſhaupt was twice or thrice at Bahrdt's Ruhe during thoſe tranſactions, and that he zealouſly promoted the formation of Reading Societies in ſeveral places.—But I am rather of the opinion that Weiſhaupt made thoſe viſits in order to keep Dr. Bahrdt within ſome bounds of decency, and to hinder him from hurting the cauſe by his precipitancy, when ſpurred on by the want of money. Weiſhaupt could not work

in

in such an unskilful manner. But he would be very glad of such help as this coarse tool could give him—and Bahrdt gave great help; for, when he was imprisoned and his papers seized, his Archives,. as he called them, shewed that there were many Reading Societies which his project had drawn together. The Prussian States had above thirty, and the number of readers was astonishingly great—and it was found, that the pernicious books had really found their way into every hut. Bahrdt, by descending a story lower than Weishaupt, has greatly increased the number of his pupils.

But, although I cannot consider the German Union as a formal revival of the Order under another name, I must hold those *United*, and the members of those Reading Societies, as *Illuminati* and *Minervals*. I must even consider the Union as a part of Spartacus' work. The plans of Weishaupt were partly carried into effect in their different branches—they were pointed out, and the way to carry them on are distinctly described in the private correspondence of the Order—It required little genius to attempt them in imitation. Bahrdt made the attempt, and in part succeeded. Weishaupt's hopes were well founded—The leaven was not only distributed, but the management of the fermentation was now understood, and it went on apace.

It is to be remarked, that nothing was found among Bahrdt's papers to support the story he writes in his diary—no such correspondences—but enough for detecting many of these Societies. Many others however were found unconnected with Bahrdt's Ruhe, not of better character, either as to Morality or Loyalty, and some of them considerable and expensive; and many proofs were found

found of a combination to force the public to a certain way of thinking, by the management of the Reviews and Journals. The extensive dealings of Nicholai of Berlin gave him great weight in the book-making trade, which in Germany surpasses all our conceptions. The catalogues of *new* writings in sheets, which are printed twice a-year for each of the fairs at Leipzig and Frankfort, would astonish a British reader by the number. The booksellers meet there, and at one glance see the whole republic of literature, and, like Roman senators, decide the sentiments of distant provinces. By thus seeing the whole together, their speculations are national, and they really have it in their power to give what turn they please to the literature and to the sentiments of Germany. Still however they must be induced by motives. The motive of a merchant is gain, and every object appears in his eye something by which money may be made. Therefore in a luxurious and voluptuous nation, licentious and freethinking books will abound. The writers suggest, and the booksellers think how the thing will tickle. Yet it must not be inferred, from the prevalence of such books, that such is the common sense of mankind, and that the writings are not the corrupters, but the corrupted, or that they are what they ought to be, because they please the public. We need only push the matter to an extremity, and its cause appears plain. Filthy prints will always create a greater crowd before the shop window than the finest performances of Wollett. Licentious books will be read with a fluttering eagerness, as long as they are not universally permitted; and pitiable will be the state of the nation when their number makes them familiar and no longer captivating.

But

But although it muſt be confeſſed that great encouragement was given to the ſceptical, infidel, and licentious writings in Germany, we ſee that it was ſtill neceſſary to practiſe ſeduction. The *Religioniſt* was made to expect ſome engaging exhibition of his faith. The *Citizen* muſt be told that his civil connections are reſpected, and will be improved; and *all* are told that good manners or virtue is to be ſupported. Man is ſuppoſed to be, in very eſſential circumſtances, what he wiſhes to be, and feels he ought to be: and he is corrupted by means of falſehood and trick. The principles by which he is wheedled into wickedneſs in the firſt inſtance, are therefore ſuch as are really addreſſed to the general ſentiments of mankind: theſe therefore ſhould be conſidered as more expreſſive of the public mind than thoſe which he afterwards adopts, after this artificial education. Therefore Virtue, Patriotiſm, Loyalty, Veneration for true and undefiled Religion, are really acknowledged by thoſe corrupters to be the *prevailing* ſentiments; and they are good if this prevalence is to be the teſt of worth. The mind that is otherwiſe affected by them, and hypocritically uſes them in order to get hold of the uninitiated, that he may in time be made to cheriſh the contrary ſentiments, cannot be a good mind, notwithſtanding any pretenſions it may make to the love of mankind.

No man, not Weiſhaupt himſelf, has made ſtronger profeſſions of benevolence, of regard for the happineſs of mankind, and of every thing that is amiable, than Dr. Bahrdt. It may not be uſeleſs to enquire what effect ſuch principles have had on his own mind, and thoſe of his chief coadjutors. Deceit of every kind is diſhonourable; and the deceit that is profeſſedly employed in the proceedings of the Union is no exception. No pious fraud *whatever* muſt be uſed, and pure religion muſt be preſented to the view without all diſguiſe.

" The more fair Virtue's ſeen, the more ſhe charms.
" Safe, plain, and eaſy, are her artleſs ways.
" With face erect, her eyes look ſtrait before ;
" For dauntleſs is her march, her ſtep ſecure.

" Not ſo, pale Fraud—now here ſhe turns, now there,
" Still ſeeking darker ſhades, ſecure in none,
" Looks often back, and wheeling round and round,
" Sinks headlong in the danger ſhe would ſhun."

The mean motive of the Proteſtant Sceptic is as inconſiſtent with our notions of honeſty as with our notions of honour ; and our ſuſpicions are juſtly raiſed of the character of Dr. Bahrdt and his aſſociates, even although we do not ſuppoſe that their aim is the total aboliſhing of religion. With propriety therefore may we make ſome enquiry about their lives and conduct. Fortunately this is eaſy in the preſent inſtance. A man that has turned every eye upon himſelf can hardly eſcape obſervation. But it is not ſo eaſy to get fair information. The peculiar ſituation of Dr. Bahrdt, and the cauſe between him and the public, are of all others the moſt productive of miſtake, miſrepreſentation, obloquy, and injuſtice. But even here we are fortunate. Many remarkable parts of his life are eſtabliſhed by the moſt reſpectable teſtimony, or by judicial evidences; and, to make all ſure, he has written his own life. I ſhall inſert nothing here that is not made out by the two laſt modes of proof, reſting nothing on the firſt, however reſpectable the evidence may be. But I muſt obſerve, that his life was alſo written by his dear friend Pott, the partner of Walther the bookſeller.

ler. The story of this publication is curious, and it is instructive.

Bahrdt was in prison, and in great poverty. He intended to write his own life, to be printed by Walther, under a fictitious name, and in this work he intended to indulge his spleen and his dislike of all those who had offended him, and in particular all priests, and rulers, and judges, who had given him so much trouble. He knew that the strange, and many of them scandalous anecdotes, with which he had so liberally interlarded many of his former publications, would set curiosity on tiptoe, and would procure a rapid sale as soon as the public should guess that it was his own performance, by the singular but significant name which the pretended author would assume. He had almost agreed with Walther for a thousand dahlers, (about L. 200), when he was imprisoned for being the author of the farce so often named, and of the commentary on the *Religion Edict*, written by Pott, and for the proceedings of the German Union. He was refused the use of pen and ink. He then applied to Pott, and found means to correspond with him, and to give him part of his life already written, and materials for the rest, consisting of stories, and anecdotes, and correspondence. Pott sent him several sheets, with which he was so pleased, that they concluded a bargain. Bahrdt says, that Pott was to have 400 copies, and that the rest was to go to the maintenance of Bahrdt and his family, consisting of his wife, daughter, a Christina and her children who lived with them, &c. Pott gives a different account, and the truth was different from both, but of little consequence to us. Bahrdt's papers had been seized, and searched for evidence of his transactions, but the strictest attention was paid to the precise points of the

charge, and no paper was abstracted which did not relate to these. All others were kept in a sealed room. Pott procured the removal of the seals and got possession of them. Bahrdt says, that his wife and daughter came to him in prison, almost starving, and told him that now that the room was opened, Pott had made an offer to write for their support, if he had the use of these papers—that this was the conclusion of the bargain, and that Pott took away all the papers. N. B. Pott was the associate of Walther, who had great confidence in him (*Anecdotenbuch fur meinen leiben Amtsbruder, p.* 400) and had conducted the business of Stark's book, as has been already mentioned. No man was better known to Bahrdt, for they had long acted together as chief hands in the Union. He would therefore write the life of its founder *con amore*, and it might be expected to be a rare and tickling performance. And indeed it was. The first part of it only was published at this time; and the narration reaches from the birth of the hero till his leaving Leipzig in 1768. The attention is kept fully awake, but the emotions which successively occupy the mind of the reader are nothing but strong degrees of aversion, disgust, and horror. The figure set up to view is a monster, a man of talents indeed, and capable of great things; but lost to truth, to virtue, and even to the affectation of common decency—In short, a shameless profligate.—Poor Bahrdt was astonished,—stared —but, having his wits about him, saw that this life would sell, and would also sell another.— Without loss of time, he said that he would hold Pott to his bargain—but he reckoned without his host. " No, no," said Pott, " your are not the " man I took you for—your correspondence was " put into my hands—I saw that you had de-
" ceived

"ceived me, and it was my duty, as a man
"*who loves truth above all things*, to hinder you
"from deceiving the world. I have not writ-
"ten the book you defired me. I did not work
"for you, but for myfelf—therefore you get
"not a grofchen." "Why, Sir," faid Bahrdt, we
"both know that this won't do. You and I have
"already tried it. You received Stark's manu-
"fcript, to be printed by Walther—Walther and
"you fent it hither to Michaelis, that I might fee
"it during the printing. I wrote an illuftratino
"and a key, which made the fellow very ridicu-
"lous, and they were printed together, with one
"title page.—You know that we were caft in
"court.—Walther was obliged to print the work
"as Stark firft ordered, and we loft all our la-
"bour.—So fhall you now, for I will commence
"an action this inftant, and let me fee with what
"face you will defend yourfelf, within a few
"weeks of your laft appearance in court." Pott
faid, "You may try this. My work is already fold,
"and difperfed over all Germany—and I have
"no objection to begin yours to-morrow—believe
"me, it will fell." Bahrdt pondered—and refolved to write one himfelf.

This is another fpecimen of the *Union*.

DR. CARL FREDERICK BAHRDT was born in 1741. His father was then a parifh minifter, and afterwards Profeffor of Theology at Leipzig, where he died, in 1775. The youth, when at College, enlifted in the Pruffian fervice as a huffar, but was bought off by his father. He was M. A. in 1761. He became catechift in his father's church, was a popular preacher, and publifhed fermons in 1765, and fome controverfial writings, which did him honour—But he then began to indulge in conviviality, and in anonymous pafqui-
nades,

nades, uncommonly bitter and offensive. No person was safe—Professors—Magistrates—Clergymen, had his chief notice—also students—and even comrades and friends. (Bahrdt says, that these things might cut to the quick but they were all just.) Unluckily his temperament was what the atomical philosophers (who can explain every thing by æthers and vibrations) call sanguine. He *therefore* (his own word) was a passionate admirer of the ladies. Coming home from supper he frequently met a young Miss in the way to his lodgings, neatly dressed in a rose-coloured silk jacket and train, and a sable bonnet, costly, and like a lady. One evening (after some old Renish, as he says,) he saw the lady home. Some time after, the mistress of the house, Madam Godschusky, came into his room, and said that the poor maiden was pregnant. He could not help that—but it was very unfortunate, and would ruin him if known.—He therefore gave the old lady a bond for 200 dahlers, to be paid by instalments of twenty-five.———
" The girl was sensible, and good, and as he had
" already paid for it, and her conversation was
" agreeable, he did not discontinue his acquaint-
" ance." A comrade one day told him, that one Bel, a magistrate, whom he had lampooned, knew the affair, and would bring it into court, unless he immediately retrieved the bond. This bond was the only evidence, but it was enough. Neither Bahrdt nor his friend could raise the money. But they fell on another contrivance. They got Madam Godschusky to meet them at another house, in order to receive the money. Bahrdt was in a closet, and his comrade wore a sword. The woman could not be prevailed on to produce the bond till Bahrdt should arrive, and the money be put into her hands, with a present to herself. The
comrade

comrade tried to flutter her, and, drawing his
sword, shewed her how men fenced—made passes
at the wall—and then at her—but she was too
firm—he then threw away his sword, and began
to try to force the paper from her. She defended
herself a good while, but at length he got the paper out of her pocket, tore it in pieces, opened the
closet door, and said, " There you b——, there
" is the honourable fellow whom you and your
" wh— have bullied—but it is with me you have
" to do now, and you know that I can bring you
" to the gallows." There was a great squabble to
be sure, says Bahrdt, but it ended, and I thought
all was now over.—But Mr. Bel had got word of
it, and brought it into court the very day that
Bahrdt was to have made some very reverend appearance at church. In short, after many attempts
of his poor father to save him, he was obliged to
send in his gown and band, and to quit the place.
It was some comfort, however, that Madam
Godschusky and the young Miss did not fare much
better. They were both imprisoned. Madam G.
died sometime after of some shocking disease.
The court records give a very different account of
the whole, and particularly of the scuffle; but
Bahrdt's story is enough.

Bahrdt says, that his father was severe---but acknowledges that his own temperament was hasty,
(why does not his father's temperament excuse something? *Vibratiunculæ* will explain every thing or
nothing. " *Therefore* (again) I sometimes forgot
myself. One day I laid a loaded pistol on the table,
and told him that he should meet with that if he went
on so. But I was only seventeen."

Dr. Bahrdt was, of course, obliged to leave the
place. His friends, and Semler in particular, an
eminent theological writer, who had formed a very
favourable

favourable opinion of his uncommon talents, were affiduous in their endeavours to get an eftablifhment for him. But his high opinion of himfelf, his temper, impetuous, precipitant, and overbearing, and a bitter fatirical habit which he had freely indulged in his outfet of life, made their endeavours very ineffectual.

At laft he got a profefforfhip at Erlangen, then at Erfurth, and in 1771, at Gieffen. But in all thefe places he was no fooner fettled than he got into difputes with his colleagues and with the eftablifhed church, being a ftrenuous partizan of the innovations which were attempted to be made in the doctrines of chriftianity. In his anonymous publications, he did not truft to rational difcuffion alone, but had recourfe to ridicule and perfonal anecdotes, and indulged in the moft cutting farcafms and grofs fcurrility. Being fond of convivial company, his income was infufficient for the craving demand, and as foon as he found that anecdote and flander always procured readers, he never ceafed writing. He had wonderful readinefs and activity, and fpared neither friends nor foes in his anonymous performances. But this could not laft, and his avowed theological writings were fuch as could not be fuffered in a Profeflor of Divinity. The very ftudents at Gieffen were fhocked with fome of his liberties. After much wrangling in the church judicatories he was juft going to be difmiffed, when he got an invitation to Marfchlins in Switzerland to fuperintend an academy. He went thither about the year 1776, and formed the feminary after the model of Bafedow's Philanthropine, or academy, at Deffau, of which I have already given fome account. It had acquired fome celebrity, and the plan was peculiarly fuited to Bahrdt's tafte, becaufe it left him at liberty to introduce any fyftem of religious or irreligious

opinions

opinions that he pleafed. He refolved to avail himfelf of this liberty, and though a clergyman and Doctor of Theology, he would outftrip even Bafedow, who had no ecclefiaftical orders to reftrain him. But he wanted the moderation, the prudence and the principle of Bafedow. He had, by this time, formed his opinion of mankind, by meditating on the feelings of his own mind. His theory of human nature was fimple—" The leading propenfities, fays he, of the human mind are three—Inftinctive liberty (Freyheitftriebe)—inftinctive activity (Triebe fur Thatigkeit)----and inftinctive love (Liebes triebe)." I do not wifh to mifunderftand him, but I can give no other tranflation.---" If a man is ob-
" ftructed in the exercife of any of thefe propenfi-
" ties he fuffers an injury.—The bufinefs of a good
" education therefore is to teach us how they are to
" be enjoyed in the higheft degree."

We need not be furprifed although the Doctor fhould find it difficult to manage the Cyclopedia in his Philanthropine in fuch a manner as to give fatisfaction to the neighbourhood, which was habituated to very different fentiments,—Accordingly he found his fituation as uncomfortable as at Gieffen. He fays, in one of his lateft performances,
" that the Grifons were a ftrong inftance of the
" immenfe importance of education. They knew
" nothing but their handicrafts, and their minds
" were as coarfe as their perfons." He quarrelled with them all, and was obliged to abfcond after lying fometime in arreft.

He came to Durkheim or Turkheim, where his father was or had been minifter. His literary talents were well known.—After fome little time he got an affociation formed for erecting and fupporting a Philanthropine or houfe of education. A large fund was collected, and he was enabled to travel into Holland and England, to engage pupils, and was furnished with proper recommendations.—On his return the plan was carried into execution. The caſtle or reſidence of Count Leining Hartzburgh, at Heideſheim, having gardens, park, and every handſome accommodation, had been fitted up for it, and it was conſecrated by a ſolemn religious feſtival in 1778.

But his old misfortunes purſued him. He had indeed no colleagues to quarrel with, but his avowed publications became every day more obnoxious—and when any of his anonymous pieces had a great run, he could not ſtifle his vanity and conceal the author's name. Of theſe pieces, ſome were even ſhocking to decency. It was indifferent to him whether it was friend or foe that he abuſed; and ſome of them were ſo horribly injurious to the characters of the moſt reſpectable men in the ſtate, that he was continually under the correction of the courts of juſtice. There was hardly a man of letters that had ever been in his company who did not ſuffer by it. For his conſtant practice was to father every new ſtep that he took towards Atheiſm on ſome other perſon; and, whenever the reader ſees, in the beginning of a book, any perſon celebrated by the author for ſound ſenſe, profound judgment, accurate reaſoning, or praiſed for acts of friendſhip and kindneſs to himſelf, he may be aſſured that, before the cloſe of the book, this man will convince Dr. Bahrdt in ſome private converſation, that ſome doctrine, cheriſhed and venerated by all Chriſtians, is a piece of knaviſh ſuperſtition. So loſt was Dr. Bahrdt to all ſenſe of ſhame. He ſaid that he held his own opinions independent of all mankind, and was indifferent about their praiſe or their reproach.

Bahrdt's

Bahrdt's licentious, very licentious life, was the cause of most of these enormities. No income could suffice and he wrote for bread. The artful manner in which the literary manufacture of Germany was conducted, made it impossible to hinder the rapid dispersion of his writings over all Germany; and the indelicate and coarse maw of the public was as ravenous as the sensuality of Dr. Bahrdt, who really battened in the Epicurean sty. The consequence of all this was that he was obliged to fly from Heidesheim, leaving his sureties in the *Philanthropine* to pay about 14,000 dahlers, besides debts without number to his friends. He was imprisoned at Dienheim, but was released I know not how, and settled at Halle. There he sunk to be a keeper of a tavern and billiard-table, and his house became the resort and the bane of the students in the University.—He was obliged therefore to leave the city. He had somehow got funds which enabled him to buy a little vineyard, prettily situated in the neighbourhood. This he fitted up with every accommodation that could invite the students, and called it *Bahrdt's Ruhe*. We have already seen the occupations of Dr. B. in this *Buen Retiro*—Can we call it *otium cum dignitate*? Alas, no! He had not lived two years here, bustling and toiling for the German Union, sometimes without a bit of bread—when he was sent to prison at Halle, and then to Magdeburg, where he was more than a year in jail. He was set at liberty, and returned to *Bahrdt's Ruhe*, not, alas, to live at ease, but to lie down on a sick-bed, where, after more than a year's suffering increasing pain, he died on the 23d of April 1793, the most wretched and loathsome victim of unbridled sensuality. The account of his case is written by a friend, a Dr. Jung, who professes to defend his memory

memory and his principles. The medical description melted my heart, and I am certain would make his bitterest enemy weep. Jung repeatedly says, that the case was not venereal—calls it the vineyard disease---the quicksilver disease, (he was dying of an unconquerable salivation,) and yet, through the whole of his narration, relates symptoms and sufferings, which, as a medical man, he could not possibly mean to be taken in any other sense than as effects of pox. He meant to please the enemies of poor Bahrdt, knowing that such a man could have no friends, and being himself ignorant of what friendship or goodness is. The fate of this poor creature affected me more than any thing I have read of a great while. All his open enemies put together have not said so much ill of him as his trusted friend Pott, and another confident, whose name I cannot recollect, who published in his lifetime an anonymous book called *Bahrdt with the Iron Brow*.---and this fellow Jung, under the absurd mask of friendship, exhibited the loathsome carcase for a florin, like a malefactor's at Surgeon's Hall. Such were the fruits of the German Union, of that Illumination that was to refine the heart of man, and bring to maturity the seeds of native virtue, which are choaked in the hearts of other men by superstition and despotism. We see nothing but mutual treachery and base desertion.

I do not concern myself with the gradual perversion of Dr. Bahrdt's moral and religious opinions. But he affected to be the enlightener and reformer of mankind; and affirmed that all the mischiefs in life originated from despotism supported by superstition. " In vain," says he, " do " we complain of the inefficacy of religion. All " positive religion is founded on injustice. No
" Prince

" Prince has a right to prefcribe or fanction any
" fuch fyftem. Nor would he do it, were not
" the priefts the firmeft pillars of his tyranny,
" and fuperftition the ftrongeft fetters for his fub-
" jects. He dares not fhow Religion as fhe is—
" pure and undefiled----She would charm the eyes
" and the hearts of mankind, would immediately
" produce true morality, would open the eyes
" of freeborn man, would teach him what are
" his rights, and who are his oppreffors, and
" Princes would vanifh from the face of the
" earth."

Therefore, without troubling ourfelves with the truth or falfehood of his religion of Nature, and affuming it as an indifputable point, that Dr. Bahrdt has feen it in this natural and fo effective purity, it is furely a very pertinent queftion, " Whether has the fight produced on his mind " an effect fo far fuperior to the acknowledged " faintnefs of the impreffion of Chriftianity on " the bulk of mankind, that it will be prudent to " adopt the plan of the German Union, and at " once put an end to the divifions which fo un- " fortunately alienate the minds of profeffing " Chriftians from each other?" The account here given of Dr. Bahrdt's life feems to decide the queftion.

But it will be faid, that I have only related fo many inftances of the quarrels of Priefts and their flavifh adherents, with Dr. Bahrdt. Let us view him in his ordinary conduct, not as the champion and martyr of Illumination, but as an ordinary citizen, a hufband, a father, a friend, a teacher of youth, a clergyman.

When Dr. Bahrdt was a parifh-minifter, and prefident of fome inferior ecclefiaftical diftrict, he was empowered to take off the cenfures of the church

from

from a young woman who had born a baſtard child. By violence he again reduced her to the ſame condition, and eſcaped cenſure, by the poor girl's dying of a fever before her pregnancy was far advanced, or even legally documented. Alſo, on the night of the ſolemn farce of conſecrating his Philanthropine, he debauched the maid-ſervant, who bore twins, and gave him up for the father. The thing, I preſume, was not judicially proved, otherwiſe he would have ſurely been diſgraced; but it was afterwards made evident, by the letters which were found by Pott, when he undertook to write his life. A ſeries of theſe letters had paſſed between him and one Graf, a ſteward, who was employed by him to give the woman the ſmall pittance by which ſhe and the infants were maintained. Remonſtrances were made when the money was not advanced; and there are particularly letters about the end of 1779, which ſhow that Bahrdt had ceaſed giving any thing. On the of February 1780, the infants (three years old) were taken away in the night, and were found expoſed, the one at Uſſtein, and the other at Worms, many miles diſtant from each other, and almoſt frozen to death. The firſt was diſcovered by its moans, by a ſhoemaker in a field by the road-ſide, about ſix in the morning; the other was found by two girls between the hedges in a lane, ſet between two great ſtones, paſt all crying. The poor mother travelled up and down the country in queſt of her infants, and hearing theſe accounts, found them both, and took one of them home; but not being able to maintain both, when Bahrdt's commiſſioner refuſed contributing any more, it remained with the good woman who had taken it in*.

* This is worſe than Rouſſeau's conduct, who only ſent his children to the Foundling hoſpital, that he might never know them again. (See his Confeſſions.)

Bahrdt

Bahrdt was married in 1772, while at Gieſſen; but after waſting the greateſt part of his wife's little fortune left her by a former huſband, he was provoked by loſing 1000 florins (about 110*l.*) in the hands of her brother who would not pay it up. After this he uſed her very ill, and ſpeaks very contemptuouſly of her in his own account of his life, calling her a dowdy, jealous, and every thing contemptible. In two infamous novels, he exhibits characters, in which ſhe is repreſented in a moſt cruel manner; yet this woman (perhaps during the honey-moon) was enticed by him one day into the bath, in the pond of the garden of the Philanthropine at Heideſheim, and there, in the ſight of all the pupils did he (alſo undreſſed) toy with his naked wife in the water. When at Halle, he uſed the poor woman extremely ill, keeping a miſtreſs in the houſe, and giving her the whole command of the family, while the wife and daughter were confined to a ſeparate part of it. When in priſon at Magdeburgh, the ſtrumpet lived with him, and bore him two children. He brought them all to his houſe when he was at liberty. Such barbarous uſage made the poor woman at laſt leave him and live with her brother. The daughter died about a year before him, of an overdoſe of laudanum given by her father, to procure ſleep, when ill of a fever. He ended his own wretched life in the ſame manner, unable, poor man, to bear his diſtreſs, without the ſmalleſt compunction or ſorrow for his conduct; and the laſt thing he did was to ſend for a bookſeller, (Vipink of Halle, who had publiſhed ſome of his vile pieces,) and recommend his ſtrumpet and her children to his protection, without one thought of his injured wife.

I ſhall end my account of this profligate monſter with a ſpecimen of his way of uſing his friends.

" Of

"Of all the acquisitions which I made in England, Mr. ------(the name appears at full length) was the most important. This person was accomplished in the highest degree. With sound judgment, great genius, and correct taste, he was perfectly a man of the world. He was my friend, and the only person who warmly interested himself for my institution. To his warm and repeated recommendations I owe all the pupils I got in England, and many most respectable connections; for he was universally esteemed as a man of learning and of the most unblemished worth. He was my friend, my conductor, and I may say my preserver; for when I had not bread for two days, he took me to his house, and supplied all my wants. This gentleman was a clergyman, and had a small but genteel and selected congregation, a flock which required strong food. My friend preached to them pure natural religion, and was beloved by them. His sermons were excellent, and delivered with native energy and grace, because they came from the heart. I had once the honour of preaching for him. But what a difference—I found myself afraid---I feared to speak too boldly, because I did not know where I was, and thought myself speaking to my crouching countrymen. But the liberty of England opens every heart, and makes it accessible to morality. I can give a very remarkable instance.

"The women of the town in London do not, to be sure, meet with my unqualified approbation in all respects. But it is impossible not to be struck with the propriety and decency of their manners, so unlike the clownish impudence of our German wh—. I could not distinguish them from modest women, otherwise than by their greater attention and eagerness to shew me civility. My friend
"used

" ufed to laugh at my miftakes, and I could not be-
" lieve him when he told me that the lady who had
" kindly fhewed the way to me, a foreigner, was a
" votary of Venus. He maintained that Englifh li-
" berty naturally produced morality and kindnefs.
" I ftill doubted, and he faid that he would con-
" vince me by my own experience. Thefe girls
" are to be feen in crowds every evening in every
" quarter of the town. Although fome of them
" may not have even a fhift, they come out in the
" evening dreffed like princeffes, in hired clothes,
" which are entrufted to them without any fear of
" their making off with them. Their fine fhape,
" their beautiful fkin, and dark brown hair, their
" bofoms, fo prettily fet off by their black filk drefs,
" and above all, the gentle fweetnefs of their man-
" ners, makes an impreffion in the higheft degree
" favourable to them. They civilly offer their arm
" and fay, " My dear, will you give me a glafs of
" wine." If you give them no encouragement, they
" pafs on, and give no farther trouble. I went with
" my friend to Covent Garden, and after admiring
" the innumerable beauties we faw in the piazzas,
" we gave our arm to three very agreeable girls, and
" immediately turned into a temple of the Cythere-
" an Goddefs, which is to be found at every fecond
" door in the city, and were fhewn into a parlour
" elegantly carpeted and furnifhed, and lighted with
" wax, with every other accommodation at hand.—
" My friend called for a pint of wine, and this was
" all the expence for which we received fo much
" civility. The converfation and other behaviour
" of the ladies was agreeable in the higheft degree,
" and *not a word* paffed that would have diftinguifh-
" ed them from nuns, or that was not in the higheft
" degree mannerly and elegant. We parted in the
" ftreet—and fuch is the liberty of England, that

"my friend ran not the fmalleft rifk of fuffering either in his honour or ufefulnefs.—Such is the effect of freedom."

We may be fure, the poor man was aftonifhed when he faw his name before the public as one of the enlighteners of Chriftian Europe. He is really a man of worth, and of the moft irreproachable character, and knew that whatever might be the protection of Britifh liberty, fuch conduct would ruin him with his own hearers, and in the minds of all his refpectable countrymen. He therefore fent a vindication of his character from this flanderous abufe to the publifhers of the principal newfpapers and literary journals in Germany. The vindication is complete, and B. is convicted of having related what he *could not poffibly have feen*. It is worthy of remark, that the vindication did not appear in the *Berlin Monatfchrift*, nor in any of the journals which made favorable mention of the performances of the Enlighteners.

"Think not, indignant reader," fays Arbuthnot, "that this man's life is ufelefs to mortals." It fhews in a ftrong light the falfity of all his declamations in favour of his fo much praifed natural religion and univerfal kindnefs and humanity. No man of the party writes with more perfuafive energy, and, though his petulance and precipitant felf-conceit lead him frequently aftray, no man has occafionally put all the arguments of thefe philofophers in a clearer light; yet we fee that all is falfe and hollow. He is a vile hypocrite, and the real aim of all his writings is to make money, by foftering the fenfual propenfities of human nature, although he fees and feels that the completion of the plan of the German Union would be an event more deftructive and lamentable than any that can be pointed out in the annals of fuperftition. I will not fay that all partifans

of

of Illumination are hogs of the fty of Epicurus like this wretch. But the reader muft acknowledge that, in the inftitution of Weifhaupt, there is the fame train of fenfual indulgence laid along the whole, and that purity of heart and life is no part of the morality that is held forth as the perfection of human nature. The final abolition of Chriftianity is undoubtedly one of its objects—whether as an end of their efforts, or as a mean for the attainment of fome end ftill more important. Purity of heart is perhaps the moft diftinctive feature of Chriftian morality. Of this Dr. Bahrdt feems to have had no conception; and his inftitution, as well as his writings, fhew him to have been a very coarfe fenfualift. But his tafte, though coarfe, accorded with what Weifhaupt confidered as a ruling propenfity, by which he had the beft chance of fecuring the fidelity of his fubjects.—Craving defires, beyond the bonds of our means, were the natural confequences of indulgence; and fince the purity of Chriftian morality ftood in his way, his firft care was to clear the road by rooting it out altogether—What can follow but general diffolutenefs of manners?

Nothing can more diftinctly prove the crooked politics of the Reformers than this. It may be confidered as the main-fpring of their whole machine. Their pupils were to be led by means of their fenfual appetites, and the aim of their conductors was not to inform them, but merely to lead them; not to reform, but to rule the world. —They would reign, though in hell, rather than ferve in heaven.—Dr. Bahrdt was a true Apoftle of Illuminatifm; and though his torch was made of the groffeft materials, and " ferved only to dif- " cover fights of woe," the horrid glare darted into every corner, roufing hundreds of filthy vermin, and directing their flight to the rotten carrion

rion where they could beft depofit their poifon and their eggs; in the breafts, to wit, of the fenfual and profligate, there to fefter and burft forth in a new and filthy progeny; and it is aftonifhing what numbers were thus roufed into action. The fcheme of Reading Societies had taken prodigioufly, and became a very profitable part of the literary trade of Germany. The bookfellers and writers foon perceived its importance, and acted in concert.

I might fill a volume with extracts from the criticifms which were publifhed on the *Religion Edict* fo often mentioned already. The Leipzig catalogue for one year contained 173. Although it concerned the Pruffian States alone, thefe appeared in every corner of Germany; nay, alfo in Holland, in Flanders, in Hungary, in Switzerland, in Courland, and in Livonia. This fhows it to have been the operation of an Affociated Band, as was intimated to the King, with fo much petulance by Mirabeau. There was (paft all doubt) fuch a combination among the innumerable fcribblers who fupplied the fairs of Leipzig and Frankfort. Mirabeau calls it a *Conjuration des Philofophes*, an expreffion very clear to himfelf, for the myriads of gareteers who have long fed the craving mouth of Paris (" always thirfting after fome " new thing") called themfelves philofophers, and, like the gangs of St. Giles's, converfed with each other in a cant of their own, full of *morale*, of *energie*, of *bienvillance*, &c. &c. &c. unintelligible or mifunderftood by other men, and ufed for the purpofe of deceit. While Mirabeau lived too, they formed a *Conjuration*. The 14th of July 1790, the moft folemn invocation of the Divine prefence ever made on the face of this earth, put an end to the propriety of this appellation; for it

became

became neceffary (in the progrefs of political Illumination) to declare that oaths were nonfenfe, becaufe the invoked was a creature of the imagination, and the grand federation, like Wiefhaupt and Bahrdt's Mafonic Chriftianity, is declared, to thofe initiated into the higher myfteries, to be a lie. But if we have no longer a *Conjuration des Philofophes*, we have a gang of fcribblers that has got poffeffion of the public mind by their management of the literary Journals of Germany, and have made licentious fentiments in politics, in morals, and in religion, as familiar as were formerly the articles of ordinary news. All the fceptical writings of England put together will not make half the number that have appeared in Proteftant Germany during the laft twelve or fifteen years. And, in the Criticifms on the Edict, it is hard to fay whether infidelity or difloyalty fills the moft pages.

To fuch a degree had the Illuminati carried this favourite and important point that they obtained the direction even of thofe whofe office it was to prevent it. There is at Vienna, as at Berlin, an office for examining and licenfing writings before they can have their courfe in the market. This office publifhes annually an index of forbidden books. In this index are included the accouut of the laft *Operations of Spartacus and Philo in the Order of Illuminati*, and a differtation on *The Final Overthrow of Free Mafonry*, a moft excellent performance, fhowing the gradual corruption and final perverfion of that fociety to a feminary of fedition. Alfo the Vienna *Magazine of Literature and Arts*, which contains many accounts of the interferences of the Illuminati in the difturbances of Europe. The Cenfor who occafioned this prohibition was an *Illuminatus* named *Retzer*.

He

He makes a moſt pitiful and Jeſuitical defence, ſhowing himſelf completely verſant in all the chicane of the *Illuminati*, and devoted to their Infidel principles. (See *Rel. Begebenh.* 1795, p. 493.)

There are two performances which give us much information reſpecting the ſtate of moral and political opinions in Germany about this time. One of them is called, *Proofs of a hidden Combination to deſtroy the Freedom of Thought and Writing in Germany.* Theſe proofs are general, taken from many concurring circumſtances in the condition of German literature. They are convincing to a thinking mind, but are too abſtracted to be very impreſſive on ordinary readers. The other is the *Appeal to my Country*, which I mentioned in page 84. This is much more ſtriking, and in each branch of literature, gives a progreſſive account of the changes of ſentiment, all ſupported by the evidence of the books themſelves. The author puts it paſt contradiction, that in every ſpecies of literary compoſition into which it was poſſible, without palpable abſurdity, to introduce licentious and ſeditious principles, it was done. Many romances, novels, journeys through Germany and other countries*, are written on purpoſe to attach praiſe or reproach to certain ſentiments, characters, and pieces of conduct. The Prince, the nobleman, is made deſpotic, oppreſſive, unfeeling or ridiculous—the poor, and the man of talents, are unfortunate and neglected—and here and there a fictitious Graff or Baron is

---

* A plan adopted within theſe few years in our own country, which, if proſecuted with the ſame induſtry with which it has been begun, will ſoon render our circulating Libraries ſo many Nurſeries of Sedition and Impiety. (See *Travels into Germany* by Eſte.)

made

made a divinity, by philanthropy expressed in romantic charity and kindness, or oftentatious indifference for the little honours which are so precious in the eyes of a German.—In short, the system of Weishaupt and Knigge is carried into vigorous effect over all. In both these performances, and indeed in a vast number of other pieces, I see that the influence of Nicholai is much commented on, and considered as having had the chief hand in all those innovations.

Thus I think it clearly appears, that the suppression of the Illuminati in Bavaria and of the Union in Brandenburgh, were insufficient for removing the evils which they had introduced. The Elector of Bavaria was obliged to issue another proclamation in November 1790, warning his subjects of their repeated machinations, and particularly enjoining the magistrates to observe carefully the assemblies in the Reading Societies, which were multiplying in his States. A similar proclamation was made and repeated by the Regency of Hanover, and it was on this occasion that Mauvillon impudently avowed the most anarchical opinions.—But Weishaupt and his agents were still busy and successful. The habit of plotting had formed itself into a regular system. Societies now acted every where in secret, in correspondence with similar societies in other places. And thus a mode of co-operation was furnished to the discontented, the restless, and the unprincipled in all places. without even the trouble of formal initiations, and without any external appearances by which the existence and occupations of the members could be distinguished. The hydra's teeth were already sown, and each grew up, independent of the rest, and soon sent out its own offsets.—In all places where such secret practices were

were going on, there did not fail to appear fome individuals of more than common zeal and activity, who took the lead, each in his own circle. This gave a confiftency and unity to the operations of the reft, and they, encouraged by this co-operation, could now attempt things which they would not otherwife have ventured on. It is not till this ftate of things obtains, that this influence becomes fenfible to the public. Philo, in his public declaration, unwarily lets this appear. Speaking of the numerous little focieties in which their principles were cultivated, he fays, " we thus be-" gin to be formidable." It may now alarm—but it is now too late. The fame germ is now fprouting in another place.

I muft not forget to take notice that about this time (1787 or 1788,) there appeared an invitation from a Baron or Prince S———, Governor of the Dutch fortrefs H———, before the troubles in Holland, to form a fociety *for the Protection of Princes.* —The plan is expreffed in very enigmatical terms, but fuch as plainly fhew it to be merely an odd title, to catch the public eye; for the Affociation is of the fame feditious kind with all thofe already fpoken of, viz. profeffing to enlighten the minds of men, and making them imagine that all their hardfhips proceed from fuperftition, which fubjects them to ufelefs and crafty priefts; and from their own indolence and want of patriotifm, which make them fubmit to the mal-adminiftration of minifters. The Sovereign is fuppofed to be innocent, but to be a cypher, and every magiftrate, who is not chofen by the people actually under him, is held to be a defpot, and is to be bound hand and foot.—Many circumftances concur to prove that the projector of this infidious plan is the Prince Salms, who fo affiduoufly fomented all the difturbances in the Dutch and Auftrian Netherlands.

lands. He had, before this time, taken into his service Zwack, the Cato of the Illuminati. The project had gone some length when it was discovered and suppressed by the States.

Zimmerman, who had been President of the Illuminati in Manheim, was also a most active person in propagating their doctrines in other countries. He was employed as a missionary, and erected some Lodges even in Rome—also at Neufchatel—and in Hungary. He was frequently seen in the latter place by a gentleman of my acquaintance, and preached up all the ostensible doctrines of Illuminatism in the most public manner, and made many proselytes. But when it was discovered that their real and fundamental doctrines were different from those which he professed in order to draw in proselytes, Zimmerman left the country in haste.—Some time after this he was arrested in Prussia for seditious harangues—but he escaped, and has not been heard of since.—When he was in Hungary he boasted of having erected above an hundred Lodges in different parts of Europe, some of which were in England.

———

That the Illuminati and other hidden Cosmo-political societies had some influence in bringing about the French Revolution, or at least in accelerating it, can hardly be doubted. In reading the secret correspondence, I was always surprised at not finding any reports from France, and something like a hesitation about establishing a mission there; nor am I yet able thoroughly to account for it. But there is abundant evidence that they interfered, both in preparing for it in the same manner as in Germany, and in accelerating its progress. Some letters in the

Brunſwick Journal from one *Campe*, who was an inſpector of the ſeminaries of education, a man of talents, and an *Illuminatus*, put it beyond doubt. He was reſiding in Paris during its firſt movements, and gives a minute account of them, lamenting their exceſſes, on account of their imprudence, and the riſk of ſhocking the nation, and thus deſtroying the project, but juſtifying the motives, on the true principles of Coſmo-politiſm. The Vienna Zeitſchrift and the Magazine of Literature and Fine Arts for 1790, and other pamphlets of that date, ſay the fame thing in a clearer manner. I ſhall lay together ſome paſſages from ſuch as I have met with, which I think will ſhew beyond all poſſibility of doubt that the Illuminati took an active part in the whole tranſaction, and may be ſaid to have been its chief contrivers. I ſhall premiſe a few obſervations, which will give a clearer view of the matter.

CHAP. IV.

The French Revolution.

DURING thefe diffenfions and difcontents, and this general fermentation of the public mind in Germany, political occurrences in France gave exercife and full fcope for the operation of that fpirit of revolt which had long growled in fecret in the different corners of that great empire. The Cofmo-political and fceptical opinions and fentiments fo much cultivated in all the Lodges of the *Philalethes* had by this time been openly profeffed by many of the fages of France, and artfully interwoven with their ftatiftical economics. The many contefts between the King and the Parliament of Paris about the regiftration of his edicts, had given occafion to much difcuffion, and had made the public familiarly acquainted with topics altogether unfuitable to the abfolute monarchy of France.

This acquaintance with the natural expectations of the fubject, and the expediency of a candid attention on the part of Government to thefe expectations, and a view of Legiflation and Government founded on a very liberal interpretation of all thefe things, was prodigioufly promoted by the rafh interference of France in the difpute between Great Britain and her colonies. In this attempt to ruin Britain, even the court of France was obliged to preach the doctrines of Liberty, and to take its chance that Frenchman would confent to be the only flaves. But their officers and foldiers, who returned from America, imported the American principles, and in every company found hearers who liftened with delight and regret to their fafcinating tale of American independence.

independence. During the war, the Minifter, who had too confidently pledged himfelf for the deftruction of Britain, was obliged to allow the Parifians to amufe themfelves with theatrical entertainments, where Englifh law was reprefented as oppreffion, and every fretful extravagance of the Americans was applauded as a noble ftruggle for native freedom.— All wifhed for a tafte of that liberty and equality which they were allowed to applaud on the ftage; but as foon as they came from the theatre into the ftreet, they found themfelves under all their former reftraints. The fweet charm had found its way into their hearts, and all the luxuries of France became as dull as common life does to a fond girl when fhe lays down her novel.

In this irritable ftate of mind a fpark was fufficient for kindling a flame. To import this dangerous delicacy of American growth, France had expended many millions, and was drowned in debts. The mad prodigality of the Royal Family and the Court had drained the treafury, and foreftalled every livre of the revenue. The edicts for new taxes and forced loans were moft unwelcome and oppreffive.

The *Avocats au parlement* had nothing to do with ftate-affairs, being very little more than barrifters in the higheft court of juftice; and the higheft claim of the Prefidents of this court was to be a fort of humble counfellors to the King in common matters. It was a very ftrange inconfiftency in that ingenious nation to permit fuch people to touch on thofe ftate-fubjects; for, in fact, the King of France was an abfolute Monarch, and the fubjects were flaves. This is the refult of all their painful refearch, notwithftanding that glimmerings of natural juftice and of freedom are to be met with in their records. There could not be found in their hiftory fo much as a tolerable account of the manner of
calling

calling the nation together, to learn from the people how their chains would beſt pleaſe their fancy. But all this was againſt nature, and it was neceſſary that it ſhould come to an end, the firſt time that the monarch confeſſed that he could not do every thing unleſs they put the tools into his hands. As things were approaching gradually but rapidly to this condition, the impertinent interference (for ſo a Frenchman, ſubject of the Grand Monarch, *muſt* think it) of the advocates of the Parliament of Paris was popular in the higheſt degree; and it muſt be confeſſed, that in general it was patriotic, however inconſiſtent with the conſtitution. They felt themſelves pleading the cauſe of humanity and natural juſtice. This would embolden honeſt and worthy men to ſpeak truth, however unwelcome to the court. In general, it muſt alſo be granted that they ſpoke with caution and with reſpect to the ſovereign powers; and they had frequently the pleaſure of being the means of mitigating the burdens of the people. The Parliament of Paris, by this conduct, came to be looked up to as a ſort of mediator between the King and his ſubjects; and as the avocats ſaw this, they naturally roſe in their own eſtimation far above the rank in which the conſtitution of their government had placed them. For it muſt always be kept in mind, that the robe was never conſidered as the dreſs of a Nobleman, although the caſſock was. An advocate was merely not a rotourier; and though we can hardly conceive a profeſſion more truly honourable than the diſpenſing of diſtributive juſtice, nor any ſkill more congenial to a rational mind than that of the practical morality which we, in theory, conſider as the light by which they are always conducted; and although even the artificial conſtitution of France had long been obliged to bow to the dictates of nature and humanity, and confer nobility, and even title,

title, on such of the professors of the municipal law as had, by their skill and their honourable character, risen to the first offices of their profession, yet the Noblesse de la Robe never could incorporate with the Noblesse du Sang, nor even with the Noblesse de l'Epee. The descendants of a Marquis de la Robe never could rise to certain dignities in the church and at court. The avocats de la parlement felt this, and smarted under the exclusion from court-honours; and though they eagerly courted such nobility as they could attain, they seldom omitted any opportunity that occurred during their junior practice, of exposing the arrogance of the Noblesse, and the dominion of the court. This increased their popularity, and in the present situation of things, being certain of support, they went beyond their former cautious bounds, and introduced in their pleadings, and particularly in their joint remonstrances against the registration of edicts, all the wiredrawn morality, and cosmo-political jurisprudence, which they had so often rehearsed in the Lodges, and which had of late been openly preached by the economists and philosophers.

A signal was given to the nation for engaging "en masse" in political discussion. The *Notables* were called upon to come and advise the King; and the points were laid before them, in which his Majesty, (infallible till now) acknowledged his ignorance or his doubts. But who were the Notables? Were they more knowing than the King, or less in need of instruction? The nation thought otherwise; nay, the court thought otherwise; for in some of the royal proclamations on this occasion, men of letters were invited to assist with their counsels, and to give what information their reading and experience should suggest as to the best method of convoking the States General, and of conducting their deliberations. When a Minister thus

solicits

solicits advice from all the world how to govern, he most assuredly declares his own incapacity, and tells the people that now they must govern themselves. This however was done, and the Minister, Neckar the Philosopher and Philanthropist of Geneva, set the example, by sending in *his* opinion, to be laid on the council-table with the rest. On this signal, counsel poured in from every garret, and the press groaned with advice in every shape. Ponderous volumes were written for the Bishop or the Duke; a handsome 8vo for the *Notable* Officer of eighteen; pamphlets and single sheets for the loungers in the *Palais Royal*. The fermentation was astonishing; but it was no more than should have been expected from the most cultivated, the most ingenious, and the least bashful nation on earth. All wrote, and all read. Not contented with bringing forth all the fruits which the Illumination of these bright days of reason had raised in such abundance in the conservatories of the *Philalethes*, and which had been gathered from the writings of Voltaire, Diderot, Rousseau, Raynal, &c. the patriotic counsellors of the Notables had ransacked all the writings of former ages. They discovered THAT FRANCE HAD ALWAYS BEEN FREE! One would have thought, that they had travelled with Sir John Mandeville in that country where even the speeches of former times had been frozen, and were now thawing apace under the beams of the sun of Reason. For many of these essays were as incongruous and mal a-propos as the broken sentences recorded by Mr. Addison in the Spectator. A gentleman who was in Paris at this time, a person of great judgment, and well informed in every thing respecting the constitution and present condition of his country, assured me that this invitation, followed by the memorial of Mr. Neckar, operated

operated like an electrical shock. In the course of four or five days, the appearance of Paris was completely changed. Every where one saw crowds staring at papers pasted on the walls—breaking into little parties—walking up and down the streets in eager conversation—adjourning to coffee-houses —and the conversation in all companies turned to politics alone ; and in all these conversations a new vocabulary, where every second word was Morality, Philanthropy, Toleration, Freedom, and Equalisation of property. Even at this early period persons were listened to without censure, or even surprise, who said that it was nonsense to think of reforming their government, and that it must be completely changed. In short, in the course of a month, a spirit of licentiousness and a rage for innovation had completely pervaded the minds of the Parisians. The most conspicuous proof of this was the unexpected fate of the Parliament. It met earlier than usual, and to give greater eclat to its patriotic efforts, and completely to secure the gratitude of the people, it issued an arret on the present state of the nation, containing a number of resolutions on the different leading points of national liberty. A few months ago these would have been joyfully received as the Magna Charta of Freedom, and really contained all that a wise people should desire; but because the Parliament had sometime before given it as their opinion as the constitutional counsel of the Crown, that the States should be convoked on the principles of their last meeting in 1614, which preserved the distinctions of rank, all their past services were forgotten —all their hard struggle with the former administration, and their unconquerable courage and perseverance, which ended only with their downfal, all were forgotten ; and those distinguished members

members whose zeal and sufferings ranked them with the most renowed heroes and martyrs of patriotism, were now regarded as the contemptible tools of Aristocracy. The Parliament now set, in a fiery troubled sky—to rise no more.

Of all the barristers in the Parliament of Paris, the most conspicuous for the display of the enchanting doctrines of Liberty and Equality was Mr. Duval, son of an Avocat in the same court, and ennobled about this time under the name of Despresmenil. He was member of a Lodge of the *Amis Reunis* at Paris, called the *Contract Social*, and of the Lodge of *Chevaliers Bienfaisants* at Lyons. His reputation as a barrister had been prodigiously increased about this time by his management of a cause, where the descendant of the unfortunate General Lally, after having obtained the restoration of the family honours, was striving to get back some of the estates. Mr. Lally Tollendahl had even trained himself to the profession, and pleaded his own cause with astonishing abilities. But Desprefmenil had near connections with the family which was in possession of the estates, and opposed him with equal powers, and more address. He was on the side which was most agreeable to his favourite topics of declamation, and his pleadings attracted much notice both in Paris and in some of the provincial Parliaments. I mention these things with some interest, because this was the beginning of that marked rivalship between Lally Tollendahl and Desprefmenil, which made such a figure in the Journals of the National Assembly. It ended fatally for both. Lally Tollendahl was obliged to quit the Assembly, when he saw it determined on the destruction of the monarchy and of all civil order, and at last to emigrate from his country with the loss of all his property, and to subsist on the kindness of England. Dsepresmenil attained his meridian of popularity by his discovery of the secret plan of the Court to establish the *Cour pleniere*, and ever after this took the lead in all the strong measures of the Parliament of Paris, which was now overstepping all bounds of moderation or propriety, in hopes of preserving its influence after it had rendered itself impotent by an unguarded stroke. Despresmenil was the first martyr of that Liberty and Equality which it was now boldly preaching, having voluntarily surrendered himself a prisoner to the officer sent to demand him from the Parliament. He was also a martyr to any thing that remained of the very shadow of liberty after the Revolution, being guillotined by Robespierre.

I have already mentioned the intrigues of Count Mirabeau at the Court of Berlin, and his seditious preface and notes on the anonymous letters on the Rights of the Prussian States. He also, while at Berlin, published an *Essai sur la Secte des Illumines*, one of the strangest and most impudent performances that ever appeared. He there describes a sect existing in Germany, called the *Illuminated*, and says, that they are the most absurd and gross fanatics imaginable, waging war with every appearance of Reason, and maintaining the most ridiculous superstitions. He gives some account of these, and of their rituals, ceremonies, &c. as if he had seen them all. His sect is a confused mixture of Christian superstitions, Rosycrucian nonsense, and every thing that can raise contempt and hatred. But no such Society ever existed, and Mirabeau confided in his own powers of deception, in order to screen from observation those who were known to be Illuminati, and to hinder the rulers from attending to their real

real machinations, by means of this Ignis fatuus of his own brain. He knew perfectly that the Illuminati were of a ftamp diametrically oppofite; for he was illuminated by Mauvillon long before. He gained his point in fome meafure, for Nicholai and others of the junto immediately adopted the whim, and called them *Obfcurantem*, and joined with Mirabeau in placing on the lift of *Obfcurantem* feveral perfons whom they wifhed to make ridiculous.

Mirabeau was not more difcontented with the Court of Berlin for the fmall regard it had teftified for his eminent talents, than he was with his own Court, or rather with the minifter Calonne, who had fent him thither. Calonne had been greatly diffatisfied with his conduct at Berlin, where his felf-conceit, and his private projects, had made him act in a way almoft contrary to the purpofes of his miffion. Mirabeau was therefore in a rage at the minifter, and publifhed a pamphlet, in which his celebrated memorial on the ftate of the nation, and the means of relieving it, was treated with the utmoft feverity of reproach; and in this conteft his mind was wrought up to that violent pitch of oppofition which he ever after maintained. To be noticed, and to lead, were his fole objects—and he found, that taking the fide of the difcontented was the beft field for his eloquence and reftlefs ambition.—Yet there was no man that was more devoted to the principles of a court than count Mirabeau, provided he had a fhare in the adminiftration; and he would have obtained it, if any thing moderate would have fatisfied him—but he thought nothing worthy of him but a place of active truft, and a high department. For fuch offices all knew him to be totally unfit. He wanted knowledge of great things, and was learned only in the bustling detail of intrigue, and at any time would sacrifice every thing to have an opportunity of exercising his brilliant eloquence, and indulging his passion for satire and reproach.—The greatest obstacle to his advancement was the abject worthlessness of his character. What we usually call profligacy, viz. debauchery, gaming, impiety, and every kind of sensuality, were not enough—he was destitute of decency in his vices—tricks which would disgrace a thief-catcher, were never boggled at in order to supply his expences. For instance,—His father and mother had a process of separation—Mirabeau had just been liberated from prison for a gross misdemeanour, and was in want of money.—He went to his father, sided with him in invectives against his mother, and, for 100 guineas, wrote his father's memorial for the court.—He then went to his mother, and by a similar conduct got the same sum from her—and both memorials were presented. Drinking was the only vice in which he did not indulge—his exhausted constitution did not permit it. His brother, the Viscount, on the contrary, was apt to exceed in jollity. One day the Count said to him, " How can you, Brother, so " expose yourself?"——" What!" says the Viscount, " how insatiable you are—Nature has " given you every vice, and having left me only " this one, you grudge it me."—When the elections were making for the States-General, he offered himself a candidate in his own order at Aix—But he was so abhorred by the Noblesse, that they not only rejected him but even drove him from their meetings. This affront settled his measures, and he determined on their ruin. He went to the Commons, disclaimed his being a gentleman, sat up a little shop in the market place of

Aix

Aix, and fold trifles—and now, fully refolved what line he fhould purfue, he courted the Commons, by joining in all their exceffes againſt the Nobleffe, and was at laſt returned a member of the Affembly.

From this account of Mirabeau we can eafily foretel the ufe he would make of the Illumination which he had received in Germany. Its grand truths and juſt morality feem to have had the fame effects on his mind as on that of Weifhaupt or Bahrdt.

In the year 1768, Mirabeau, in conjunction with the duke de Lauzun and the Abbe Perigord, afterwards Bifhop of Autun (the man fo puffed in the National Affemblies as the brighteſt pattern of humanity) reformed a Lodge of Philalethes in Paris, which met in the Jacobin College or Convent. It was one of the *Amis Reunis*, which had now rid itfelf of all the infignificant myfticifm of the fect. This was now become troublefome, and took up the time which would be much better employed by the *Chevaliers du Soliel*, and other ſtill more refined champions of reafon and univerfal citizenfhip. Mirabeau had imparted to it fome of that Illumination which had beamed upon him when he was in Berlin. In 1788, he and the Abbe were wardens of the lodge. They found that they had not acquired all the dexterity of management that he underſtood was practifed by his Brethren in Germany, for keeping up their connection, and conducting their corefpondence. A letter was therefore fent from this Lodge, figned by thefe two gentlemen, to the Brethren in Germany, requeſting their affiftance and inftruction. In the courfe of this year, and during the fitting of the Notables, A DEPUTATION WAS SENT from the German Illuminati to catch this glorious

ous opportunity of carrying their plan into full execution with the greatest eclat.

Nothing can more convincingly demonstrate the early intentions of a party, and this a great party, in France to overturn the constitution completely, and plant a democracy or oligarchy on its ruins. The Illuminati had no other object.— They accounted all Princes usurpers and tyrants, and all privileged orders their abettors. They intended to establish a government of Morality, as they called it, *(Sittenregiment)* where talents and character (to be estimated by their own scale, and by themselves) should alone lead to preferment. They meant to abolish the laws which protected property accumulated by long continued and successful industry, and to prevent for the future any such accumulation. They intended to establish universal Liberty and Equality, the imprescriptible Rights of Man, (at least they pretended all this to those who were neither Magi or Regentes.) And, as necessary preparations for all this, they intended to root out all religion and ordinary morality, and even to break the bonds of domestic life, by destroying the veneration for marriage-vows, and by taking the education of children out of the hands of the parents. *This was all that the Illuminati could teach*, and THIS WAS PRECISELY WHAT FRANCE HAS DONE.

I cannot proceed in the narration without defiling the page with the detested name of *Orleans*, stained with every thing that can degrade or disgrace human nature. He only wanted Illumination, to shew him in a system all the opinions, dispositions, and principles which filled his own wicked heart. This contemptible being was illuminated by Mirabeau, and has shown himself the most zealous disciple of the Order. In his oath of allegiance he
declares

declares, "That the interests and the object of the Order shall be rated by him above all other relations, and that he will serve it with his honour, his fortune, and his blood."—He has kept his word, and has sacrificed them all—And he has been treated in the true spirit of the Order—used as a mere tool, cheated and ruined.—For I must now add, that the French borrowed from the Illuminati a maxim, unheard of in any other association of banditti, viz. that of cheating each other. As the managers had the sole possession of the higher mysteries, and led the rest by principles which they held to be false, and which they employed only for the purpose of securing the co-operation of the inferior Brethren, so Mirabeau, Sieyes, Pethion, and others, led the Duke of Orleans at first by his wicked ambition, and the expectation of obtaining that crown which they intended to break in pieces, that they might get the use of his immense fortune, and of his influence on the thousands of his depending sycophants, who ate his bread and pandered to his gross appetites. Although we very soon find him acting as an *Illuminatus*, we cannot suppose him so lost to common sense as to contribute his fortune, and risk his life, merely in order that the one should be afterwards taken from him by law, and the other put on a level with that of his groom or his pimp. He surely hoped to obtain the crown of his indolent relation. And indeed Mirabeau said to Bergasse, that "when the project was mentioned to the Duke of Orleans, he received it with all possible graciousness," (*avec toute la grace imaginable.*) During the contests between the Court and the Parliament of Paris, he courted popularity with an indecency and folly that nothing can explain but a mad and fiery ambition which blinded his eyes to all consequences. This is put out of doubt by his behaviour

our at Versailles on the dreadful 5th and 6th of October, 1789. The depositions at the Chatelet prove in the most incontestible manner, that during the horrors of those two days he was repeatedly seen, and that whenever he was recognized by the crowd, he was huzzaed with *Vive Orleans, Vive notre Roi Orleans, &c.*—He then withdrew, and was seen in other places. While all about the unfortunate Royal Family were in the utmost concern for their fate, he was in gay humour, chatting on indifferent subjects. His last appearance in the evening of the 5th was about nine o'clock, conversing in a corner with men disguised in mean dress, and some in women's clothes; among whom were Mirabeau, Barnave, Duport, and other deputies of the Republican party —and these men were seen immediately after, concealed among the lines of the regiment de Flandre, the corruption of which they had that day compleated. He was seen again next morning, conversing with the same persons in women's dress. And when the insulted Sovereign was dragged in triumph to Paris, Orleans was again seen skulking in a balcony behind his children, to view the procession of devils and furies; anxiously hoping all the while that some disturbance would arise in which the King might perish.—I should have added that he was seen in the morning at the top of the stairs, pointing the way with his hand to the mob, where they should go, while he went by another road to the King. In short, he went about trembling like a coward, waiting for the explosion which might render it safe for him to shew himself. Mirabeau said of him, "The fellow carries a loaded pistol in his bosom, but will never dare to pull the trigger." He was saved, notwithstanding his own folly, by being joined in the accusation with Mirabeau, who could not rescue himself without striving also for Orleans, whom he despised, pifed, while he made ufe of his fortune.—In fhort, Orleans was but half illuminated at this time, and hoped to be King or Regent.

Yet he was deeply verfed in the preparatory leffons of Illuminatifm, and well convinced of its fundamental truths. He was well affured of the great influence of the women in fociety, and he employed this influence like a true difciple of Weifhaupt.—Above three hundred nymphs from the purlieus of the Palais Royal were provided with ecus and Louis d'ors, by his grand procureur the Abbe Sieyes, and were fent to meet and to illuminate the two battalions of the Regiment de Flandre, who were coming to Verfailles for the protection of the Royal Family. The privates of one of thefe regiments came and informed their officers of this attempt made on their loyalty.—45,000l. livres were given them at St. Denys, to make them difband themfelves—and the poor lads were at firft dazzled by the name of a fum that was not familiar to them—but when fome thinking head among them told them that it only amounted to two Louis d'ors a piece, they difclofed the bribery. They were then offered 90,000, but never faw it. (Depofitions at the Chatelet No. 317.) Mademoifelle Therouane, the *favorita* of the day, at the Palais Royal, was the moft active perfon of the armed mob from Paris, dreffed *en Amazonne*, with all the elegance of the opera, and turned many young heads that day which were afterwards taken off by the guillotine. The Duke of Orleans acknowledged, before his death, that he had expended above 50,000l. fterling in corrupting the *Gardes Francoifes*. The armed mob which came from Paris to Verfailles on the 5th of October, importuning the King for bread, had their pockets filled with crown pieces—and Orleans was feen on that day by two gentlemen, with a bag of money fo heavy that it was faftened to his

his clothes with a ſtrap, to hinder it from being oppreſſive, and to keep it in ſuch a poſition that it ſhould be acceſſible in an inſtant. (See the Depoſitions at the Chatelet, No. 177.)

But ſuch was the contempt into which his groſs profligacy, his cowardice, and his niggardly diſpoſition, had brought him with all parties, that, if he had not been quite blinded by his wicked ambition, and by his implacable reſentment of ſome bitter taunts he had gotten from the King and Queen, he muſt have ſeen very early that he was to be ſacrificed as ſoon as he had ſerved the purpoſes of the faction. At preſent, his aſſiſtance was of the utmoſt conſequence. His immenſe fortune, much above three millions ſterling, was almoſt exhauſted during the three firſt years of the Revolution. But (what was of more conſequence) he had almoſt unbounded authority among the Free Maſons.

In this country we have no conception of the authority of a National Grand Maſter. When Prince Ferdinand of Brunſwick, by great exertions among the jarring ſects in Germany, had got himſelf elected Grand Maſter of the *Strict Obſervanz*, it gave ſerious alarm to the Emperor, and to all the Princes of Germany, and contributed greatly to their connivance at the attempts of the *Illuminati* to diſcredit that party. In the great cities of Germany, the inhabitants paid more reſpect to the Grand Maſter of the Maſons than to their reſpective Princes. The authority of the D. of Orleans in France was ſtill greater, in conſequence of his employing his fortune to ſupport it. About eight years before the Revolution he had (not without much intrigue and many bribes and promiſes) been elected Grand Maſter of France, having under his directions all the *Improved* Lodges. The whole Aſſociation was called the *Grand Orient de la la France*, and in 1785 contained 266 of thefe Lodges; (fee *Freymaurerifche Zeitung, Neuwied* 1787.) Thus he had the management of all thofe Secret Societies; and the licentious and irreligious fentiments which were currently preached there, were fure of his hearty concurrence. The fame intrigue which procured him the fupreme chair, muft have filled the Lodges with his dependents and emiffaries, and thefe men could not better earn their pay, than by doing their utmoft to propagate infidelity, immorality, and impurity of manners.

But fomething more was wanted: Difrefpect for the higher Orders of the State, and difloyalty to the Sovereign.—It is not fo eafy to conceive how thefe fentiments, and particularly the latter, could meet with toleration, and even encouragement, in a nation noted for its profeffions of veneration for its Monarch, and for the pride of its Nobleffe. Yet I am certain that fuch doctrines were habitually preached in the Lodges of *Philalethes*, and *Amis Reunis de la Verite*. That they fhould be very current in Lodges of low-born Literati, and other Brethren in inferior ftations, is natural, and I have already faid enough on this head. But the French Lodges contained many gentlemen in eafy, and affluent circumftances. I do not expect fuch confidence in my affertions, that even in thefe the fame opinions were very prevalent. I was therefore much pleafed with a piece of information which I got while thefe fheets were printing off, which corroborates my affertions.

This is a performance called *La voile retiree, ou le Secret de la Revolution explique par la Franc Maconnerie*. It was written by a Mr. Lefranc, Prefident of the Seminary of the *Eudifts* at Caen in Normandy, and a fecond edition was publifhed at Paris in 1792.

1792. The author was butchered in the maſſacre of September. He ſays, that on the death of a friend, who had been a very zealous Maſon, and many years Maſter of a reſpectable Lodge, he found among his papers a collection of Maſonic writings, containing the rituals, catechiſms, and ſymbols of every kind, belonging to a long train of degrees of Free Maſonry, together with many diſcourſes delivered in different Lodges, and minutes of their proceedings. The peruſal filled him with aſtoniſhment and anxiety. For he found that doctrines were taught, and maxims of conduct were inculcated, which were ſubverſive of religion and of all good order in the ſtate; and which not only countenanced diſloyalty and ſedition, but even invited to it. He thought them ſo dangerous to the ſtate, that he ſent an account of them to the Archbiſhop of Paris long before the Revolution, and always hoped that that Reverend Prelate would repreſent the matter to his Majeſty's Miniſters, and that they would put an end to the meetings of this dangerous Society, or would at leaſt reſtrain them from ſuch exceſſes. But he was diſappointed, and therefore thought it his duty to lay them before the public*.

Mr. Lefranc ſays expreſsly, that this ſhocking perverſion of Free Maſonry to ſeditious purpoſes

---

* Had the good man been ſpared but a few months, his ſurpriſe at this neglect would have ceaſed. For, on the 19th of November 1793, the Archbiſhop of Paris came to the Bar of the Aſſembly, accompanied by his Vicar and eleven other Clergymen, who there renounced their Chriſtianity and their clerical vows; acknowledging that they had played the villain for many years againſt their conſciences, teaching what they knew to be a lie, and were now reſolved to be honeſt men. The Vicar indeed had behaved like a true *Illuminatus* ſome time before, by running off with another man's wife and his ſtrong box.—None of them, however, ſeem to have attained the higher myſteries, for they were all guillotined not long after.

was,

was, in a great meafure, but a late thing, and was chiefly brought about by the agents of the Grand Mafter, the Duke of Orleans. He was, however, of opinion that the whole Mafonic Fraternity was hoftile to Chriftianity and to good morals, and that it was the contrivance of the great fchifmatic Fauftus Socinus, who being terrified by the fate of Servetus, at Geneva, fell on this method of promulgating his doctrines among the great in fecret. This opinion is but ill fupported, and is incompatible with many circumftances in Free Mafonry— But it is out of our way at prefent. Mr. Lefranc then takes particular notice of the many degrees of Chivalry cultivated in the Lodges, and fhows how, by artful changes in the fucceffive explanations of the fame fymbols, the doctrines of Chriftianity, and of all revealed religion, are completely exploded, and the *Philofophe Inconnu* becomes at laft a profeffed Atheift.—He then takes notice of the political doctrines which are in like manner gradually unfolded, by which " patriot-
" ifm and loyalty to the prince are declared to be
" narrow principles, inconfiftent with univerfal
" benevolence, and with the native and impre-
" fcriptible rights of man ; civil fubordination is
" actual oppreffion, and Princes are *ex officio* ufur-
" pers and tyrants." Thefe principles he fairly deduces from the Catechifms of the *Chevalier du Soliel*, and of the *Philofophe Inconnu*. He then proceeds to notice more particularly the intrigues of the Duke of Orleans. From thefe it appears evident that his ambitious views and hopes had been of long ftanding, and that it was entirely by his fupport and encouragement that feditious doctrines were permitted in the Lodges. Many noblemen and gentlemen were difgufted and left thefe Lodges, and advantage was taken of their abfence

abſence to *improve* the Lodges ſtill more, that is to make them ſtill more anarchical and ſeditious. Numbers of paltry ſcribblers who haunted the Palace Royal, were admitted into the Lodges, and there vented their poiſonous doctrines. The Duke turned his chief attention to the French guards, introducing many of the privates and inferior officers into the obſcure and even the more reſpectable Lodges, ſo that the officers were frequently diſguſted in the Lodges by the inſolent behaviour of their own ſoldiers under the maſk of Maſonic Brotherhood and Equality—and this behaviour became not unfrequent even out of doors. He aſſerts with great confidence that the troops were much corrupted by theſe intrigues—and that when they ſometimes declared, on ſervice, that they would not fire *on their Brethren*, the phraſe had a particular reference to their Maſonic Fraternity, becauſe they recogniſed many of their Brother Maſons in every crowd.—And the corruption was by no means confined to Paris and its neighbourhood, but extended to every place in the kingdom where there was a Municipality and a Maſon Lodge.

Mr. Lefranc then turns our attention to many peculiarities in the Revolution, which have a reſemblance to the practices in Free Maſonry. Not only was the arch rebel the Duke of Orleans, the Grand Maſter, but the chief actors in the Revolution, Mirabeau, Condorcet, Rochefoucault, and others, were diſtinguiſhed office-bearers in the great Lodges. He ſays that the diſtribution of France into departments, diſtricts, circles, cantons, &c. is perfectly ſimilar, with the ſame denominations, to a diſtribution which he had remarked in the correſpondence of the Grand Orient[*].

ent*. The President's hat in the National Assembly is copied from that of a *Tres Venerable Grand Maitre*.—The scarf of a Municipal Officer is the same with that of a Brother Apprentice.—When the Assembly celebrated the Revolution in the Cathedral, they accepted of the highest honours of Masonry by passing under the *Arch of Steel*, formed by the drawn swords of two ranks of Brethren.—Also it is worthy of remark, that the National Assembly protected the meetings of Free Masons, while it preremptorily prohibited every other private meeting. The obligation of laying aside all stars, ribbands, crosses, and other honourable distinctions, under the pretext of Fraternal Equality, was not merely a prelude, but was intended as a preparation for the destruction of all civil distinctions, which took place almost at the beginning of the Revolution,—*and the first proposal of a surrender*, says Mr. Lefranc, *was made by a zealous Mason*.—He farther observes, that the horrible and sanguinary oaths, the daggers, death-heads, cross-bones, the imaginary combats with the murderers of Hiram, and many other gloomy ceremonies, have a natural tendency to harden the heart, to remove its natural disgust at deeds of horror, and have paved the way for those shocking barbarities which have made the name of Frenchmen abhorred over all Europe. These deeds were indeed perpetrated by a mob of fanatics; but the principles were promulgated and fostered by persons who style themselves philosophers.

I see more evidence of these important facts in another book just published by an emigrant gen-

---

* I cannot help observing, that it is perfectly similar to the arrangement and denominations which appear in the secret correspondence of the Bavarian Illuminati.

tleman (Mr. Latocnaye). He confirms my repeated aſſertions, that all the irreligious and ſeditious doctrines were the ſubjects of repeated harangues in the Maſon Lodges, and that all the principles of the Revolution, by which the public mind was as it were ſet on fire, were nothing but enthuſiaſtic amplifications of the common-place cant of Free Maſonry, and aroſe naturally out of it. He even thinks " that this *muſt of neceſſity* be the caſe
" in every country where the minds of the lower
" claſſes of the State are in any way conſiderably
" fretted or irritated ; it is almoſt impoſſible to
" avoid being drawn into this vortex, whenever
" a diſcontented mind enters into a Maſon Lodge.
" The ſtale ſtory of brotherly love, which at an-
" other time would only lull the hearer aſleep,
" now makes him prick up his ears, and liſten
" with avidity to the ſilly tale, and he cannot
" hinder fretting thoughts from continually rank-
" ling in his mind."

Mr. Latocnaye ſays expreſsly, " That notwith-
" ſtanding the general contempt of the public for
" the Duke of Orleans, his authority as Grand
" Maſter of the Maſons gave him the greateſt
" opportunity that a ſeditious mind could deſire
" for helping forward the Revolution. He had
" ready to his hand a connected ſyſtem of hidden
" Societies, protected by the State, habituated to
" ſecrecy and artifice, and already tinged with
" the very enthuſiaſm he wiſhed to inſpire. In
" theſe he formed political committees, into which
" only his agents were admitted. He filled the
" Lodges with the French guards, whom he cor-
" rupted with money and hopes of preferment;
" and by means of the Abbe Sieyes, and other
" emiſſaries, they were harangued with all the ſo-
" phiſtical declamation, or cant of Maſonry."

Mr.

Mr. Latocnaye says, that all this was peculiar to the Lodges of the Grand Orient; but that there were many (not very many, if we judge by the Neuwied almanac, which reckons only 289 in all France in 1784, of which 266 were of the Grand Orient) Lodges who continued on the old plan of amusing themselves with a little solemn trifling. He coincides with Mr. Lefranc in the opinion that the awful and gloomy rituals of Masonry, and particularly the severe trials of confidence and submission, must have a great tendency to harden the heart, and fit a man for attrocious actions. No one can doubt of this who reads the following instance:

" A candidate for reception into one of the
" highest Orders, after having heard many threat-
" enings denounced against all who should betray
" the Secrets of the Order, was conducted to a
" place where he saw the dead bodies of several
" who were said to have suffered for their trea-
" chery. He then saw his own brother tied hand
" and foot, begging his mercy and intercession.
" He was informed that this person was about to
" suffer the punishment due to this offence, and
" that it was reserved for him (the candidate) to
" be the instrument of this just vengeance, and
" that this gave him an opportunity of manifest-
" ing that he was completely devoted to the Or-
" der. It being observed that his countenance
" gave signs of inward horror, (the person in
" bonds imploring his mercy all the while) he
" was told that in order to spare his feelings, a
" bandage should be put over his eyes. A dagger
" was then put into his right hand, and being
" hood-winked, his left hand was laid upon the
" palpitating heart of the criminal, and he was
" then ordered to strike. He instantly obeyed;
" and when the bandage was taken from his eyes,

he

" he faw that it was a lamb that he had ftabbed.
" Surely fuch trials and fuch wanton cruelty are
" fit only for training confpirators."

Mr. Latocnaye adds, that " when he had been
" initiated, an old gentleman afked him what he
" thought of the whole?" He anfwered, " A great
" deal of noife, and much nonfenfe." " Nonfenfe."
faid the other, " don't judge fo rafhly, young man;
" I have worked thefe twenty-five years, and the
" farther I advanced, it interefted me the more ;
" but I ftopped fhort, and nothing fhall prevail on
" me to advance a ftep farther." In another converfation the gentleman faid, " I imagine that my
" ftoppage was owing to my refufal about nine years
" ago, to liften to fome perfons who made to me,
" out of the Lodge, propofals which were feditious
" and horrible; for ever fince that time I have re-
" marked, that my higher Brethren treat me with a
" much greater referve than they had done before,
" and that, under the pretext of further inftruction;
" they have laboured to confute the notions which
" I had already acquired, by giving fome of the
" moft delicate fubjects a different turn. I faw
" that they wanted to remove fome fufpicions which
" I was beginning to form concerning the ultimate
" fcope of the whole."

I imagine that thefe obfervations will leave no
doubt in the mind of the reader with refpect to the
influence of the fecret Fraternity of Free Mafonry
in the French Revolution, and that he will allow it
to be highly probable that the infamous Duke of Orleans had, from the beginning, entertained hopes of
mounting the throne of France. It is not my province to prove or difprove this point, only I think
it no lefs evident, from many circumftances in the
tranfactions of thofe tumultuous days, that the
active leaders had quite different views, and were

impelled

impelled by fanatical notions of democratic felicity, or, more probably, by their own ambition to be the movers of this vast machine, to overturn the ancient government, and erect a republic, of which they hoped to be the managers*. Mirabeau had learned when in Germany that the principles of anarchy had been well digested into a system, and therefore wished for some instruction as to the subordinate detail of the business, and for this purpose requested a deputation from the *Illuminati*.

In such a cause as this, we may be certain that no ordinary person would be sent. One of the deputies was Amelius, the next person in the order to Spartacus and Philo. His worldly name was Johann. J. C. Bode, at Weimar, privy-counsellor to the Prince of Hesse-Darmstadt. (See *Fragmente der Biographie des verstorbenes Freyherr Bode in Weimar, mit zuverlaßigen Urkunder*, 8vo. *Riom*. 1795. See also *Endliche Shickfall der Freymaurerey*, 1794; also *Wiener Zeitschrift fur* 1793.)—This person has played a principal part in the whole scheme of Illumination. He was a person of considerable and showy talents as a writer. He had great talents for conversation, and had kept good company. With

---

* The depositions at the Chatelet, which I have already quoted, give repeated and unequivocal proofs, that he, with a considerable number of the deputies of the National Assembly, had formed this plot before the 5th of October 1789. That trial was conducted in a strange manner, partly out of respect for the Royal Family, which still had some hearts affectionately attached to it, and to the monarchy, and partly by reason of the fears of the members of this court. There was now no safety for any person who differed from the opinion of the frantic populace of Paris. The chief points of accusation were written in a schedule which is not published, and the witnesses were ordered to depose on these in one general Yes or No; so that it is only the least important part of the evidence that has been printed. I am well informed that the whole of it is carefully preserved, and will one day appear.

respect

respect to his myftical character, his experience was great. He was one of the Templar Mafons, and among them was *Eques a Liliis Convallium.* He had fpeculated much about the origin and hiftory of Mafonry, and when at the Willemfbad convention, was converted to Illuminatifm. He was the great inftigator of Nicholai, Gedicke, and Biefter, to the hunt after Jefuits which fo much occupied them, and fuggefted to Nicholai his journey through Germany. Leuchtfenring whom I mentioned before, was only the letter-carrier between Bode and thefe three authors. He was juft fuch a man as Weifhaupt wifhed for; his head filled with Mafonic fanaticifm, attaching infinite importance to the frivolities of Mafonry, and engaged in an enthufiaftic and fruitlefs refearch after its origin and hiftory. He had collected, however, fuch a number of archives (as they were called) of Free Mafonry, that he fold his manufcript to the Duke of Saxe Gotha, (into whofe fervice Weifhaupt engaged himfelf when he was driven from Bavaria), for 150 dahlers. This little anecdote fhows the high importance attributed to thofe matters by perfons of whom we fhould expect better things. Bode was alfo a moft determined and violent materialift. Befides all thefe qualities, fo acceptable to the Illuminati, he was a difcontented Templar Mafon, having been repeatedly difappointed of the preferment which he thought himfelf entitled to. When he learned that the firft operations of the Illuminati were to be the obtaining the fole direction of the Mafon Lodges, and of the whole Fraternity, his hopes revived of rifing to fome of the Commanderies, which his enthufiafm, or rather fanaticifm, had made him hope to fee one day regained by the Order:—but when he found that the next and favourite object was to root out the *Strict Obfervanz* altogether, he ftarted back. But Philo faw that the
underftanding

CHAP. IV.   THE FRENCH REVOLUTION.   289

underſtanding (ſhall we call it?) that can be dazzled with one whim, may be dazzled with another, and he now attached him to Illuminatiſm, by a magnificent diſplay of a world ruled by the Order, and conducted to happineſs by means of Liberty and Equality. This did the buſineſs, as we ſee by the private correſpondence, where Philo informs Spartacus of his firſt difficulties with Amelius. Amelius was gained over in Auguſt 1782, and we ſee by the ſame correſpondence, that the greateſt affairs were ſoon entruſted to him—he was generally employed to deal with the great. When a Graf or a Baron was to be wheedled into the Order, Amelius was the agent.—He was alſo the chief operator in all their conteſts with the Jeſuits and the Roſycrucians. It was alſo Bode that procured the important acceſſion of Nicholai to the Order. This he brought about through Leuchtſenring; and laſtly, his numerous connections among the Free Maſons, together with Knigge's influence among them, enabled the Illuminati to worm themſelves into every Lodge, and at laſt gave them almoſt the entire command of the Fraternity.

Such was the firſt of the deputies to France. The other was a Mr. Buſſche, called in the Order Bayard; therefore probably a man of reſpectable character; for moſt of Spartacus's names were ſignificant like his own. He was a military man, Lieutenant-Colonel in the ſervice of Heſſe Darmſtadt.— This man alſo was a diſcontented Templar Maſon, and his name in that Fraternity had been *Eques a Fontibus Eremi.* He was illuminated by Knigge. He had alſo been unſucceſsful both at court and in the field, in both of which ſituations he had been attempting to make a diſtinguiſhed figure. He, as well as Bode, were immerſed in debts. They were therefore

fore juſt in the proper temper for Cofmo-political enterprife.

They went to Paris in the end of 1788, while the Notables were fitting, and all Paris was giving advice. The alarm that was raifed about Animal Magnetifm, which was indeed making much noife at that time, and particularly at Paris, was affigned by them as the great motive of the journey. Bode alfo faid that he was anxious to learn what were the corrections made on the fyftem of the *Chevaliers Bienfaifants*. They had taken that name at firft, to fcreen themfelves from the charges againſt them under the name of Templars. They had corrected fomething in their fyftem when they took the name *Philalethes*. And now when the Schifms of the *Philalethes* were healed, and the Brethren again united under the name of *Amis Reunis*, he fufpected that Jefuits had interfered; and becaufe he had heard that the principles of the *Amis Reunis* were very noble, he wifhed to be more certain that they were purged of every thing Jefuitical.

The deputies accordingly arrived at Paris, and immediately obtained admiffion into thefe two Fraternities*. They found both of them in the ripeſt

---

* To prevent interruptions, I may juſt mention here the authorities for this journey and co-operation of the two deputies.
1. *Ein wichtiger Auffchlufs über en noch wenig bekannte Veranlaſſung der Franzöfchen Revolution*, in the Vienna Zeitfchrift for 1793, p. 145.
2. *Endliche Shickfall des Freymaurer Ordens*, 1794, p. 19.
3. *Neueſte Arbeitung des Spartacus and Philo*, Munich, 1793. p. 151—54.
4. *Hiſtoriſche Nachrichten über die Franc Revolution* 1792, von Girtanner, var. loc.
5. *Revolutions Almanach für* 1792—4, Gottingen, var. loc.
6. *Beytrage zur Biographie des verſtorbenes Frey-Herr v. Bode*, 1794.
7. *Magazin des Literatur et Kunſt*, for 1792, 3, 4, &c. &c.

ſtate

state for Illumination, having shaken off all the cabalistical, chemical, and myslical whims that had formerly disturbed them, and would now take up too much of their time. They were now cultivating with great zeal the philosophico political doctrines of universal citizenship. Their leaders, to the number of twenty, are mentioned by name in the Berlin Monatschrift for 1785, and among them are several of the first actors in the French Revolution. But this is nothing distinctive, because persons of all opinions were Masons.

The Amis Reunis were little behind the Illuminati in every thing that was irreligious and anarchical, and had no inclination for any of the formalities of ritual, &c. They were already fit for the higher mysteries, and only wanted to learn the methods of business which had succeeded so well in spreading their doctrines and maxims over Germany. Besides, their doctrines had not been digested into a system, nor had the artful methods of leading on the pupils from bad to worse been practised. For hitherto, each individual had vented in the Lodges his own opinions, to unburden his own mind, and the Brethren listened for instruction and mutual encouragement. Therefore, when Spartacus's plan was communicated to them, they saw at once its importance, in all its branches; such as the use of the Mason Lodges, to fish for Minervals—the rituals and ranks to entice the young, and to lead them by degrees to opinions and measures which, at first sight, would have shocked them. The firm hold which is gotten of the pupils, and indeed of all the inferior classes, by their reports in the course of their pretended training in the knowledge of themselves and of other men—and, above all, the provincial arrangement of the order, and the clever subordination and entire dependence on a select band or Pandæmonium at
Paris,

Paris, which should inspire and direct the whole.—I think (altho' I have not express assertions of the fact) from the subsequent conduct of the French revolters, that even at this early period, there were many in those societies who were ready to go every length proposed to them by the Illuminati, such as the abolition of royalty, and of all privileged orders, as tyrants by nature, the annihilation and robbery of the priesthood, the rooting out of Christianity, and the introduction of Atheism, or a philosophical chimera which they were to call Religion. Mirabeau had often spoken of the last branch of the Illuminated principles, and the conversations held at Versailles during the awful pauses of the 5th of October, (which are to be seen in the evidence before the Chatelet in the Orleans process,) can hardly be supposed to be the fancies of an accidental mob.

Mirabeau was, as I have said, at the head of this democratic party, and had repeatedly said, that the only use of a King was to serve as a pageant, in order to give weight to public measures in the opinion of the populace.—And Mr. Latocnaye says, that this party was very numerous, and that immediately after the imprudent or madlike invitation of every scribbler in a garret to give his advice, the party did not scruple to speak their sentiments in public, and that they were encouraged in their encomiums on the advantages of a virtuous republican government by Mr. Neckar, who had a most extravagant and childish predilection for the constitution of Geneva, the place of his nativity, and was also much tinged with the Cosmo-political philosophy of the times. The King's brothers, and the Princes of the blood, presented a memorial to his Majesty, which concluded by saying, that " the effervesence of the " public opinions had come to such a height that

" the

" the moſt dangerous principles, imported from
" foreign parts, were avowed in print with per-
" fect impunity—that his majeſty had unwarily
" encouraged every fanatic to dictate to him,
" and to ſpread his poiſonous ſentiments, in which
" the rights of the throne were not only diſre-
" ſpected, but were even diſputed—that the rights
" of the higher claſſes in the ſtate ran a great riſk
" of being ſpeedily ſuppreſſed, and that nothing
" would hinder the ſacred right of property from
" being ere long invaded, and the unequal diſtri-
" bution of wealth from being thought a proper
" ſubject of reform."

When ſuch was the ſtate of things in Paris; it is plain that the buſineſs of the German deputies would be eaſily tranſacted. They were received with open arms by the *Philalethes*, the *Amis de la Verite*, the *Social Contract*, &c. and in the courſe of a very few weeks in the end of 1788, and the beginning of 1789, (that is, before the end of March) the whole of the Grand Orient, including the *Philalethes*, *Amis Reunis*, *Martiniſtes*, &c. had the ſecrets of Illumination communicated to them. The operation naturally began with the Great National Lodge of Paris, and thoſe in immediate dependence on it. It would alſo ſeem, from many circumſtances that occurred to my obſervation, that the Lodges in Alſace and Lorraine were Illuminated at this time, and not long before as I had imagined. Straſburg I know had been Illuminated long ago, while Philo was in the Order. A circumſtance ſtrikes me here as of ſome moment. The ſects of *Philalethes*, and *Amis Reunis* were refinements engrafted on the ſyſtem of the *Chevaliers Beinfaiſants* at Lyons. Such refinements never fail to be conſidered as a ſort of hereſy, and the profeſſors will be held with a jealous and unfriendly eye by fome, who will pride themfelves on adhering to the old faith. And the greater the fuccefs of the herefy, the greater will be the animofity between the parties.—May not this help to explain the mutual hatred of the Parifians and the Lyonnois, which produced the moft dreadful attrocities ever perpetrated on the face of the earth, and made a fhambles and a defert of the fineft city of France?

The firft proceeding by the advice of the deputies was the formation of a political committee in every Lodge. This committee correfponded with the diftant Lodges, and in it were difcufsed and fettled all the political principles which were to be inculcated on the members. The author of the *Neuefte Arbeitung* fays exprefsly, that " he " was thoroughly inftructed in this; that it was " given in charge to thefe committees to frame " general rules, and to carry through the great " plan *(grand auvre)* of a general overturning " of religion and government." The principal leaders of the fubfequent Revolution were members of thefe committees. Here were the plans laid, and they were tranfmitted through the kingdom by the Correfponding Committees.

Thus were the ftupid Bavarians (as the French were once pleafed to call them) their inftructors in the art of overturning the world. The French were indeed the firft who put it in practice. Thefe committees arofe from the Illuminati in Bavaria, who had by no means given over working; and thefe committees produced the Jacobin Club. It is not a frivolous remark, that the Mafonic phrafe of the perfons who wifh to addrefs the Brethren, " *(F. S. je demande la parole,* which the F. S. re-
" ports to the V. G. M. and which he announces
" to the Brethren thus, " *Mes freres, frere tel
" demande*

"*demande la parole, la parole lui est accordee,"*) is exactly copied by the Jacobin Club. There is surely no natural connection between Free Masonry and Jacobinism—but we seek the link—Illuminatism.—

The office-bearers of one of the Lodges of Philalethes in Paris were *Martin, Willermooz,* (who had been deputy from the *Chevaliers Beinfaifants* to the Willemsbad Convention) *Chappe, Minet*, de la Henriere,* and *Savatier de l'Ange.* In another (the *Contrat Social*) the Political Committee consisted of *La Fayette, Condorcet, Pethion, d'Orleans, Abbe Bartholis, d'Aiguillon, Bailly, Marq. de la Salle, Desprefmenil.* This particular Lodge had been founded and conducted by one *De Leutre,* an adventurer and cheat of the first magnitude, who sometimes made a figure, and at other times was without a shilling. At this very time he was a spy attached to the office of the police of Paris†. The *Duke of Orleans* was Warden

---

* Minet was, I think, at this time a player. He was son of a surgeon at Nantes—rob'ed his father and fled—enlisted in Holland—deserted and became smuggler—was taken and burnt in the hand—became player and married an actress—then became priest—a d was made Bishop of Nantes by Couftard in discharge of a debt of 500l. Mr. Latocnaye often saw Couftard kneel to him for benediction. It cannot be suppo'ed that he was much venerated in his pontificals in his native city.—It seems Minet, Minet, is the call of the children to a kitten—This was prohibited at Nantes, and many persons whipped for the freedom used with his name.

† I am told that he now (or very lately) keeps the best company, and lives in elegance and affluence in London.

> *Augur, fchænobates, medicus, magus omnia novit*
> *Græculus efuriens; in cælum jufforis, ibit‡.*
> *Ingenium volex audacia perdita, fermo*
> *Promptus.*——

‡ All sciences a hungry Frenchman knows,
  And bid him go to hell—to hell he goes.
                    Johnson's Translation.

of the Lodge. The *Abbe Sieyes* was a Brother Orator, but not of this Lodge, nor, I think, of the former. It was probably of the one conducted by Mirabeau and the Abbe Perigord. But it appears from the piece from which I am at prefent borrowing, that Sieyes was prefent in the meetings of both Lodges, probably as vifiting Brother, employed in bringing them to common meafures. I muft obferve, that the fubfequent conduct of fome of thefe men does not juft accord with my conjecture, that the principles of the Illuminati were adopted in their full extent. But we know that all the Bavarian Brethren were not equally Illuminated, and it would be only copying their teachers if the clevereft of thefe their fcholars fhould hold a *fanctum fanctorum* among themfelves, without inviting all to the conference. Obferve too that the chief leffon which they were now taking from the Germans was *the method of doing bufinefs*, of managing their correfpondence, and of procuring and training pupils. A Frenchman does not think that he needs inftruction in any thing like principle or fcience. He is ready on all occafions to be the inftructor.

Thus were the Lodges of France converted in a very fhort time into a fet of fecret affiliated focieties, correfponding with the mother Lodges of Paris, receiving from thence their principles and inftructions, and ready to rife up at once when called upon to carry on the great work of overturning the ftate.

Hence it has arifen that the French aimed, in the very beginning, at overturning the whole world. In all the revolutions of other countries, the fchemes and plots have extended no farther than the nation where they took their rife. But here we have feen that they take in the whole world

world. They have repeatedly declared this in their manifeſtos, and they have declared it by their conduct—This is the very aim of the Illuminati. Hence too may be explained how the revolution took place in a moment in every part of France. The revolutionary ſocieties were early formed, and were working in ſecret before the opening of the National Aſſembly, and the whole nation changed, and changed again, and again, as if by beat of drum. Thoſe duly initiated in this myſtery of iniquity were ready every where at a call. And we ſee Weiſhaupt's wiſh accompliſhed in an unexpected degree, and the debates in a club giving laws to ſolemn aſſemblies of the nation, and all France bending the neck to the city of Paris. The members of the club are Illuminati, and ſo are a great part of their correſpondents.— Each operates in the ſtate as a Minerval would do in the Order, and the whole goes on with ſyſtematic regularity. The famous Jacobin Club was juſt one of thoſe Lodges, as has been already obſerved; and as, among individuals one commonly takes the lead, and contrives for the reſt, ſo it has happened on the preſent occaſion, that this Lodge, ſupported by Orleans and Mirabeau, was the one that ſtepped forth and ſhewed itſelf to the world and thus became the oracle of the party; and all the reſt only echoed its diſcourſes, and at laſt allowed it to give law to the whole, and even to rule the kingdom. It is to be remarked too that the founders of the club at Mentz were Illuminati, *(Relig. Begebenh.* 1793. p. 448.) before the Revolution, and correſponded with another Lodge at Straſburg; and theſe two produced mighty effects during the year 1790. In a performance called *Memoires Poſthumes de Cuſtine* it is ſaid, that when that general was bending his courſe to Holland,

land, the Illuminati at Strasburg, Worms, and Spire, immediately formed clubs, and invited him into that quarter, and, by going to Mentz and encouraging their brethren in that city, they raised a party against the garrison, and actually delivered up the place to the French army.

A little book, just now printed with the title *Paragraphan*, says, that Zimmerman, of whom I have spoken more than once, went to France to preach liberty. He was employed as a missionary of Revolution in Alsace, where he had formerly been a most successful missionary of Illuminatism. Of his former proceedings the following is a curious anecdote. He connected himself with a highly accomplished and beautiful woman, whose conversation had such charms, that he says she gained him near a hundred converts in Spire alone. Some persons of high rank, and great exterior dignity of character, had felt more tender impressions— and when the lady informed them of certain consequences to their reputation, they were glad to compound matters with her friend Mr. Zimmerman, who either passed for her husband or took the scandal on himself. He made above 1500 Louis d'ors in this way. When he returned, as a preacher of Revolution, he used to mount the pulpit with a sabre in his hand, and bawl out, " Behold, Frenchmen, this is your God. This " alone can save you." The author adds, that when Custine broke into Germany, Zimmerman got admission to him, and engaged to deliver Manheim into his hands. To gain this purpose, he offered to set some corners of the city on fire, and assured him of support. Custine declined the offer.—Zimmerman appeared against him before the Revolutionary Tribunal, and accused him of treachery to his cause.—Custine's answer is re-

remarkable,

markable. " Hardly," faid he, " had I fet my
" foot in Germany, when this man, and all the
" fools of his country, befieged me, and would
" have delivered up to me their towns and vil-
" lages—What occafion had I to do any thing to
" Manheim, when the Prince was neutral?" Zimmerman found his full account in Robefpierre's
bloody fway—but the fhort term of his attrocities
was alfo the whole of Zimmerman's carreer. He
was arrefted, but again liberated, and foon after
again imprifoned, after which I can learn no more
of him. The fame thing is pofitively afferted in
another performance, called *Cri de la Raifon*, and
in a third, called *Les Mafques Arrachees*. Obferve too, that it is not the clubs merely that are
accufed of this treachery, but the Illuminati. *De
la Metherie* alfo, in his preface to the *Journal de
Phyfique* for 1790, fays exprefsly, that " the caufe
" and arms of France were powerfully fupported
" in Germany by a fect of philofophers called the
" Illuminated." In the preface to the *Journal* for
1792, he fays, that " Letters and deputations were
" received by the Affembly from feveral Corref-
" ponding Societies in England, felicitating them
" on the triumph of Reafon and Humanity, and
" promifing them their cordial affiftance."——
He read fome of thefe manifeftos, and fays,
that " one of them recommended ftrongly the
" political education of the children, who fhould
" be taken from the parents and trained up
" for the ftate."——Another lamented the baleful influence of property, faying, that " the ef-
" forts of the Affembly would be fruitlefs, till the
" fence was removed with which the laws fo
" anxioufly fecured inordinate wealth. They
" fhould rather be directed to the fupport of ta-
" lents and virtue; becaufe property would al-
" ways

"ways support itself by the too great influence
"which it had in every corrupted state. The
"laws should prevent the too great accumulation
"of it in Particular families."——In short, the
counsel was almost verbatim what the Abbe Cossandey declared to have been preached in the meetings of the Illuminati, which terrified him and his colleagues, and made them quit the association. Anarcharsis Cloots, born in Prussian Westphalia, a keen Illuminatus, came to Paris for the express purpose of forwarding the *great work*, and by intriguing in the style of the Order, he got himself made one of the Representatives of the Nation. He seems to have been one of the completest fanatics in Cosmo-politism, and just such a tool as Weishaupt would choose to employ for a coarse and arduous job. He broke out at once into all the silly extravagance of the unthinking herd, and his whole language is just the jargon of Illumination. Citizen of the world—Liberty and Equality, the imprescriptible Rights of Man——Morality, dear Morality—Kings and Priests are useless things—they are Despots and Corrupters, &c.—He declared himself an atheist, and zealously laboured to have atheism established by law. He conducted that farcical procession in the true style of the most childish ritual of Philo, where counterfeited deputies from all quarters of the world, in the dresses of their countries, came to congratulate the nation for its victory over Kings and Priests. It is also worthy of remark, that by this time Leuchtsenring, whom we have seen so zealous an *Illuminatus*, after having been as zealous a Protestant, tutor of Princes, Hofrath and Hofmeister, was now a secretary or clerk in one of the Bureaus of the National Assembly of France.

I may

I may add as a finifhing touch, that the National Affembly of France was the only body of men that I have ever heard of who openly and fyftematically propofed to employ affaffination, and to inftitute a band of patriots, who fhould exercife this profeffion either by fword, piftol, or poifon;—and though the propofal was not carried into execution, it might be confidered as the fentiments of the meeting; for it was only delayed till it fhould be confidered how far it might not be imprudent, becaufe they might expect reprifals. The Abbe Dubois engaged to poifon the Comte d'Artois; but was himfelf robbed and poifoned by his accomplices.—There were ftrong reafons for thinking that the Emperor of Germany was poifoned—and that Mirabeau was thus treated by his pupil Orleans,—alfo Madame de Favras and her fon.—This was copying the Illuminati very carefully.

After all thefe particulars, can any perfon have a doubt that the Order of Illuminati formally interfered in the French Revolution, and contributed greatly to its progrefs? There is no denying the infolence and oppreffion of the Crown and the Nobles, nor the mifery and flavery of the people, nor that there were fufficient provocation and caufe for a total change of meafures and of principles. But the rapidity with which one opinion was declared in every corner, and that opinion as quickly changed, and the change announced every where, and the perfect conformity of the principles, and famenefs of the language, even in arbitrary trifles, can hardly be explained in any other way. It may indeed be faid " *que les beaux genies fe rencontrent*,—that
" wits jump. The principles are the fame, and
" the conduct of the French has been fuch as the
" Illuminati would have exhibited; but this is all
" —the Illuminati no longer exifted." Enough has been

been said on this point already.—The facts are as have been narrated. The Illuminati continued *as an Order*, and even held assemblies, though not so frequently nor so formally as before, and though their *Areopagus* was no longer at Munich. But let us hear what the French themselves thought of the matter.

In 1789, or the beginning of 1790, *a manifesto was sent from the* GRAND NATIONAL LODGE *of Free Masons* (so it is entitled) *at Paris, signed by the Duke of Orleans as Grand Master, addressed and sent to the Lodges in all the respectable cities of Europe, exhorting them to unite for the support of the French Revolution, to gain it friends, defenders, and dependents; and according to their opportunities, and the practicability of the thing, to kindle and propagate the spirit of revolution through all lands.* This is a most important article, and deserves a very serious attention. I got it first of all in a work called, *Hochste wichtige Erinnerungen zur rechten Zeit uber einige der allerernsthaftesten Angelegenheiten dieses Zeitalters, von L. A. Hoffmann*, Vienna, 1795*.

· The author of this work says, " That every thing
" he advances in these memorandums is consistent
" with his own personal knowledge, and that he is
" ready to give convincing proofs of them to any
" respectable person who will apply to him person-
" ally. He has already given such convincing do-
" cuments to the Emperor, and to several Princes,
" that many of the machinations occasioned by this
" manifesto have been detected and stopped; and
" he would have no scruple at laying the whole be-
" fore the public, did it not unavoidably involve
" several worthy persons who had suffered them-
" selves to be misled, and heartily repented of their

---

* Most important Memorandums, in proper Season, concerning one of the most serious Occurrences of the present Age, by L. A. Hoffmann, Vienna, 1795.

" errors."

"errors." He is naturally (being a Catholic) very severe on the Proteſtants, (and indeed he has much reaſon,) and by this has drawn on himſelf many bitter retorts. He has however defended himſelf againſt all that are of any conſequence to his good name and veracity, in a manner that fully convinces any impartial reader, and turns to the confuſion of the ſlanderers.

Hoffmann ſays, that "he ſaw ſome of thoſe mani-
"feſtos; that they were not all of one tenor, ſome
"being addreſſed to friends, of whoſe ſupport they
"were already aſſured." One very important article of their contents is *Earneſt exhortations to eſtabliſh in every quarter ſecret ſchools of political education, and ſchools for the public education of the children of the people, under the direction of well-principled maſters; and offers of pecuniary aſſiſtance for this purpoſe, and for the encouragement of writers in favour of the Revolution, and for indemnifying the patriotic bookſellers who ſuffer by their endeavours to ſuppreſs publications which have an oppoſite tendency.* We know very well that the immenſe revenue of the Duke of Orleans was ſcattered among all the rabble of the *Palais Royal.* Can we doubt of its being employed in this manner? Our doubts muſt vaniſh, when we ſee that not long after this was publicly ſaid in the National Aſſembly, "that this method was the moſt effectual for accompliſhing their purpoſe of ſetting Europe in a flame." "But much expence," ſays the ſpeaker, "will attend it, and much has al-
"ready been employed, which cannot be named
"becauſe it is given in ſecret." The Aſſembly' had given the Illumination war-hoop—" *Peace with
"cottages, but war with palaces*"—A *pouvoir revolutionnaire* is mentioned, which ſuperſedes all narrow thoughts, all ties of morality. Lequinio publiſhes the moſt deteſtable book that ever iſſued from a
printing

printing prefs, *Les Prejuges vaincus,* containing all the principles, and expreſſed in the very words of Illuminatifm.

Hoffmann fays, that the French *Propaganda* had many emiſſaries in Vienna, and many friends whom he could point out. Mirabeau in particular had many connections in Vienna, and to the certain knowledge of Hoffmann, carried on a great correfpondence in cyphers. The progreſs of Illumination had been very great in the Auſtrian States, and a ſtatefman gave him an account of their proceedings, *(qui font redreſſer les cheveux)* which makes one's hair ſtand on end. " I no lon-
" ger wonder," fays he, " that the *Neuefte Arbei-*
" *tung des Spartacus und Philo* was forbidden.
" O ye almighty *Illuminati,* what can you not
" accompliſh by your ſerpent-like infinuation and
" cunning!" Your leaders fay, " This book is
" dangerous, becaufe it will teach wicked men
" the moſt refined methods of rebellion, and it
" muſt never get into the hands of the common
" people. They have faid with the moſt impu-
" dent face to fome Princes, who did not per-
" ceive the deeper-laid reaſon for fuppreſſing the
" book. The leaders of the *Illuminati* are, not
" without reafon, in anxiety, leſt the inferior
" claſſes of their own Society ſhould make juſt
" reprifals for having been fo bafely tricked, by
" keeping them back and in profound ignorance
" of their real defigns; and for working on
" them by the very goodneſs of their hearts, to
" their final ruin; and left the Free Mafons,
" whom they have alfo abuſed, ſhould think of
" revenging themfelves, when the matchlefs vil-
" lainy of their deceivers has been fo clearly ex-
" pofed. It is in vain for them to talk of the danger
" of inſtructing the people in the methods of fo-
" menting

" menting rebellion by this book. The aims are
" too apparent, and even in the neighbourhood of
" Regenſburg, where the ſtrength of the *Illumi-*
" *nati* lay, every perſon ſaid aloud, that the Illu-
" minatiſm diſcovered by this book was High
" Treaſon, and the moſt unheard of attempt to
" annihilate every religion and every civil go-
" vernment." He goes on: " In 1790 I was as
" well acquainted with the ſpirit of the Illumina-
" tion-ſyſtem as at preſent, but only not ſo docu-
" mented by their conſtitutional acts, as it is now
" by the *Neueſte Arbeitung des Spartacus und*
" *Philo.* My Maſonic connections were formerly
" extenſive, and my publication entitled *Eighteen*
" *Paragraphs Concerning Free Maſonry,* procured
" me more acquaintance with Free Maſons of
" the greateſt worth, and of *Illuminati* equally
" upright, perſons of reſpectability and know-
" ledge, who had diſcovered and repented the
" trick and inveigling conduct of the Order. All
" of us jointly ſwore oppoſition to the *Illuminati,*
" and my friends conſidered me as a proper in-
" ſtrument for this purpoſe. To whet my zeal,
" they put papers into my hands which made me
" ſhudder, and raiſed my diſlike to the higheſt
" pitch. I received from them liſts of the mem-
" bers, and among them ſaw names which I la-
" mented exceedingly. Thus ſtood matters in
" 1790, when the French Revolution began to
" take a ſerious turn. The intelligent ſaw in the
" open ſyſtem of the Jacobins the complete hid-
" den ſyſtem of the Illuminati. We knew that
" this ſyſtem included the whole world in its
" aims, and France was only the place of its firſt
" exploſion. The Propaganda works in every
" corner to this hour, and its emiſſaries run about
" in all the four quarters of the world, and are to
" be

"be found in numbers in every city that is a seat of government."

" He farther relates how they in Vienna wanted to enlist him, and, as this failed, how they have abused him even in the foreign newspapers.

" I have personal knowledge (continues he) that in Germany a second Mirabeau, Mauvillon, had proposed in detail a plan of revolution, entirely and precisely suited to the present state of Germany. This he circulated among several Free Mason Lodges, among all the Illuminated Lodges which still remained in Germany, and through the hands of all the emissaries of the Propaganda, who had been already dispatched to the frontiers *(vorpoften)* of every district of the empire, with means for stirring up the people." (N. B. In 1792, Mauvillon, finding abundant support and encouragement in the appearance of things round him, when the French arms had penetrated every where, and their invitations to revolt had met with so hearty a reception from the discontented in every state, came boldly forward, and, in the Brunswick Journal for March 1792, declared that " he heartily rejoiced in the French Revolution, wished it all success, and thought himself liable to no reproach when he declared his hopes that a similar Revolution would speedily take place in Germany.")

In the Hamburgh Political Journal, August, September, and October 1790, there are many proofs of the machinations of emissaries from the *Mason Lodges* of Paris among the German Free Masons—See pages 836, 963, 1087, &c. It appears that a club has taken the name of *Propaganda,* and meets once a week at least, in the form of a

Mason

Mason Lodge. It consists of persons of all nations, and is under the direction of the Grand Master, the Duke of Orleans. De Leutre is one of the Wardens. They have divided Europe into colonies, to which they give revolutionary names, such as the *Cap*, the *Pike*, the *Lantern*, &c. They have ministers in these colonies. (One is pointed out in Saxony, by marks which I presume are well understood.) A secret press was found in Saxe Gotha, furnished with German types, which printed a seditious work called the *Journal of Humanity*. This Journal was found in the mornings lying in the streets and highways. The house belonged to an *Illuminatus* of the name of Duport, a poor schoolmaster—he was associated with another in Strasburg, who was also an *Illuminatus*.—His name was Meyer, the writer of the Strasburg Newspaper. He had been some time a teacher in Salzmann's accademy, who we see was also an *Illuminatus*, but displeased with their proceedings almost at first. (Private Correspondence.)

"I have personal knowledge (continues Professor Hoffman) that in 1791, during the temporary dearth at Vienna, several of these emissaries were busy in corrupting the minds of the poor, by telling them that in like manner the court had produced a famine in Paris in 1789. I detected some of them, and exposed them in my *Patriotic Remarks on the Present Dearth*, and had the satisfaction of seeing my endeavours of considerable effect."

Surely these facts show that the Anarchists of France knew of the German Illuminati, and confided in their support. They also knew to what particular Lodges they could address themselves with safety and confidence.—But what need is there of more argument, when we know the zeal

of

of the Illuminati, and the unhoped for opportunity that the Revolution had given them of acting with immediate effect in carrying on their great and darling work? Can we doubt that they would eagerly put their hand to the Plough? And, to complete the proof, do we not know from the lists found in the secret correspondence of the Order, that they already had Lodges in France, and that in 1790 and 1791 many Illuminated Lodges in Germany, viz. Mentz, Worms, Spire, Frankfort, actually interfered, and produced great effects. In Switzerland too they were no less active. They had Lodges at Geneva and at Bern. At Bern two Jacobins were sentenced to several years imprisonment, and among their papers were found their patents of Illumination. I also see the fate of Geneva ascribed to the operations of Illuminati residing there, by several writers—particularly by Girtanner, and by the Gottingen editor of the Revolution Almanac.

I conclude this article with an extract or two from the proceedings of the National Assembly and Convention, which make it evident that their principles and their practice are precisely those of the Illuminati, on a great scale.

When the assumption of the Duchy of Savoy as an 84th Department was debated, Danton said to the Convention.

" In the moment that we send freedom to a
" nation on our frontier, we must say to them you
" must have no more Kings—for if we are surrounded by tyrants, their coalition puts our
" own freedom in danger.—When the French
" nation sent us hither, it created a great committee for the general insurrection of the people."

On the 19th of November 1792 it was decreed, " That the Convention, in the name of " the French nation, tenders help and fraternity " to all people who would recover their liberty."

On the 21ſt of November, the Preſident of the Convention ſaid to the pretended deputies of the Duchy of Savoy, " Repreſentatives of an inde-
" pendent people, important to mankind was the
" day when the National Convention of France
" pronounced its ſentence, *Royal dignity is abo-*
" *liſhed.*—-From that day many nations will, in
" future, reckon the era of their political exiſt-
" ence.—From the beginning of civil eſtabliſh-
" ments Kings have been in oppoſition to their
" nations—-but now they riſe up to annihilate
" Kings.—Reaſon, when ſhe darts her rays into
" every corner, lays open eternal truths——She
" alone enables us to paſs ſentence on deſpots, hi-
" therto the ſcare-crow of other nations."

But the moſt diſtinct exhibition of principle is to be ſeen in a report from the diplomatic committee, who were commiſſioned to deliberate on the conduct which France was to hold with other nations. On this report was founded the decree of the 15th of December 1793. The Reporter addreſſes the Convention as follows:

" The Committees of Finance and War aſk in
" the beginning—What is the object of the war
" which we have taken in hand? Without all
" doubt the object is THE ANNIHILATION OF
" ALL PRIVILEGES, WAR WITH THE PALACES,
" PEACE WITH THE COTTAGES. Theſe are the
" principles on which *your declaration of war* is
" founded. All tyranny, all privilege, muſt be
" treated as an enemy in the countries where we
" ſet our foot. This is the genuine reſult of our
" principles.—But it is not with Kings alone that
" we

" we are to wage war—were thefe our fole ene-
" mies, we fhould only have to bring down ten
" or twelve heads. We have to fight with all
" their accomplices, with the privileged orders,
" who devour and have oppreffed the people dur-
" ing many centuries.

" We muft therefore declare ourfelves for a
" revolutionary power in all the countries into
" which we enter—(Loud applaufes from the Af-
" fembly)—Nor need we put on the cloak of hu-
" manity—we difdain fuch little arts.—We muft
" clothe ourfelves with all the brilliancy of rea-
" fon, and all the force of the nation. We need
" not mafk our principles——the defpots know
" them already. The firft thing we muft do is to
" ring the alarum bell, for infurrection and up-
" roar.——We muft, in a folemn manner, let the
" people fee the banifhment of their tyrants and
" privileged cafts——otherwife, the people, ac-
" cuftomed to their fetters, will not be able to
" break their bonds.—It will effect nothing, mere-
" ly to excite a rifing of the people—this would
" only be giving them words inftead of ftanding
" by them.

" And fince, in this manner, we ourfelves are
" the Revolutionary Adminiftration, all that is
" againft the rights of the people muft be over-
" thrown at our entry—We muft difplay our prin-
" ciples by actually deftroying all tyranny; and
" our generals after having chafed away the ty-
" rants and their fatellites, muft proclaim to the
" people that they have brought them happinefs;
" and then, on the fpot, they muft fupprefs tithes,
" feudal rights, and every fpecies of fervitude."

" But we fhall have done nothing if we ftop
" here. Ariftocracy ftill domineers—we muft
" therefore fupprefs all authorities exifting in the
" hands

"hands of the upper claſſes.—When the Revo-
"lutionary Authority appears, there muſt nothing
"of the old eſtabliſhment remain.—A popular
"ſyſtem muſt be introduced—every office muſt
"be occupied by new functionaries—and the
"Sans Cullottes muſt every where have a ſhare
"in the Adminiſtration.

"Still nothing is done, till we declare aloud
"the *preciſion* of our principles to ſuch as want
"only half freedom.—We muſt ſay to them—If
"you think of compromiſing with the privileged
"caſts, we cannot ſuffer ſuch dealing with ty-
"rants—They are our enemies, and we muſt treat
"them as enemies, becauſe they are neither for
"Liberty nor Equality.—Show yourſelves diſ-
"poſed to receive a free conſtitution—and the
"Convention will not only ſtand by you, but will
"give you permanent ſupport; we will defend
"you againſt the vengeance of your tyrants—
"againſt their attacks, and againſt their return.
"—Therefore aboliſh from among you the No-
"bles, and every eccleſiaſtical and military in-
"corporation. They are incompatable with Equa-
"lity.—Henceforward you are citizens, all equal
"in rights—equally called upon to rule, to de-
"fend, and to ſerve your country.—The agents
"of the French Republic will inſtruct and aſſiſt
"you in forming a free conſtitution, and aſſure
"you of happineſs and fraternity."

This Report was loudly applauded, and a decree formed in preciſe conformity to its principles. Both were ordered to be tranſlated into
all languages, and copies to be furniſhed to their
generals, with orders to have them carefully diſ-
perſed in the countries which they invaded.

And, in completion of theſe decrees, their ar-
mies found it eaſy to collect as many diſcontented
or

or worthless perfons in any country as fufficed for fetting up a tree of liberty. This they held as a fufficient call for their interference.----Sometimes they performed this ceremony themfelves—a reprefentation was eafily made up in the fame way—and then, under the name of a free conftitution, the nation was forced to acquiefce in a form dictated at the point of the bayonet, in which they had not the fmalleft liberty to choofe—and they were plundered of all they had, by way of compenfating to France for the trouble fhe had taken.—-And this they call Liberty.—It needs no comment.—

Thus have I attempted to prove that the prefent awful fituation of Europe, and the general fermentation of the public mind in all nations, have not been altogether the natural operations of difcontent, oppreffion, and moral corruption, although thefe have been great, and have operated with fatal energy; but that this political fever has been carefully and fyftematically heightened by bodies of men, who profeffed to be the phyficians of the State, and, while their open practice employed cooling medicines, and a treatment which all approved, adminiftered in fecret the moft inflammatory poifons, which they made up fo as to flatter the difeafed fancy of the patient. Although this was not a plan begun, carried on, and completed by the fame perfons, it was undoubtedly an uniform and confiftent fcheme, proceeding on the fame unvaried principle, and France undoubtedly now fmarts under all the woes of German Illumination.

I beg leave to fuggeft a few thoughts, which may enable us to draw fome advantage from this fhocking mafs of information.

General

General Reflections.

I. I may observe, in the *first* place, and I beg it may be particularly attended to, that in all those villainous machinations against the peace of the world, the attack has been first made on the principles of Morality and Religion. The conspirators saw that till these are extirpated, they have no chance of success; and their manner of proceeding shews that they consider Religion and Morality as inseparably connected together. We learn much from this—*Fas est et ab hoste doceri.*—They endeavour to destroy our religious sentiments, by first corrupting our morals. They try to inflame our passions, that when the demands from this quarter become urgent, the restraints of Religion may immediately come in sight, and stand in the way. They are careful, on this occasion, to give such a view of those restraints, that the real origin of them does not appear.—We are made to believe that they have been altogether the contrivance of Priests and despots, in order to get the command of us. They take care to support these assertions by facts, which, to our great shame, and greater misfortune, are but too numerous. Having now the passions on their side, they find no difficulty in persuading the voluptuary, or the discontented, that tyranny, actually exerted, or resolved on in future, is the sole origin of religious restraint. He seeks no further argument, and gives himself no trouble to find any. Had he examined the matter with any care, he would find himself just brought back to those very feelings of moral excellence and moral depravity that he wishes to get rid of altogether; and these would tell him that pure Religion does not lay a single restraint on us that a noble nature would not have laid on itself—nor enjoins a single duty which an ingenuous and warm heart would not be ashamed to find itself deficient in. He would then see that all the sanctions of Religion are fitted to his high rank in the scale of existence. And the more he contemplates his future prospects, the more they brighten upon his view, the more attainable they appear, and the more he is able to know what they may probably be. Having attained this happy state of mind, (an attainment in the power of any kind heart that is in earnest in the enquiry) he will think that no punishment is too great for the unthankful and groveling soul which can forego such hopes, and reject these noble proffers, for the comparatively frivolous and transitory gratifications of life. He is not frightened into worthy and virtuous conduct by fears of such merited punishment; but, if not enticed into it by his high expectations, he is, at least, retained in the paths of virtue by a kind of manly shame.

But all this is overlooked, or is kept out of sight, in the instructions of Illuminatism. In these the eye must be kept always directed to the Despot. This is the bugbear, and every thing is made to connect with present or future tyranny and oppression——Therefore Religion is held out as a combination of terrors---the invention of the state-tools, the priests. But it is not easy to stifle the suggestions of Nature— therefore no pains are spared to keep them down, by encreasing the uncertainty and doubts which arise in the course of all speculations on such subjects. Such difficulties occur in all scientific discussions.—Here they must be numerous and embarrassing--- for in this enquiry we come near the first principles of things, and the first principles of human knowledge. The geometer does not wonder at mistakes

takes even in *his* science, the most simple of all others.----Nor does the mechanic or the chemist reject all his science, because he cannot attain clear conceptions of some of the natural relations which operate in the phenomena under his consideration.—Nor do any of these students of nature brand with the name of fool, or knave, or bigot, another person who has drawn a different conclusion from the phenomenon.——In one point they all agree—they find themselves possessed of faculties which enable them to speculate, and to discover; and they find, that the operation of those faculties is quite unlike the things which they contemplate by their means—*and they feel a satisfaction in the possession of them*, and in this distinction.——But this seems a misfortune to our Illuminators. I have long been struck with this. If by deep meditation I have solved a problem which has baffled the endeavours of others, I should hardly thank the person who convinced me that my success was entirely owing to the particular state of my health, by which my brain was kept free from many irritations to which other persons are exposed. Yet this is the conduct of the Illuminated—They are abundantly self-conceited; and yet they continually endeavour to destroy all grounds of self-estimation.---They rejoice in every discovery that is reported to them of some resemblance, unnoticed before, between mankind and the inferior creation, and would be happy to find that the resemblance is complete. It is very true, Mr. Pope's " Poor Indian, with untutor'd " mind," had no objection to his dog's going to heaven with him:

" And thinks, admitted to that equal sky,
" His faithful dog shall bear him company."

This

This is not an abject, but it is a modest sentiment. But our high-minded philosophers, who, with Beatrice in the play, "cannot brook obedience to a "wayward piece of marl," if it be in the shape of a Prince, have far other notions of the matter. Indeed they are not yet agreed about it. Mr. de la Metherie hopes, that before the enlightened Republic of France has got into its teens, he shall be able to tell his fellow-citizens, in his *Journal de Physique*, that particular form of crystallization which men have been accustomed to call God.---Dr. Priestley again deduces all intelligence from elastic undulations, and will probably think, that his own great discoveries have been the quiverings of some fiery marsh *miasma*. While Pope's poor Indian hopes to take his dog to heaven with him, these Illuminators hope to die like dogs, and that both soul and body shall be as if they never had been.

Is not this a melancholy result of all our Illumination? It is of a piece with the termination of the ideal Philosophy, viz. professed and total ignorance. Should not this make us start back and hesitate, before we pout like wayward children at the hardships of civil subordination, and before we make a sacrifice to our ill humour of all that we value ourselves for? Does it not carry ridicule and absurdity in its forehead?---Such assertions of personal worth and dignity, (always excepting Princes and Priests,) and such abject acknowledgments of worthlessness.--- Does not this, of itself, show that there is some radical fault in the whole? It has all arisen from what they have called *Illumination*, and this turns out to be worse than darkness---But we also know that it has all arisen from self-conceited discontent, and that it has been brought to its present state by the rage of speculation. We may venture to put the question to any man's conscience---whether discontent

tent did not precede his doubts about his own nature and whether he has not *encouraged* the train of argument that tended to degrade him? " Thy wifh " was father, Harry, to that thought."---Should not this make us diftruft, at leaft, the operations of this faculty of our mind, and try to moderate and check this darling propenfity.---It feems a misfortune of the age---for we fee that it is a natural fource of difturbance and revolution.

But here it will be immediately faid, " What, " muft we give over thinking---be no longer ration- " al creatures, and believe every lie that is told us?" By no means.---Let us be *really* rational creatures--- and, taught by experience, let us, in all our fpeculations on fubjects which engage the paffions, guard ourfelves with the moft anxious care againft the rifk of having our judgments warped by our defires.--- There is no propenfity of our nature of which the proper and modeft indulgence is not beneficial to man, and which is not hurtful, when this indulgence is carried too far.---And if we candidly perufe the page of hiftory, we fhall be convinced that the abufe is great in proportion as the fubject is important. What has been fo ruinoufly perverted as the religious principle?---What horrid fuperftition has it not produced? The Reader will not, I hope, take it amifs that I prefume to direct his attention to fome maxims which ought to conduct a prudent man in his indulgence of a fpeculative difpofition, and apply them to the cafe in hand.

Whoever will for a while call off his attention from the common affairs of life, the *Curæ hominum, et rerum pondus inane*, and will but reflect a little on that wonderful principle within him, which carries him over the whole univerfe, and fhows him its various relations---Whoever alfo remarks how very fmall a proportion his own individual exiftence bears to this immeasurable scene, cannot but feel an inexpressible pleasure in the contemplation of his own powers---He must rise in his own estimation, and be disposed to cherish with fondness this principle which so eminently raises him above all around him. Of all the sources of human vanity this is surely the most manly, the most excusable, and the most likely to be extravagantly indulged.—We may be certain that it will be so indulged, and that men will frequently speculate for the sake of speculation alone, and that they will have too much confidence in the results of this favourite occupation,---As there have been ages of indolent and abject credulity and superstition, it is next to certain that there are also times of wild and extravagant speculation---and when we see it becoming a sort of general passion, we may be certain that this is a case in point.

This can hardly be denied to be the character of the present day. It is not denied. On the contrary it is gloried in as the prerogative of the eighteenth century. All the speculations of antiquity are considered as glimmerings (with the exceptions of a few brighter flashes) when compared with our present meridian splendor. We should therefore listen with caution to the inferences from this boasted Illumination. Also when we reflect on what passes in our own minds, and on what we observe in the world, of the mighty influence of our desires and passions on our judgments, we should carefully notice whether any such warping of the belief is probable in the present case. That it is so is almost certain---for the general and immediate effect of this Illumination is to lessen or remove many restraints which the sanctions of religion lay on the indulgence of very strong passions, and to diminish our regard for a certain purity or correctness of manners, which religion recommends as the only conduct

duct suited to our noble natures, and as absolutely necessary for attaining that perfection and happiness of which we are capable.——For surely if we take away religion, it will be wisdom " to eat and " to drink, since to-morrow we die." If, moreover, we see this Illumination extolled above all science, as friendly to virtue, as improving the heart, and as producing a just morality, which will lead to happiness both for ourselves and others, but perceive at the same time that these assertions are made at the expence of principles, which our natural feelings force us to venerate as supreme and paramount to all others, we may then be certain that our informer is trying to mislead and deceive us.——For all virtue and goodness both of heart and conduct, is in perfect harmony, and there is no jarring or inconsistency. But we must pass this sentence on the doctrines of this Illumination. For it is a melancholy truth that they have been preached and recommended, for the most part, by clergymen, parish-ministers, who, in the presence of invoked Deity, and in the face of the world, have set their solemn seal to a system of doctrines directly opposite to those recommended in their writings; which doctrines they solemnly profess to believe, and solemnly swear to inculcate. Surely the informations and instructions of such men should be rejected. Where shall we find their real opinions? In their solemn oaths? —or in these infidel dissertations?—In either case, they are deceivers, whether misled by vanity or by the mean desire of church-emoluments; or they are prostitutes, courting the society of the wealthy and sensual. Honesty, like justice, admits of no degrees. A man is honest, or he is a knave, and who would trust a knave? But such men are unsuitable instructors for another reason—they are

unwise;

unwife; for, whatever they may think, they are not refpected as men of worth, but are inwardly defpifed as parafites, by the rich, who admit them into their company, and treat them with civility, for their own reafons. We take inftructions not merely from the knowing, the learned, but from the wife—not therefore from men who give fuch evidences of weaknefs.

Such would be the conduct of a prudent man, who liftens to the inftructions of another with the ferious intention of profiting by them. In the prefent cafe he fees plain proofs of degraded felf eftimation, of difhonefty, and of mean motives. But the prudent man will go further—he will remark that diffolute manners, and actions which are inevitably fubverfive of the peace and order, nay, of the very exiftence of fociety, are the natural and neceffary confequences of irreligion. Should any doubt of this remain in his mind; fhould he fometimes think of an Epictetus, or one or two individuals of antiquity, who were eminently virtuous, without the influence of religious fanctions, he fhould recollect, that the Stoics were animated by the thought, that while the wife man was playing the game of life, the gods were looking on, and pleafed with his fkill. Let him read the beautiful account given by Dr. Smith of the rife of the Stoic philofophy, and he will fee that it was an artificial but noble attempt of a few exalted minds, enthufiafts in virtue, aiming to fteel their fouls againft the dreadful but unavoidable misfortunes to which they were continually expofed by the daily recurring revolutions in the turbulent democracies of ancient Greece. There, a philofopher was this day a magiftrate, and the next day a captive and a flave. He would fee that this fair picture of mental happinefs and independence was
fitted

fitted for the contemplation of only a few choice spirits, but had no influence on the bulk of mankind. He must admire the noble characters who were animated by this manly enthusiasm, and who have really exhibited some wonderful pictures of virtuous heroism; but he will regret, that the influence of these manly, these natural principles, was not more extensive. He will say to himself, "How will a whole nation act when re-
"ligious sanctions are removed, and men are ac-
"tuated by reason alone?"—He is not without instruction on this important subject. France has given an awful lesson to surrounding nations, by shewing them what is the natural effect of shaking off the religious principle, and the veneration for that pure morality which characterises Christianity. By a decree of the Convention, (June 6, 1794) it is declared, that there is nothing criminal in the promiscuous commerce of the sexes, and therefore nothing that derogates from the female character, when woman forgets that she is the depositary of all domestic satisfaction——that her honour is the sacred bond of social life——that on her modesty and delicacy depend all the respect and confidence that will make a man attach himself to her society, free her from labour, share with her the fruits of all his own exertions, and work with willingness and delight, that she may appear on all occasions his equal, and the ornament of all his acquisitions. In the very argument which this selected body of senators has given for the propriety of this decree, it has degraded woman below all estimation. "It is to prevent her
"from murdering the fruit of unlawful love, by re-
"moving her shame, and by relieving her from the
"fear of want." The senators say, "the Republic
"wants citizens, and therefore must not only re-
"move

" move this temptation of fhame, but muft take care
" of the mother while fhe nurfes the child. It is
" the property of the nation, and muft not be loft."
The woman all the while is confidered only as the
fhe-animal, the breeder of Sans Culottes. This is
the *juſt* morality of Illumination. It is really amuſ-
ing (for things revolting to nature now amuſe) to
obſerve with what fidelity the principles of the Illuminati have expreſſed the ſentiments which take poſſeſſion of a people who have ſhaken off the ſanctions
of Religion and morality. The following is part of
the addreſs to *Pſycharion* and the company mentioned in page 257 : " Once more, Pſycharion, I in-
" dulge you with a look behind you to the flowery
" days of childhood. Now look forwards, *young*
" *woman!* the holy circle of the marriageable,
" (*mannbaren*) welcome you. Young men, honour
" the young woman, the future breeder (*gebaere-*
" *rin*) !" Then, to all.—" Rejoice in the dawn of
" Illumination and of Freedom. Nature at laſt en-
" joys her ſacred never-fading rights. Long was
" her voice kept down by civil ſubordination; but
" the days of your majority now draw nigh, and you
" will no longer, under the authority of guardians,
" account it a reproach to confider with enlighten-
" ed eyes the ſecret workſhops of nature, and to en-
" joy your work and duty." Minos thought this
very fine, but it raiſed a terrible diſturbance and
broke up the aſſembly.

Such are the effects of this boaſted enlightening of
the human mind with reſpect to religion and morality. Let us next conſider what is the reſult of the
mighty informations which we have got in reſpect
of our ſocial or political connections.

II. We have learned the ſum total of this political Illumination, and ſee that, if true, it is melancholy, deſtructive of our preſent comforts, numerous as
they

CHAP. iv.   THE FRENCH REVOLUTION.   323

they are, and affords no profpect of redrefs from which we can profit, but, on the contrary, plunges mankind into diffention, mutual injury, and univerfal mifery, and all this for the *chance* only of prevailing in the conteft, and giving our pofterity a *chance* of going on in peace, if no change fhall be produced, as in former times, by the efforts of ambitious men. But the Illumination appears to be partial, nay falfe. What is it? It holds out to the prince nothing but the refignation of all his poffeffions, rights and claims, fanctioned by the quiet poffeffion of ages, and by all the feelings of the human heart which give any notion of right to his loweft fubject. All thefe poffeffions and claims are difcovered to have arifen from ufurpations, *and are therefore tyranny*. It has been difcovered, that all fubordinate fubjections were enforced, *therefore their continuance is flavery*. But both of thefe hiftorical affertions are in a great degree falfe, and the inferences from them are unreafonable. The world has gone on as we fee it go on at prefent. Moft principalities or fovereignties have arifen as we fee perfonal authorities and influence arife every day among ourfelves. Bufinefs for the whole muft be done. Moft men are fufficiently occupied by their private affairs, and they are indolent even in thefe—they are contented when another does the thing for them. There is not a little village, nor a fociety of men, where this is not feen every day. Some men have an enjoyment in this kind of vicarious employment. Other men like influence and power, and thus are compenfated for their trouble. Thus many petty managers of public affairs arife in every country. The mutual animofities of individuals, and ftill more, the animofities of tribes, clans, and different affociations, give rife to another kind of fuperiors—to leaders, who direct the ftruggles of the reft,

whether

whether for offence or defence. The descendants of Israel said, " they wanted a man to go out before " the people, like other nations." As the small business of a few individuals requires a manager or a leader, so do some more general affairs of these petty superiors.---Many of these also are indolent enough to wish this trouble taken off their hands; and thus another rank of superiors arises, and a third, and so on, till a great State may be formed; and in this gradation each class is a competent judge of the conduct of that class only which is immediately above it.

All this may arise, and has often arisen, from voluntary concession alone. This concession may proceed from various causes,—from confidence in superior talents—from confidence in great worth,---most generally from the respect or deference which all men feel for great possessions. This is frequently founded in self-interest and expectations of advantage; but it is natural to man, and perhaps springs from our instinctive sympathy with the satisfactions of others---we are unwilling to disturb them, and even wish to promote them.

But this subordination may arise, and has often arisen, from other causes---from the love of power and influence, which makes some men *eager* to lead others, or even to manage their concerns. We see this every day, and it may be perfectly innocent. It often arises from the desire of gain of one kind or another.---This also may frequently be indulged with perfect innocence, and even with general advantage. Frequently, however, this subordination is produced by the love of power or of gain pushed to an immoderate degree of ambition, and rendered unjust. Now there arise oppression, tyranny, sufferings, and slavery. Now appears an opposition between the rights or claims of the ruler and of the

people.

people. Now the rulers come to confider themſelves as a different claſs, and their tranſactions are now only with each other.---Prince becomes the rival or the enemy of Prince; and in their conteſts one prevails, and the dominion is enlarged. This rivalſhip may have begun in any rank of ſupériors; even between the firſt managers of the affairs of the ſmalleſt communities; and it muſt be remarked that they only are the immediate gainers or loſers in the conteſt, while thoſe below them live at eaſe, enjoying many advantages of the delegation of their own concerns.

No human ſociety has ever proceeded purely in either of theſe two ways, but there has always been a mixture of both.---But this proceſs is indiſpenſably neceſſary for the formation of a great nation, and for all the conſequences that reſult only from ſuch a coalition.---Therefore it is neceſſary for giving riſe to all thoſe comforts, and luxuries, and elegances; which are to be found only in great and cultivated ſtates. It is neceſſary for producing ſuch enjoyments as we ſee around us in Europe, which we prize ſo highly, and for which we are making all this ſtir and diſturbance. I believe that no man who expects to be believed will poſitively aſſert that human nature and human enjoyments are not meliorated by this cultivation.---It ſeems to be the intention of nature; and, notwithſtanding the follies and vices of many, we can have little heſitation in ſaying that there are in the moſt cultivated nations of Europe, and even in the higheſt ranks of thoſe nations, men of great virtue and worth, and of high accompliſhment---Nor can we deny that ſuch men are the fineſt ſpecimens of human nature. Roſſeau indeed wrote a whimſical pamphlet, in which he had the vanity to think that he had proved that all theſe fruits of cultivation were loſſes to humanity and virtue---Yet Rouſſeau could not be contented with the society of the rude and unpolished, although he pretended that he was almost the sole worshipper of pure virtue.—He supported himself, not by assisting the simple peasant, but by writing music and luscious novels for the pampered rich.

This is the circumstance entirely overlooked, or artfully kept out of sight, in the boasted Illumination of these days. No attention is paid to the important changes which have happened in national greatness, in national connection, in national improvement—yet we never think of parting with any of the advantages, real or imaginary, which these changes have produced—nor do we reflect that in order to keep a great nation together—to make it act with equality, or with preponderancy, among other nations, the individual exertions must be concentrated, must be directed—and that this requires a ruler vested with supreme power, and *interested by some great and endearing motive*, such as hereditary possession of this power and influence, to maintain and defend this coalition of men.—All this is overlooked, and we attend only to the subordination which is indispensably necessary. Its grievances are immediately felt, and they are heightened tenfold by a delicacy or sensibility which springs from the great improvements in the accommodations and enjoyments of life, which the gradual usurpation and subsequent subordination have produced, and continue to support. But we are determined to have the elegance and grandeur of a palace without the prince.—We will not give up any of our luxuries and refinements, yet will not support those high ranks and those nice minds which produced them, and which must continue to keep them from degenerating into barbarous simplicity and coarse sensuality. We would keep the philosophers, the poets, the artists, but not the Mæcenases. It is very true that in such a state there would be no *Conjuration des Philosophes;*

Philosophes; for in such a state this vermin of *philosophes* and scribblers would not have existed. In short, we would have what is impossible.

I have no hesitation in saying, that the British Constitution is the form of government *for a great and refined nation*, in which the ruling sentiments and propensities of human nature seem most happily blended and balanced. There is no occasion to vaunt it as the ancient rights of Britons, the wisdom of ages, &c. It has attained its present pitch of perfection by degrees, and this not by the efforts of wisdom, but by the struggles of vice and folly, working on a rich fund of good nature, and of manly spirit, that are conspicuous in the British character. I do not hesitate to say that it is the *only* form of government which will admit and give full exercise to all the respectable propensities of our nature, with the least chance of disturbance and the greatest probability of man's arriving at the highest pitch of improvement in every thing that raises him above the beasts of the field. Yet there is no part of it that may not, that is not, abused, by pushing it to an improper length, and the same watchful care is necessary for preserving our inestimable blessings that was employed in acquiring them. This is to be done, not by flying at once to an abstract theory of the rights of man. There is an evident folly in this procedure. What is this theory? It is the best general sketch that we can draw of social life, deduced from our knowledge of human nature. And what is this knowledge? It is a well digested abstract, or rather a declaration *of what we have observed* of human actions. What is the use therefore of this intermediate picture, this theory of the rights of man?—It has a chance of being unlike the original——it must certainly have imperfections,

fections, therefore it can be of no ufe to us. We fhould go at once to the original—we fhould confider how men *have acted*—what *have* been their mutual expectations—their fond propenfities—what of thefe are inconfiftent with each other—what are the degrees of indulgence which *have been* admitted in them all without difturbance.—I will venture to fay that whoever does this, will find himfelf imperceptibly led to contemplate a mixed hereditary monarchy, and will figure to himfelf a parliament of King, Lords, and Commons, all looking at each other with fomewhat of a cautious or jealous eye, while the reft of the nation are fitting, " each under his own vine and " under his own fig-tree, and there is none to " make him afraid ;"—in one word, the Conftitution of Great Britain.

A moft valuable refult of fuch contemplation will be a thorough conviction that the grievance which is moft clamoroufly infifted on is the inevitable confequence of the liberty and fecurity which we enjoy. I mean minifterial corruption, with all the difmal tale of placemen, and penfioners, and rotten boroughs, &c. &c. Thefe are never feen in a defpotic government——there they are not wanted—nor can they be very apparent in an uncultivated and poor ftate—but in a luxurious nation, where pleafures abound, where the returns of induftry are fecure; here an individual looks on every thing as his own acquifition—he does not feel his relation to the ftate—has no patriotifm—thinks that he would be much happier if the ftate would let him alone. He is fretted by the reftraints which the public weal lays on him—therefore government and governors appear as checks and hindrances to his exertions—hence a general inclination to refift adminiftration. Yet public bufinefs

bufinefs muft be done, that we may lie down and rife again in fafety and peace. Adminiftration muft be fupported---there are always perfons who wifh to poffefs the power that is exercifed by the prefent minifters, and would turn them out. How is all this to be remedied? I fee no way but by applying to the felfifh views of individuals---by rewarding the friends of adminiftration---This may be done with perfect virtue---and from this the felfifh will conceive hopes, and will fupport a virtuous miniftry---but they are as ready to help a wicked one. This becomes the greateft misfortune of a free nation. Minifters are tempted to bribe---and, if a fyftematic oppofition be confidered as a neceffary part of a practical conftitution, it is almoft indifpenfable---and it is no where fo prevalent as in a pure democracy. Laws may be contrived to make it very troublefome, but can never extirpate it nor greatly diminifh it; this can be done only by defpotifm, or by national virtue. It is a fhameful complaint----we fhould not reprobate a few minifters, but the thoufands who take the bribes. Nothing tends fo much to diminifh it in a corrupted nation as great limitations to the eligibility of reprefentatives---and this is the beauty of our conftitution.

We have not difcovered, therefore, by this boafted Illumination, that Princes and fuperiors are ufelefs, and muft vanifh from the earth; nor that the people have now attained full age, and are fit to govern themfelves. We want only to revel a little on the laft fruits of national cultivation, which we would quickly confume, and never allow to be raifed again. No matter how this progrefs began, whether from conceffion or ufurpation---We poffefs it, and, if wife, we will preferve it, by preferving its indifpenfable fupports. They

have

have indeed been frequently employed very improperly, but their moſt pernicious abuſe has been this breed of ſcribbling vermin, which have made the body politic ſmart in every limb.

Hear what opinion was entertained of the ſages of France by their Prince, the father of Louis XVI. the unfortunate martyr of Monarchy. "By "the principles of our new Philoſophers, the "Throne no longer wears the ſplendour of divi- "nity. They maintain that it aroſe from vio- "lence, and that by the ſame juſtice that force "erected it, force may again ſhake it, and over- "turn it. The people can never give up their "power. They only let it out for their own ad- "vantage, and always retain the right to reſcind "the contract, and reſume it whenever their per- "ſonal advantage, their only rule of conduct, "requires it. Our philoſophers teach in public "what our paſſions ſuggeſt only in ſecret. They "ſay to the Prince that all is permitted only "when all is in his power, and that his duty is "fulfilled when he has pleaſed his fancy. Then, "ſurely, if the laws of ſelf-intereſt, that is, the "ſelf-will of human paſſions, ſhall be ſo generally "admitted, that we thereupon forget the eternal "laws of God and of Nature, all conceptions of "right and wrong, of virtue and vice, of good "and evil, muſt be extirpated from the human "heart. The throne muſt totter, the ſubjects "muſt become unmanageable and mutinous, and "their ruler hard-hearted and inhuman. The "people will be inceſſantly oppreſſed or in an "uproar."---"What ſervice will it be if I order "ſuch a book to be burnt?---the author can write "another to-morrow." This opinion of a Prince is unpoliſhed indeed, and homely, but it is juſt.

Weiſhaupt

Weishaupt grants, that "there will be a terrible convulsion, and a storm---but this will be succeeded by a calm---the unequal will now be equal---and when the cause of dissension is thus removed, the world will be in peace."---True, when the causes of dissension are removed. Thus, the destruction of our crop by vermin is at an end when a flood has swept every thing away---but as new plants will spring up in the waste, and, if not instantly devoured, will again cover the ground with verdure, so the industry of man, and his desire of comfort and consideration, will again accumulate in the hands of the diligent a greater proportion of the good things of life. In this infant state of the emerging remains of former cultivation, comforts, which the present inhabitants of Europe would look on with contempt, will be great, improper, and hazardous acquisitions. The principles which authorise the proposed dreadful equalisation will as justly entitle the idle or unsuccessful of future days to strip the possessor of his advantages, and things must ever remain on their savage level.

III. I think that the impression which the insincerity of conduct of those instructors will leave on the mind, must be highly useful. They are evidently teaching what they do not believe themselves----and here I do not confine my remark to their preparatory doctrines, which they afterwards explode. I make it chiefly with respect to their grand ostensible principle, which pervades the whole, a principle which they are obliged to adopt against their will.--They know that the principles of virtue are rooted in the heart, and that they can only be smothered----but did they pretend to eradicate them and proclaim *hominem homini lupum*, all would spurn at their
instruction

instruction. We are wheedled, by tickling our fancy with a notion that sacred virtue is not only secure, but that it is only in such hearts that it exerts its native energy. Sensible that the levelling maxims now spoken of are revolting to the mind, the Illuminators are under the necessity of keeping us from looking at the shocking picture, by displaying a beautiful scene of Utopian happiness—and they rock us asleep by the eternal lullaby of morality and universal philanthropy. Therefore the foregoing narration of the personal conduct of these instructors and reformers of the world, is highly useful. All this is to be brought about by the native loveliness of pure virtue, purged of the corruptions which superstitious fears have introduced, and also purged of the selfish thoughts which are avowed by the advocates of what their opponents call true religion. This is said to hold forth eternal rewards to the good, and to threaten the wicked with dreadful punishment. Experience has shown how inefficient such motives are. Can they be otherwise? say our Illuminators. Are they not addressed to a principle that is ungenerous and selfish? But our doctrines, say they, touch the hearts of the worthy. Virtue is beloved for her own sake, and all will yield to her gentle sway. But look, Reader, look at Spartacus the murderer, at Cato the keeper of poisons and the thief---Look at Tiberius, at Alcibiades, and the rest of the Bavarian Pandemonium. Look at poor Bahrdt. Go to France---look at Lequinio, at Condorcet*. Look

---

* De la Metherie says, *(Journ. de Phys. Nov.* 1792,) that Condorcet was brought up in the house of the old Duke of Rochefoucault, who treated him as his son—got Turgot to create a lucrative office for him, and raised him to all his eminence—yet he pursued him with malicious reports—and actually employed ruffians to assassinate him Yet is Condorcet's writing a model of humanity and tenderness.

at the Monster Orleans.———All were liars. Their divinity had no influence on their profligate minds. They only wanted to wheedle you, by touching the strings of humanity and goodness which are yet braced up in your heart, and which still yield sweet harmony if you will accompany their notes with those of religion, and neither clog them with the groveling pleasures of sense, nor damp the whole with the thought of eternal silence.

A most worthy and accomplished gentleman, who took refuge in this country, leaving behind him his property, and friends to whom he was most tenderly attached, often said to me that nothing so much affected him as the revolution in the hearts of men.—Characters which were unspotted, hearts thoroughly known to himself, having been tried by many things which search the inmost folds of selfishness or malevolence—in short, persons whose judgments were excellent, and on whose worth he could have rested his honour and his life, so fascinated by the contagion, that they came at last to behold, and even to commit the most atrocious crimes with delight.— He used sometimes to utter a sigh which pierced my heart, and would say, that it was caused by some of those things that had come across his thoughts. He breathed his last among us, declaring that it was impossible to recover peace of mind, without a total oblivion of the wickedness and miseries he had beheld. —What a valuable advice, " Let him that thinketh he standeth, take heed lest he fall."---When the prophet told Hazael that he would betray his Prince, he exclaimed, " Is thy servant a dog, that he should do such a thing ?" Yet next day he murdered him.

Never since the beginning of the world, has true religion received so complete an acknowledgment of her excellence, as has been extorted from the fanatics who have attempted to destroy her. Religion

stood in their way, and the wretch Marat, as well as the steady villain Weishaupt, saw that they could not proceed till they had eradicated all sentiments of of the moral government of the universe. Human nature, improved as it has been by religion, shrunk from the tasks that were imposed, and it must therefore be brutalized---The grand confederation was solemnly sworn to by millions in every corner of France---but, as Mirabeau said of the declaration of the Rights of Man, it must be made only the " Almanack of the bygone year"---Therefore Lequinio must write a book, declaring oaths to be nonsense, unworthy of San Culottes, and all religion to be a farce. Not long after, they found that they had some use for a God---but he was gone---and they could not find another. Their constitution was gone--- and they have not yet found another. What is now left them on which they can depend for awing a man into a respect for truth in his judicial declarations ? what but the honour of a Citizen of France, who laughs at all engagements, which he has broken again and again ? Religion has taken off with her every sense of human duty. What can we expect but villainy from an Archbishop of Paris and his chapter, who made a public profession that they had been playing the villains for many years, teaching what they thought to be a bundle of lies ? What but the very thing which they have done, cutting each other's throats ?---Have not the enlightened citizens of France applauded the execution of their fathers ? Have not the furies of Paris denounced their own children ? But turn your eyes from the horrifying spectacle, and think on your own noble descent and alliance. You are not the accidental productions of a fatal chaos, but the work of a Great Artist, creatures that are cared for, born to noble prospects, and conducted to them by the plainest
and

and most simple precepts, " to do justly, to love
" mercy, and to walk humbly before God," not be-
wildered by the false and fluttering glare of French
Philosophy, but conducted by this clear, single light,
perceivable by all, " Do to others what you should
" reasonably expect them to do to you."

Think not the Muse whose sober voice you hear,
  Contracts with bigot frown her sullen brow,
Casts round Religion's orb the mists of Fear,
  Or shades with horror what with smiles should glow.

No—she would warn you with seraphic fire,
  Heirs as ye are of Heaven's eternal day,
Would bid you boldly to that Heaven aspire,
  Not sink and slumber in your cells of clay.

Is this the bigot's rant? Away, ye vain,
  Your doubts, your fears, in gloomy dulness steep;
Go—soothe your souls in sickness, death, or pain,
  With the sad solace of eternal sleep.

Yet know, vain sceptics, know, th' Almighty Mind,
  Who breath'd on man a portion of his fire,
Bade his free soul, by earth nor time confin'd,
  To Heaven, to immortality aspire.

Nor shall this pile of hope his bounty rear'd,
  By vain philosophy be e'er destroy'd;
Eternity, by all or hop'd or fear'd,
  Shall be by all or suffer'd or enjoy'd.
                              MASON.

    The unfortunate Prince who has taken refuge in
this kingdom, and whose situation among us is an
illustrious mark of the generosity of the nation, and
of the sovereignty of its laws, said to one of the
Gentleman about him, that " if this country was to
" escape the general wreck of nations, it would
" owe its preservation to Religion."—When this
was doubted, and it was observed, that there had
not been wanting many Religionists in France;
                                      " True,"

" True," said the Prince, " but they were not in
" earneſt.—I ſee here a ſerious intereſt in the thing,
" The people know what they are doing when they
" go to church—they underſtand ſomething of it,
" and take an intereſt in it." May his obſervation
be juſt, and his expectations be fulfilled!

IV. I would again call upon my countrywomen
with the moſt earneſt concern, and beſeech them to
conſider this ſubject as of more particular importance
to themſelves than even to the men.---While woman is conſidered as a reſpectable moral agent, training along with ourſelves for endleſs improvement;
then, and only then, will ſhe be conſidered by lordly man as his equal;---then, and only then, will ſhe
be allowed to have any rights, and thoſe rights be
reſpected. Strip women of this prerogative, and
they become the drudges of man's indolence, or the
pampered playthings of his idle hours, ſubject to
his caprices, and ſlaves to his mean paſſions. Soon
will their preſent empire of gallantry be over. It
is a refinement of manners which ſprang from
Chriſtianity; and when Chriſtianity is forgotten,
this artificial diadem will be taken from their heads,
and unleſs they adopt the ferocious ſentiments of
their Gallic neighbours, and join in the general
uproar, they will ſink into the inſignificance of the
women in the turbulent republics of Greece,
where they are never ſeen in the buſy haunts of
men, if we except four or five, who, during the
courſe of as many centuries, emerged from the
general obſcurity, and appear in the hiſtoric page,
by their uncommon talents, and by the ſacrifice
of what my fair countrywomen ſtill hold to be
the ornament of their ſex. I would remind them,
that they have it in their power to retain their
preſent honourable ſtation in ſociety. They are
our early inſtructors; and while mothers in the
reſpectable

respectable stations of life continued to inculcate on the tender minds of their sons a veneration for the precepts of Religion, their pliant children, receiving their instructions along with the affectionate caresses of their mothers, got impressions which long retained their force, and which protected them from the impulses of youthful passions, till ripening years fitted their minds for listening to serious instruction from their public teachers. Sobriety and decency of manners were then no slur on the character of a youth, and he was thought capable of struggling for independence, or pre-eminence, fit either for supporting or defending the state, although he was neither a toper nor a rake. I believe that no man who has seen thirty or forty years of life will deny that the manners of youth are sadly changed in this respect. And, without presuming to say that this has proceeded from the neglect, and almost total cessation of the moral education of the nursery, I think myself well warranted, from my own observation, to say that this education and the sober manners of young men have quitted us together.

Some will call this prudery, and croaking. But I am almost transcribing from Cicero, and from Quintilian. Cornelia, Aurelia, Attia, and other ladies of the first rank, are praised by Cicero only for their *eminence* in this respect; but not because they were *singular*. Quintilian says, that in the time immediately prior to his own, it had been the general practice of the ladies of rank to superintend the moral education both of sons and daughters. But of late, says he, they are so engaged in continual and corrupting amusements, such as the shows of gladiators, horse-racing, and deep play, that they have no time, and have yielded their places to Greek governesses and tutors, out

cast-

casts of a nation more subdued by their own vices than by the Roman arms.——I dare say this was laughed at, as croaking about the corruption of the age. But what was the consequence of all this?—The Romans became the most abandoned voluptuaries, and, to preserve their mean pleasures, they crouched as willing slaves to a succession of the vilest tyrants that ever disgraced humanity.

What a noble fund of self-estimation would our fair partners acquire to themselves, if, by reforming the manners of the young generation, they should be the means of restoring peace to the world! *They have it in their power*, by the renewal of the good old custom of early instruction, and perhaps still more, by impressing on the minds of their daughters the same sentiments, and obliging them to respect sobriety and decency in the youth, and pointedly to withhold their smiles and civilities from all who transgress these in the smallest degree. This is a method of proceeding that *will most certainly be victorious*. Then indeed will the women be the saviours of their country. While therefore the German fair have been repeatedly branded with having welcomed the French invaders*, let our ladies stand up for the honour of free-born Britons, by turning against the pretended enlighteners of the world, the arms which nature has put into their hands, and which those profligates have presumptuously expected to

---

* I have met with this charge in many places; and one book in particular, written by a Prussian General Officer, who was in the country over-run by the French troops, gives a detail of the conduct of the women that is very remarkable. He also says, that infidelity has become very prevalent among the ladies in the higher circles. Indeed this melancholy account is to be found in many passages of the private correspondence of the Illuminati.

employ

employ in extending their influence over mankind. The empire of beauty is but fhort, but the empire of virtue is durable ; nor is there an inftance to be met with of its decline. If it be yet poffible to reform the world, it is poffible for the fair. By the conftitution of human nature, they muft always appear as the ornament of human life, and be the objects of fondnefs and affection ; fo that if any thing can make head againft the felfifh and overbearing difpofitions of man, it is his refpectful regard for the fex. But mere fondnefs has but little of the rational creature in it, and we fee it harbour every day in the breaft that is filled with the meaneft and moft turbulent paffions. No where is it fo ftrong as in the harems of the eaft; and as long as the women afk nothing of the men but fondnefs and admiration, they will get nothing elfe—they will never be refpected. But let them roufe themfelves, affert their dignity, by fhewing their own elevated fentiments of human nature, and by acting up to this claim, and they may then command the world.

V. Another good confequence that fhould refult from the account that has been given of the proceedings of this confpiracy is, that fince the fafcinating picture of human life, by which men have been wheedled into immediate anarchy and rebellion, is infincere, and a mere artificial creature of the imagination, it can have no fteadinefs, but muft be changed by every freak of fancy, or by every ingenious fophift, who can give an equal plaufibility to whatever fuits his prefent views. It is as much an airy phantom as any other whim of Free Mafonry, and has no prototype, no original pattern in human nature, to which recourfe may always be had, to correct miftakes, and keep things in a conftant tenor. Has not France given the moft most unequivocal proofs of this? Was not the declaration of the Rights of Man, the production of their moſt brilliant Illuminators, a picture, *in abſtracto*, where man was placed at a diſtance from the eye, that no falſe light of local ſituation might pervert the judgment or engage the paſſions? Was it not declared to be the maſter-piece of human wiſdom? Did not the nation conſider it at leiſure? and, having it continually before their eyes, did they not, ſtep by ſtep, give their aſſent to the different articles of their Conſtitution, derived from it, and fabricated by their moſt choice Illuminators? And did not this Conſtitution draw the applauſes of the bright geniuſes of other nations, who by this time were buſy in perſuading, each his countrymen, that they were ignoramuſes in ſtatiſtics, and patient ſlaves of oppreſſion or of ancient prejudices? Did not panegyrics on it iſſue from every garret in London? Where is it now? where is its ſucceſſor? Has any one plan of government ſubſiſted, except while it was ſupported by the incontroulable and inexorable power of the guillotine? Is not the preſent adminiſtration of France as much as ever the object of diſcontent and of terror, and its coercions as like as ever to the ſummary juſtice of the Pariſian mob? Is there any probability of its permanency in a ſtate of peace, when the fears of a foreign enemy no longer give a conſolidation to their meaſures, and oblige them either to agree among themſelves, or immediately to periſh?

VI. The above accounts evince in the moſt uncontrovertible manner the dangerous tendency of all myſtical ſocieties, and of all aſſociations who hold ſecret meetings We ſee that their uniform progreſs has been from frivolity and nonſenſe to wickedneſs and ſedition. Weiſhaupt has been

at

at great pains to shew the good effects of secrecy in the Association, and the arguments are valid for this purpose. But all his arguments are so many dissuasive advices to every thinking and sober mind. The man who really wishes to discover an abstruse truth will place himself, if possible in a *calm* situation, and will by no means expose himself to the impatient hankering for secrets and wonders—and he will always fear that a thing which resolutely conceals itself cannot bear the light. All who have seriously employed themselves in the discovery of truth have found the great advantages of open communication of sentiment. And it is against common sense to imagine that there is any thing of vast importance to mankind which is yet a secret, and which must be kept a secret in order to be useful. This is against the whole experience of mankind—And surely to hug in one's breast a secret of such mighty importance, is to give the lie to all our professions of brotherly love. What a solecism! a secret to enlighten and reform the whole world. We render all our endeavours impotent when we grasp at a thing beyond our power. Let an association be formed with a serious plan for reforming its own members, and let them extend in numbers in proportion as they succeed—this might do some good. But must the way of doing this be a secret?—It may be to many—who will not look for it where it is to be found—It is this:

" Do good,—seek peace,—and pursue it."

But it is almost affronting the reader to suppose arguments necessary on this point. If there be a necessity for secrecy, the purpose of the association is either frivolous, or it is selfish.

Now, in either case, the danger of such secret assemblies is manifest. Mere frivolity can never seriously occupy men come to age. And accordingly we see that in every quarter of Europe where Free Masonry has been established, the Lodges have become seed-beds of public mischief. I believe that no ordinary brother will say that the occupations in the Lodges are any thing better than frivolous, very frivolous indeed. The distribution of charity needs be no secret, and it is but a very small part of the employment of the meeting. This being the case it is in human nature that the greater we suppose the frivolity of such an association to be, the greater is the chance of its ceasing to give sufficient occupation to the mind, and the greater is the risk that the meetings may be employed to other purposes which require concealment. When this happens, self-interest alone must prompt and rule, and now there is no length that some men will not go, when they think themselves in no danger of detection and punishment. The whole proceedings of the secret societies of Free Masons on the Continent (and I am authorised to say, of some Lodges in Britain) have taken one turn, and this turn is perfectly natural. In all countries there are men of licentious morals. Such men wish to have a safe opportunity of indulging their wits in satire and sarcasm; and they are pleased with the support of others. The desire of making proselytes is in every breast—and it is whetted by the restraints of society. And all countries have discontented men, whose grumblings will raise discontent in others, who might not have attended to some of the trifling hardships and injuries they met with, had they not been reminded of them. To be discontented, and not to think of schemes of redress,

is

is what we cannot think natural or manly—and where can fuch fentiments and fchemes find fuch fafe utterance and fuch probable fupport as in a fecret fociety? Free Mafonry is innocent of all thefe things; but Free Mafonry has been abufed, and at laft totally perverted—and fo will and muft any fuch fecret affociation, as long as men are licentious in their opinions or wicked in their difpofitions.

It were devoutly to be wifhed therefore that the whole fraternity would imitate the truly benevolent conduct of thofe German Lodges who have formally broken up, and made a patriotic facrifice of their amufement to the fafety of the ftate. I cannot think the facrifice great or coftly. It can be no difficult matter to find as pleafing a way of paffing a vacant hour——and the charitable deeds of the members need not diminifh in the fmalleft degree. Every perfon's little circle of acquaintance will give him opportunities of gratifying his kind difpofitions, without the chance of being miftaken in the worth of the perfon on whom he beftows his favours. There is no occafion to go to St. Peterfburg for a poor Brother, nor to India for a convert to Chriftianity, as long as we fee fo many fufferers and infidels among ourfelves.

But not only are fecret focieties dangerous, but all focieties whofe object is myfterious. The whole hiftory of man is a proof of this pofition. In no age or country has there ever appeared a myfterious affociation which did not in time become a public nuifance. Ingenious or defigning men of letters have attempted to fhow that fome of the ancient myfteries were ufeful to mankind, containing rational doctrines of natural religion. This was the ftrong hold of Weifhaupt, and he quotes the Eleufinian, the Pythagorean, and other myfteries,

teries. But surely their external signs and tokens were every thing that is shocking to decency and civil order. It is uncommon presumption for the learned of the eighteenth century to pretend to know more about them than their contemporaries, the philosophers, the lawgivers of antiquity. These give no such account of them. I would desire any person who admires the ingenious dissertations of Dr. Warburton to read a dull German book, called *Caracteristik der Mysterien der Altern*, published at Frankfort in 1787. The author contents himself with a patient collection of every scrap of every ancient author who has said any thing about them. If the reader can see any thing in them but the most absurd and immoral polytheism and fable, he must take words in a sense that is useless in reading any other piece of ancient composition. I have a notion that the Dionysiacs of Iona had some scientific secrets, viz. all the knowledge of practical mechanics which was employed by their architects and engineers, and that they were really a Masonic Fraternity. But, like the *Illuminati*, they tagged to the secrets of Masonry the secret of drunkenness and debauchery; they had their Sister Lodges, and at last became rebels, subverters of the states where they were protected, till aiming at the dominion of all Ionia, they were attacked by the neighbouring states and dispersed. They were Illuminators too, and wanted to introduce the worship of Bacchus over the whole country, as appears in the account of them given by *Strabo*. Perhaps the Pythagoreans had also some scientific secrets; but they too were Illuminators, and thought it their duty to overset the State, and were themselves overset.

Nothing is so dangerous as a mystic Association. The object remaining a secret in the hands of the managers

managers, the rest simply put a ring in their own noses, by which they may be led about at pleasure; and still panting after the secret, they are the better pleased the less they see of their way. A mystical object enables the leader to shift his ground as he pleases, and to accommodate himself to every current fashion or prejudice. This again gives him almost unlimited power; for he can make use of these prejudices to lead men by troops. He finds them already associated by their prejudices, and waiting for a leader to concentrate their strength and set them in motion. And when once great bodies of men are set in motion, with a creature of their fancy for a guide, even the engineer himself cannot say, " Thus far shalt thou " go, and no farther."

VII. We may also gather from what we have seen that all declamations on universal philanthropy are dangerous. Their natural and immediate effect on the mind is to increase the discontents of the unfortunate, and of those in the laborious ranks of life. No one, even of the Illuminators, will deny that those ranks must be filled, if society exists in any degree of cultivation whatever, and that there will always be a greater number of men who have no farther prospect. Surely it is unkind to put such men continually in mind of a state in which they might be at their ease; and it is unkindness unmixed, because all the change that they will produce will be, that James will serve John, who formerly was the servant of James. Such declamations naturally tend to cause men to make light of the obligations and duties of common patriotism, because these are represented as subordinate and inferior to the greater and more noble affection of universal benevolence. I do not pretend to say that patriotism is founded in a rationally perceived pre-eminence or excellence of

the

the society with which we are connected. But if it be a fact that society will not advance unless its members take an interest in it, and that human nature improves only in society, surely this interest should be cherished in every breast. Perhaps national union arises from national animosity;—but they are plainly distinguishable, and union is not necessarily productive of injustice. The same arguments that have any force against patriotism are equally good against the preference which natural instinct gives parents for their children, and surely no one can doubt of the propriety of maintaining this in its full force, subject however to the precise laws of justice.

But I am in the wrong to adduce paternal or filial affection in defence of patriotism and loyalty, since even those natural instincts are reprobated by the *Illuminati*, as hostile to the all-comprehending philanthropy. Mr. de la Metherie says, that among the memorials sent from the clubs in England to the National Assembly, he read two, (printed,) in which the Assembly was requested to establish a community of wives, and to take children from their parents and educate them for the nation. In full compliance with this dictate of universal philanthropy, Weishaupt would have murdered his own child and his concubine,—and Orleans voted the death of his near relation.

Indeed, of all the consequences of Illumination, the most melancholy is this revolution which it seems to operate in the heart of man,—this forcible sacrifice of every affection of the heart to an ideal divinity, a mere creature of the imagination.—It seems a prodigy, yet it is a matter of experience, that the farther we advance, or vainly suppose that we do advance, in the knowledge of our mental powers, the more are our moral feelings flattened and done away.

I remember

CHAP. IV. THE FRENCH REVOLUTION. 347

I remember reading, long ago, a differtation on the nurfing of infants by a French academician, Le Cointre of Verfailles. He indelicately fupports his theories by the cafe of his own fon, a weak puny infant, whom his mother was obliged to keep continually applied to her bofom, fo that fhe rarely could get two hours of fleep during the time of fuckling him. Mr. Le Cointre fays, that fhe contracted for this infant "*une partialite toute-a-fait deraifonable.*" —Plato, or Socrates, or Cicero, would probably have explained this by the habitual exercife of pity, a very endearing emotion.---But our Academician, better illuminated, folves it by ftimuli on the *papillæ* and on the nerves of the fkin, and by the meeting of the humifying *aura*, &c. and does not feem to think that young Le Cointre was much indebted to his mother. It would amufe me to learn that this was the wretch Le Cointre, Major of the National Guards of Verfailles, who countenanced and encouraged the fhocking treafon and barbarity of thofe ruffians on the 5th and 6th of October 1789. Complete freezing of the heart would (I think) be the confequence of a theory which could perfectly explain the affections by vibrations or cryftallizations. ---Nay, any very perfect theory of moral fentiments muft have fomething of this tendency.---Perhaps the ancient fyftems of moral philofophy, which were chiefly fearches after the *fummum bonum*, and fyftems of moral duties, tended more to form and ftrengthen the heart, and produce a worthy man, than the moft perfect theory of modern times, which explains every phenomenon by means of a nice anatomy of our affections.

So far therefore as we are really more illuminated, it may chance to give us an eafier victory over the natural or inftinctive attachments of mankind, and make the facrifice to univerfal philanthropy lefs coftly

coftly to the heart. I do not however pretend to fay that this is really the cafe: but I think myfelf fully warranted to fay, that increafe of virtuous affections in general has not been the fruit of modern Illumination. I will not again ficken the reader, by calling his attention to Weifhaupt and his affociates or fucceffors. But let us candidly contemplate the world around us, and particularly the perpetual advocates of univerfal philanthropy. What have been the general effects of their continual declamations? Surely very melancholy; nor can it eafily be otherwife.—An ideal ftandard is continually referred to. This is made gigantic, by being always feen indiftinctly, as through a mift, or rather a fluttering air. In comparifon with this, every feeling that we have been accuftomed to refpect vanifhes as infignificant; and, adopting the Jefuitical maxim, that "the great end fanctifies every mean," this fum of Cofmo-political good is made to eclipfe or cover all the prefent evils which muft be endured for it. The fact now is, that we are become fo familiarifed with enormities, fuch as brutality to the weaker fex, cruelty to old age, wanton refinement on barbarity, that we now hear unmoved accounts of fcenes, from which, a few years ago, we would have fhrunk back with horror. With cold hearts, and a metaphyfical fcale, we meafure the prefent miferies of our fellow creatures, and compare them with the accumulated miferies of former times, occafioned through a courfe of ages, and afcribed to the ambition of Princes. In this artificial manner are the atrocities of France extenuated; and we ftruggle, and partly fucceed, in reafoning ourfelves out of all the feelings which link men together in fociety.—The ties of father, hufband, brother, friend—all are abandoned for an emotion which we muft even ftrive to excite,—univerfal philanthropy. But this is fad perverfion of nature.

nature. "He that loveth not his brother whom he "hath seen, how can he love God whom he hath not "seen?" Still less can he love this ideal being, of which he labours to conjure up some indistinct and fleeting notion. It is also highly absurd; for, in trying to collect the circumstances which constitute the enjoyments of this Citizen of the World, we find ourselves just brought back to the very moral feelings which we are wantonly throwing away. Weishaupt allures us by the happiness of the patriarchal life as the *summum bonum* of man. But if it is any thing more than eating and sleeping, and squabbling with the neighbouring patriarchs, it must consist in the domestic and neighbourly affections, and every other agreeable moral feeling, all which are to be had in our present state, in greater abundance.

But this is all a pretence;—the wicked corrupters of mankind have no such views of human felicity, nor would they be contented with it; they want to intrigue and to lead; and their patriarchal life answers the same purpose of tickling the fancy as the Arcadia of the poets. Horace shows the frivolity of these declamations, without formally enouncing the moral, in his pretty Ode,

> Beatus ille qui procul negotiis.

The usurer, after expatiating on this Arcadian felicity, hurries away to change, and puts his whole cash again out to usury.

Equally ineffective are the declamations of Cosmo-politism on a mind filled with selfish passions;— they just serve it for a subterfuge.—The ties of ordinary life are broken in the first place, and the Citizen of the World is a wolf of the desart.

The unhappy consequence is, that the natural progress of liberty is retarded. Had this *ignis fatuus*

tuus not appeared and misled us, the improvements which true Illumination has really produced, the increase in sciences and arts, and the improvement in our estimate of life and happiness, would have continued to work silently and gradually in all nations; and those which are less fortunate in point of government would also have improved, by little and little, without losing any sensible portion of their present enjoyments in the possession of riches, or honours, or power. Those pretensions would gradually have come to balance each other, and true liberty, such as Britons enjoy, might have taken place over all.

Instead of this, the inhabitants of every state are put into a situation where every individual is alarmed and injured by the success of another, because all pre-eminence is criminal. Therefore there must be perpetual jealousy and struggle. Princes are now alarmed, since they see the aim of the lower classes, and they repent of their former liberal concessions. All parties maintain a sullen distance and reserve;—the people become unruly, and the sovereign hard-hearted; so that liberty, such as *can* be enjoyed in peace, is banished from the country.

VIII. When we see how eagerly the Illuminati endeavoured to insinuate their Brethren into all offices which gave them influence on the public mind, and particularly into seminaries of education, we should be particularly careful to prevent them, and ought to examine with anxious attention the manner of thinking of all who offer themselves for teachers of youth. There is no part of the secret correspondence of Spartacus and his Associates, in which we see more varied and artful methods for securing pupils, than in his own conduct respecting the students in the University, and the injunctions he gives to others. There are two men, Socher and Drexl, who

who had the general infpection of the fchools in the Electorate. They are treated by Spartacus as perfons of the greateft confequence, and the inftructions given them ftick at no kind of corruption. Weifhaupt is at pains, circuitous and mean arts, to induce young gentlemen to come under his care, and, to one whom he defcribes in another letter as a little mafter who muft have much indulgence, he caufes it to be intimated, that in the quarters where he is to be lodged, he will get the key of the ftreet-door, fo that he can admit whom he will. In all this canvaffing he never quits the great object, the forming the mind of the young man according to the principles of univerfal Liberty and Equality, and to gain this point, fcruples not to flatter, aud even to excite his dangerous paffions. We may be certain, that the zeal of Cofmo-politifm will operate in the fame way in other men, and we ought therefore to be folicitous to have all that are the inftructors of youth, perfons of the moft decent manners. No queftion but fobriety and hypocrify may inhabit the fame breaft. But its immediate effect on the pupil is at leaft fafe, and it is always eafy for a fenfible parent to reprefent the reftrictions laid on the pupil by fuch a man as the effects of uncommon anxiety for his fafety. Whereas there is no cure for the lax principles that may fteal upon the tender mind that is not early put on its guard. Weifhaupt undoubtedly thought that the principles of civil anarchy would be eafieft inculcated on minds, that had already fhaken off the reftraints of Religion, and entered into habits of fenfual indulgence. We fhall be fafe if we truft his judgment in this matter.—We fhould be particularly obfervant of the character and principles of *Men of Talents*, who offer themfelves for thefe offices, becaufe *their* influence muft be very great. Indeed this anxiety fhould extend

tend to all offices which in any way give holders any remarkable influence on the minds of confiderable numbers. Such fhould always be filled by men of immaculate characters and approved principles; and, in times like the prefent, where the moft effential queftions are the fubjects of frequent difcuffion, we fhould always confider with fome diftruft the men who are very cautious in declaring their opinions on thefe queftions.

It is a great misfortune undoubtedly to feel ourfelves in a fituation which makes us damp the enjoyments of life with fo much fufpicion. But the hiftory of mankind fhows us that many great revolutions have been produced by remote and apparently frivolous caufes. When things come to a height, it is frequently impoffible to find a cure— at any rate *medicina fero paratur*, and it is much better to prevent the difeafe—*principiis obfta—venienti occurrite morbo*.

IX. Nor can it be faid that thefe are vain fears. We know that the enemy is working among us, and that there are many appearances in thefe kingdoms which ftrongly refemble the contrivance of this dangerous affociation. We know that before the Order of Illuminati was broken up by the Elector of Bavaria, there were feveral Lodges in Britain, and we may be certain that they are not all broken up. I know that they are not, and that within thefe two years fome Lodges were ignorant or affected to be fo, of the corrupted principles and dangerous defigns of the Illuminati. The conftitution of the Order fhews that this may be, for the Lodges themfelves were illuminated by degrees. But I muft remark, that we can hardly fuppofe a Lodge to be eftablifhed in any place, unlefs there be fome very zealous Brother at hand to inftruct and direct it. And I think that a perfon can hardly be advanced as far as the

rank

rank of Scotch Knight of the Order, and be a safe man either for our Church or State. I am very well informed, that there are several thousands of subscribing Brethren in London alone, and we can hardly doubt, but that many of that number are well advanced. The vocabulary also of the Illuminati is current in certain societies among us. These societies have taken the very name and constitution of the French and German societies. Corresponding---Affiliated---Provincial---Rescript---Convention-----Reading Societies---Citizen of the World---Liberty and Equality, the Imprescriptible Rights of Man, &c. &c. And must it not be acknowledged that our public arbiters of literary merit have greatly changed their manner of treatment of Theological and political writings of late years? Till Paine's Age of Reason appeared, the most sceptical writings of England kept within the bounds of decency and of argument, and we have not, in the course of two centuries, one piece that should be compared with many of the blackguard productions of the German presses. Yet even those performances generally met with sharp reproof as well as judicious refutation. This is a tribute of commendation to which my country is most justly entitled. In a former part of my life I was pretty conversant in writings of this kind, and have seen almost every English performance of note. I cannot express the surprise and disgust which I felt at the number and the gross indecency of the German dissertations which have come in my way since I began this little history,---and many of the titles which I observe in the Leipzig catalogues are such as I think no British writer would make use of. I am told that the licentiousness of the press has been equally remarkable in France, even before the Revolution.---May this sense of propriety and decency long continue to protect us, and support the na‑
tional

tional character for real good breeding, as our attainments in manly science have hitherto gained us the respect of the surrounding nations!

I cannot help thinking that British sentiment, or British delicacy, is changed; for Paine's book is treated by most of our Reviewers with an affected liberality and candour, and is laid before the public as quite new matter, and a fair field for discussion—and it strikes me as if our critics were more careful to let no fault of his opponents pass unnoticed than to expose the futility and rudeness of this indelicate writer. In the reviews of political writings we see few of those kind endeavours, which real love for our constitutional government would induce a writer to employ in order to lessen the fretful discontents of the people; and there is frequently betrayed a satisfaction at finding administration in straits, either through misconduct or misfortune. Real love for our country and its government would (I think) induce a person to mix with his criticisms some sentiments of sympathy with the embarrassment of a minister loaded with the business of a great nation, in a situation never before experienced by any minister. The critic would recollect that the minister was a man, subject to error, but not necessarily nor altogether base. But it seems to be an assumed principle with some of our political writers and reviewers that government must always be in fault, and that every thing needs a reform. Such were the beginnings on the continent, and we cannot doubt but that attempts are made to influence the public mind in this country, in the very way that has been practised abroad.—Nay,

X. The detestable doctrines of Illuminatism have been openly preached among us. Has not Dr. Priestley said, (I think in one of his letters on
the

the Birmingham riots,) "That if the condition of other nations be as much improved as that of France will be by the change in her fyftem of government, the great crifis, dreadful as it may appear, will be a confummation devoutly to be wifhed for ;—and though calamitous to many, perhaps to many innocent perfons, will be eventually glorious and happy?"—Is not this equivalent to Spartacus faying, "True—there will be a ftorm, a convulfion—but all will be calm again?"—Does Dr. Prieftley think that the Britifh will part more eafiily than their neighbours in France with their property and honours, fecured by ages of peaceable poffeffion, protected by law, and acquiefced in by all who wifh and hope that their own defcendants may reap the fruits of their honeft induftry?—Will they make a lefs manly ftruggle?—Are they lefs numerous?—Muft his friends, his patrons, whom he has thanked, and praifed, and flattered, yield up all peaceably, or fall in the general ftruggle? This writer has already given the moft promifing fpecimens of his own docility in the principles of Illuminatifm, and has already paffed through feveral degrees of initiation. He has refined and refined on Chriftianity, and boafts, like another Spartacus, that he has, at laft, hit on the true fecret.—Has he not been preparing the minds of his readers for Atheifm by his theory of mind, and by his commentary on the unmeaning jargon of Dr. Hartley? I call it unmeaning jargon, that I may avoid giving it a more appofite and difgraceful name. For, if intelligence and defign be nothing but a certain modification of the *vibratiunculæ* or undulations of any kind, what is fupreme intelligence, but a more extenfive, and (perhaps they will call it) refined undulation, pervading or mixing

ing with all others? Indeed it is in this very manner that the universal operation of intelligence is pretended to be explained. As any new or partial undulation may be superinduced on any other already existing, and this without the least disturbance or confusion, so may the inferior intelligences in the universe be only superinductions on the operations of this supreme intelligence which pervades them all,—And thus an undulation (of what? surely of something prior to and independent of this modification) is the cause of all the beings in the universe, and of all the harmony and beauty that we observe,—And this undulation is the object of love, and gratitude, and confidence (that is, of other kinds of undulations.)—Fortunately all this has no meaning.—But surely, if any thing can tend to diminish the force of our religious sentiments, and make all Dr. Priestley's discoveries in Christianity insignificant, this will do it.

Were it possible for the departed soul of Newton to feel pain, he would surely recollect with regret that unhappy hour, when provoked by Dr. Hooke's charge of plagiarism, he first threw out his whim of a vibrating ether, to shew what might be made of an hypothesis.—For Sir Isaac Newton must be allowed to have paved the way for much of the atomical philosophy of the moderns. Newton's æther is assumed as a *fac totum* by every precipitate sciolist, who, in despite of logic, and in contradiction to all the principles of mechanics, gives us theories of muscular motion, of animal sensation, and even of intelligence and volition, by the undulations of ætherial fluids. Not one of a hundred of these theorists can go through the fundamental theorem of all this doctrine, the 47th prop. of the 2d book of the Principia, and not one in a thousand know that Newton's investigation is inconclusive.—
Yet

Yet they talk of the effects and modifications of those undulations as familiarly and confidently as if they could demonstrate the propositions in Euclid's Elements.

Yet such is the reason that satisfies Dr. Priestly.—But I do not suppose that he has yet attained his acme of Illumination. His genius has been cramped by British prejudices.—These need not sway his mind any longer. He is now in that " *rará temporis (et loci) felicitate, ubi sentire quæ velis, et quæ sentias dicere licet,*"—in the country which was honoured by giving the world the first avowed edition of the *Age of Reason,* with the name of the shop and publisher. I make no doubt but that his mind will now take a higher flight,—and we may expect to see him fire " that train by which he boasted that he would " blow up the religious establishment of his stupid " and enslaved native country."—Peace be with him.—But I grieve that he has left any of his friends and abettors among us, who declaim, in the most violent and unqualified terms, against all national Establishments of Religion, and in no friendly terms of any establishments which maintain or allow any privileged Orders. Discanting much on such topics increases the dissatisfaction of the less fortunate part of mankind, who naturally repine at advantages which do not arise from the personal merit of the possessor, although they are the natural and necessary fruits of merit in their ancestors, and of the justice and security of our happy Constitution. No well informed and sensible man will deny that the greatest injury was done to pure Religion when Constantine declared Christianity to be the Religion of the Empire, and vested the Church with all the riches and power of the Heathen Priesthood. But it is false that this was the source of all or of the worst corruptions of Christianity. The merest novice in Church History knows that the errors of the Gnostics, of the Cerinthians, and others, long preceded this event, and that thousands lost their lives in those metaphysical disputes. But I cannot help thinking that, in the present condition of Europe, religion would desert the world, if the opinions of men were not directed, in some proper degree, by National Establishments. Teachers among the Independents will court popularity, as they have always courted it; by fostering some favourite and discriminating opinion of their hearers. The old subjects of debate have now lost their zest, and I should fear that the teachers would find it a successful, as it is an easy road to popularity, to lead their hearers through a series of refinements, till they are landed, much to their satisfaction, in the Materialism of Dr. Priestley, from which it is but a step to the Atheism of Diderot and Condorcet.

Seeing that there are such grounds of apprehension, I think that we have cause to be upon our guard, and that every man who has enjoyed the sweets of British liberty should be very anxious indeed to preserve it. We should discourage all secret assemblies, which afford opportunities to the disaffected, and all conversations which foster any notions of political perfection, and create hankerings after unattainable happiness. These only increase the discontents of the unfortunate, the idle, and the worthless.---Above all, we should be careful to discourage and check immorality and licentiousness in every shape. For this will of itself subvert every government, and will subject us to the vile tyranny of a profligate mob.

XI. If there has ever been a season in which it was proper to call upon the public instructors of the nation to exert themselves in the cause of Religion and Virtue, it is surely the present. It appears, from the tenor of the whole narration before the reader,

reader, that Religion and Virtue are confidered as the great obftacles to the completion of this plan for overturning the governments of Europe—and I hope that I have made it evident that thofe confpirators have prefuppofed that there is deeply rooted in the heart of man a fincere veneration for unfophifticated virtue, and an affectionate propenfity to Religion; that is, to confider this beautiful world as the production of wifdom and power, refiding in a Being different from the world itfelf, and the natural object of admiration and of love —I do not fpeak of the truth of this principle at prefent, but only of its reality, as an impreffion on the heart of man. Thefe principles muft therefore be worked on,—and they are acknowledged to be ftrong, becaufe much art is employed to eradicate them, or to overwhelm them by other powerful agents.—We alfo fee that Religion and Virtue are confidered by thofe corrupters as clofely united, and as mutually fupporting each other. This they admit as a fact, and labour to prove it to be a miftake.—And laftly, they entertain no hopes of complete fuccefs till they have exploded both.

This being the cafe, I hope that I fhall be clear of all charge of impropriety, when I addrefs our national inftructors, and earneftly defire them to confider this caufe as peculiarly theirs. The world has been corrupted under pretence of moral inftruction.——Backwardnefs, therefore, on their part, may do inconceivable harm, becaufe it will moft certainly be interpreted as an acknowledgment of defeat, and they will be accufed of indifference and infincerity. I know that a modeft man reluctantly comes forward with any thing that has the appearance of thinking himfelf wifer or better than his neighbours. But if all are fo bafhful bashful, where will it end? Must we allow a parcel of worthless profligates, whom no man would trust with the management of the most trifling concern, to pass with the ignorant and indolent for teachers of true wisdom, and thus entice the whole world into a trap? They have succeeded with our unfortunate neighbours on the continent, and, in Germany, (to their shame be it spoken) they have been assisted even by some faithless clergymen.

But I will hope better of my countrymen, and I think that our clergy have encouragement even from the native character of Britons. National comparisons are indeed ungraceful, and are rarely candid—but I think they may be indulged in this instance. It is of his own countrymen that Voltaire speaks, when he says, that " they resemble a mixed breed " of the monkey and the tiger," animals that mix fun with mischief, and that sport with the torments of their prey.—They have indeed given the most shocking proofs of the justness of his portrait. It is with a considerable degree of national pride, therefore, that I compare the behaviour of the French with that of the British in a very similar situation, during the civil wars and the usurpation of Cromwell. There have been more numerous, and infinitely more atrocious, crimes committed in France during any one half year since the beginning of the Revolution, than during the whole of that tumultuous period. And it should be remembered, that in Britain, at that period, to all other grounds of discontent was added no small share of religious fanaticism, a passion (may I call it) which seldom fails to rouse every angry thought of the heart.—Much may be hoped for from an earnest and judicious address to that rich fund of manly kindness that is conspicuous in the British character,—a fund to which I am persuaded we owe the excellence of our constitutional

al government---No where elfe in Europe are the claims of the different ranks in fociety fo generally and fo candidly admitted. All feel their force, and all allow them to others. Hence it happens that they are enjoyed in fo much peace----hence it happens that the gentry live among the yeomen and farmers with fo eafy and familiar a fuperiority:

———————Extrema per illos
Juſtitia excedens terris veſtigia fecit.

Our clergy are alfo well prepared for the taſk. For our anceſtors differed exceedingly from the prefent Illuminators in their notions, and have enacted that the clergy ſhall be well inſtructed in natural philofophy, judging that a knowledge of the fymmetry of nature, and the beautiful adjuſtment of all her operations, would produce a firm belief of a wifdom and power which is the fource of all this fair order, the Author and Conductor of all, and therefore the natural object of admiration and of love. A good heart is open to this impreſſion, and feels no reluctance, but on the contrary a pleaſure, in thinking man the fubject of his government, and the object of his care. This point being once gained, I ſhould think that the falutary truths of Religion will be highly welcome. I ſhould think that it will be eaſy to convince ſuch minds, that in the midſt of the immenfe variety of the works of God there is one great plan to which every thing feems to refer, namely, the crowding this world, to the utmoſt degree of poſſibility, with life, with beings that enjoy the things around them, each in its own degree and manner. Among thefe, man makes a moſt confpicuous figure, and the *maximum* of his enjoyments feems a capital article in the ways of Providence. It will, I think, require little trouble to ſhew that the natural dictates of Religion, or the immediate refults of the belief of God's moral

ral government of the univerſe, coincide in every circumſtance of ſentiment, diſpoſition, and conduct, with thoſe that are moſt productive of enjoyment (on the whole) in ſocial life. The ſame train of thought will ſhew, that the real improvements in the pleaſures of ſociety, are, in fact, improvements of man's rational nature, and ſo many ſteps toward that perfection which our own conſciences tell us we are capable of, and which Religion encourages us to hope for in another ſtate of being.—And thus will " the ways of Wiſdom appear to be ways of plea-" ſantneſs, and all her paths to be peace."

Dwelling on ſuch topics, there is no occaſion for any political diſcuſſion. This would be equally improper and hurtful. Such diſcuſſions never fail to produce ill-humour.—But ſurely the higheſt complacence muſt reſult from the thought that we are co-operating with the Author of all wiſdom and goodneſs, and helping forward the favourite plans of his providence. Such a thought muſt elevate the mind which thus recogniſes a ſort of alliance with the Author of nature.—Our brethren in ſociety appear brethren indeed, heirs of the ſame hopes, and travelling to the ſame country. This will be a ſort of moral patriotiſm, and ſhould, I think, produce mutual forbearance, ſince we diſcover imperfections in all creatures, and are conſcious of them in ourſelves—notwithſtanding which, we hope to be all equal at laſt in worth and in happineſs.

I ſhould gladly hope that I ſhall not be accuſed of preſumption in this addreſs. There is no profeſſion that I more ſincerely reſpect than that of the religious and moral inſtructor of my country. I am ſaying nothing here that I am not accuſtomed to urge at much greater length in the courſe of my profeſſional duty. And I do not think that I am juſtly chargeable with vanity, when I ſuppoſe that many years of delightful ſtudy of the works of God have

given

given me somewhat more acquaintance with them than is probably attained by those who never think of the matter, being continually engaged in the bustle of life. Should one of this description say that all is fate or chance, and that " the same thing " happens to all," &c. as is but too common, I should think that a prudent man will give so much preference to *my* affertion, as at leaft to think ferioufly about the thing, before he allow himfelf any indulgence in things which I affirm to be highly dangerous to his future peace and happinefs.——For this reafon I hope not to be accufed of going out of my line, nor hear any one fay " *Ne futor ultra cre-* " *pidam.*" The prefent is a feafon of anxiety, and it is the duty of every man to contribute his mite to the general good.

It is in fome fuch hopes that I have written thefe pages ; and if they have any fuch effect, I shall think myfelf fortunate in having by chance hit on fomething ufeful, when I was only trying to amufe myfelf during the tedious hours of bad health and confinement. No perfon is more fenfible of the many imperfections of this performance than myfelf. But, as I have no motive for the publication but the hopes of doing fome good, I truft that I shall obtain a favourable acceptance of my endeavours from an intelligent, a candid, and a good-natured public. I muft entreat that it be remembered that thefe fheets are not the work of an author determined to write a book. They were for the moft part notes, which I took from books I had borrowed, that I might occafionally have recourfe to them when occupied with Free Mafonry, the firft object of my curiofity. My curiofity was diverted to many other things as I went along, and when the Illuminati came in my way, I regretted the time I had thrown away on Free Mafonry.—But, obferving
their

their connection, I thought that I perceived the progress of one and the fame defign. This made me eager to find out any remains of Weifhaupt's Affociation. I was not furprized when I faw marks of its interference in the French Revolution.—In hunting for clearer proofs I found out the German Union—and, in fine, the whole appeared to be one great and wicked project, fermenting and working over all Europe.—Some highly refpected friends encouraged me in the hope of doing fome fervice by laying my informations before the public, and faid that no time fhould be loft.—I therefore fet about collecting my fcattered facts.—I undertook this tafk at a time when my official duty preffed hard on me, and bad health made me very unfit for ftudy.—The effects of this muft appear in many faults, which I fee, without being able at prefent to amend them. I owe this apology to the public, and I truft that my good intentions will procure it acceptance*.

Nothing

* While the fheet commencing p. 341 was printing off, I got a fight of a work publifhed in Paris laft year entitled *La Conjuration d'Orleans.* It confirms all that I have faid refpecting the ufe made of the Free Mafon Lodges.—It gives a particular account of the formation of the Jacobin Club, by the Club Breton. This laft appears to have been the Affociation formed with the affiftance of the German deputies. The Jacobin Club had feveral committees, fimilar to thofe of the National Affembly. Among others, it had a Committee of Enquiry and Correfpondence, whofe bufinefs it was to gain partizans, to difcover enemies, to decide on the merits of the Brethren, and to form fimilar Clubs in other places.

The author of the above-mentioned work writes as follows, (vol. iii. p. 19.) We may judge of what the D. of Orleans could do in other places, by what he did during his ftay in England. During his ftay in London, he gained over to his intereft Lord Stanhope and Dr. Price, two of the moft refpectable members of the *Revolution Society*. This Society had no other object

Nothing would give me more sincere pleasure than to see the whole proved to be a mistake;—to be convinced that there is no such plot, and that we run no risk of the contagion; but that Britain will continue, by the abiding prevalence of honour, of virtue, and of true religion, to exhibit the fairest specimen of civil government that ever was seen on earth, and a national character and conduct not unworthy of the inestimable blessings that we enjoy. Our excellent Sovereign, at his accession to the throne, declared to his Parliament that HE GLORIED IN HAVING BEEN BORN A BRITON. —Would to God that

---

object (it said) but to support the Revolution, which had driven James II. from the throne of his ancestors.

Orleans made of this association a true Jacobin Club.—It entered into correspondence with the Committee of Enquiry of our Commune, with the same Committee of our Jacobin Club, and at last with our National Assembly. It even sent to the Assembly an ostensible letter, in which we may see the following passages:

" The Society congratulate the National Assembly of France
" on the Revolution which has taken place in that country. It
" cannot but earnestly wish for the happy conclusion of so im-
" portant a Revolution, and, at the same time, express the ex-
" treme satisfaction which it feels in reflecting on the glorious
" example which France has given to the world." (The Reader will remark, that in this example are contained all the horrors which had been exhibited in France before the month of March 1790; and that before this time, the conduct of the Duke of Orleans on the 5th and 6th of October 1789, with all the shocking atrocities of those days, were fully known in England.)

" The Society resolves unanimously to invite all the people of
" England to establish Societies through the kingdom, to support
" the principles of the Revolution, to form correspondence be-
" tween themselves, and by these means to establish a great con-
" certed Union of all the true Friends of Liberty."

Accordingly (says the French author) this was executed, and Jacobin Clubs were established in several cities of England, Scotland, and Ireland.

that all and each of his fubjects had entertained the fame lofty notions of this good fortune! Then would they have laboured, as he has done for near forty years, to fupport the honour of the Britifh name by fetting as bright an example of domeftic and of public virtue.----Then would Britons have been indeed the boaft of humanity---then we fhould have viewed thefe wicked plots of our neighbours with a fmile of contempt, and of fincere pity---and there would have been no need of this imperfect but well-meant performance.

Postscript.

ALTHOUGH I saw no reason to doubt of the validity of the proofs which I have offered in the preceding pages, of a conspiracy against the dearest interests of every nation of Europe, nor of the importance of the information to my own countrymen, it gives me great satisfaction to learn that it has been received with favour and indulgence. This I may conclude from the impression's being exhausted in a few days, and because the publisher informs me that another edition is wanted immediately. I could have wished that this were deferred for some time, that I might have availed myself of the observations of others, and be enabled to correct the mistakes into which I have been led by my scanty knowledge of the German language, and the mistakes of the writers from whom I derived all my informations. I should, in that case, have attempted to make the work more worthy of the public eye, by correcting many imperfections, which the continual distraction of bad health, and my haste to bring it before the public, have occasioned. I should have made the disposition more natural and perspicuous, and have lopped off some redundances and repetitions. But the printer tells me, that this would greatly retard the publication, by changing the series of the pages. At any rate, I am not at present in a condition to engage in any work that requires dispatch. I must yield therefore to those reasons, and content myself with such corrections as can be made immediately.

I have found, after minute enquiry, that I was mistaken as to the expression of an eminent follower

follower of Dr. Prieſtley, mentioned before. The perſon alluded to diſclaims all ſanguinary proceedings, and my information aroſe from a very erroneous account which was circulated of the converſation. But I ſtill think the caution equally neceſſary, which I recommended to the hearers of the frequent and violent declamations made by thoſe alluded to, againſt all religious eſtabliſhments.

Except the anecdote of Diderot's library, I do not recollect another aſſertion in the book, for which I have not the authority of printed evidence. This ſtory was told me by ſo many perſons of credit, who were on the ſpot at the time, that I have no doubt of its truth.

I alſo find that I was miſtaken in my conjecture that Mr. *Le Franc* communicated his ſuſpicions of the horrid deſigns of the Free Maſons to Archbiſhop *Gobet*. It muſt have been to Mr. *Le Clerc de Juigne*, a moſt worthy prelate, whom the hatred of the Jacobins obliged to fly into Switzerland. The Catholic clergy were butchered or baniſhed, and the Jacobins ſubſtituted in their places ſuch as would ſecond their views. *Gobet* was worthy of their confidence, and the *Archbiſhop of Thouloufe (Brienne)* himſelf could not have ſerved the cauſe of the philoſophiſts more effectually, had they ſucceeded in their attempts to get him continued Archbiſhop of Paris.

As the poetical picture of unqualified Liberty and Equality, and the indolent pleaſures of the patriarchal life, are the charm by which the Illuminators hope to faſcinate all hearts, and as they reprobate every conſtruction of ſociety which tolerates any permanent ſubordination, and particularly ſuch as found this ſubordination on diſtinctions

tinctions of ranks, and scout all privileges allowed to particular orders of men, I hope that it will not be thought foreign to the general purpose of the foregoing Work, if, I with great deference, lay before the Reader some of my reasons for asserting, without hesitation, in a former part, that the British constitution is the only one that will give permanent happiness to a great and luxurious nation, and is peculiarly calculated to give full exercise to the best propensities of cultivated minds. I am the more desirous of doing this, because it seems to me that most of the political writers on the Continent, and many of my countrymen, have not attended to important circumstances which distinguish our constitution from the States General of France and other countries. The republicans in France have, since the Revolution, employed the pains in searching their records, which ought to have been taken before the convocation of the States, and which would probably have prevented that step altogether. They have shewn that the meetings of the States, if we except that in 1614 and 1483, were uniformly occasions of mutual contests between the different Orders, in which the interests of the nation and the authority of the Crown were equally forgotten, and the kingdom was plunged into all the horrors of a rancorous civil war. Of this they give us a remarkable instance during the captivity of King John in 1355 and 1356, the horrors of which were hardly exceeded by any thing that has happened in our days. They have shewn the same dismal consequences of the assembly of the different Orders in Brabant; and still more remarkably in Sweden and Denmark, where they have frequently produced a revolution and change of government, all of which have terminated

nated in the absolute government, either of the Crown, or of one of the contending Orders. They laugh at the simplicity of the British for expecting that the permanent fruits of our constitution, which is founded on the same jarring principles, shall be any better; and assert, that the peaceable exercise of its several powers for somewhat more than a century, (a thing never experienced by us in former times,) has proceeded from circumstances merely accidental. With much address they have selected the former disturbances, and have connected them by a sort of principle, so as to support their system, " that a States General " or Parliament, consisting of a representation of " the different classes of citizens, can never deli- " berate for the general good, but must always " occupy their time in contentions about their " mutual invasions of privilege, and will saddle " every aid to the executive power, with some " unjust and ruinous aggrandisement of the victo- " rious Order." They have the effrontery to give the MAGNA CHARTA as an instance of an usurpation of the great feudatories, and have represented it in such a light as to make it the game of their writers and of the tribunes.—All this they have done in order to reconcile the minds of the few thinking men of the nation to the abolition of the different Orders of the State, and to their National Convention in the form of a chaotic mass of Frenchmen, one and indivisible :

Non bene junctarum discordia semina rerum,
Ubi frigida puegnabant calidis, humentia siccis,
Mollia cum duris, sine pondere habentia pondus.

Their reasonings would be just, and their proofs from history would be convincing, if their pre-

mises

mises were true; if the British Parliament were really an aſſembly of three Orders, either perſonally, or by repreſentation, deliberating apart, each having a *veto* on the deciſions of the other two. And I apprehend that moſt of my countrymen, who have not had occaſion to canvas the ſubject with much attention, ſuppoſe this to be really the Britiſh Conſtitution: for, in the ordinary table converſations on the ſubject, they ſeldom go farther, and talk with great complacence of the balance of hoſtile powers, of the King as the umpire of differences, and of the peace and proſperity that reſults from the whole.

But I cannot help thinking that this is a miſconception, almoſt in every circumſtance. I do not know any oppoſite intereſts in the State, except the general one of the governor and the governed, the king and the ſubject.—If there is an umpire in our conſtitution, it is the houſe of Lords—but this is not as a repreſentation of the perſons of birth, but as a court of hereditary magiſtrates: the Peers do not meet to defend their own privileges as citizens, but either as the counſellors of the King, or as judges in the laſt reſort. The privileges for which we ſee them ſometimes contend, are not the privileges of the high-born, of the great vaſſals of the Crown, but the privileges of the Houſe of Lords, of the ſupreme Court of Judicature, or of the King's Council. In all the nations on the Continent, the different Orders, as they are called, of the State, are corporations, bodies politic, which have juriſdiction within themſelves, and rights which they can maintain at their own hand, and privileges which mark them moſt diſtinctly, and produce ſuch a complete ſeparation between the different Orders, that they can no more mix than oil and water. Yet the great

great prefident Montefquieu fays, that the Peerage of England is a *body* of Nobility ; and he ufes the term *body* in the ftrict fenfe now mentioned, as fynonymous to corporation. He has repeatedly ufed this term to denote the fecond order of Frenchmen, perfons of noble birth, or ennobled, (that is, vefted in the privileges and diftinctions of the nobly born,) united by law, and having authority to maintain their privileges. The hiftory of France, nay of our own country, fhows us that this body may enjoy all its diftinctions of nobility, and that the Great Barons may enjoy the prerogatives of their baronies, although the authority of the Crown is almoft annihilated.—We have no cogent reafon, therefore, for thinking that they will be conftantly careful to fupport the authority of the Crown ; and much lefs to believe that they will, at the fame time, watch over the liberties of the people. In the election of their reprefentatives, (for the whole body of the gentlemen muft appear by reprefentation,) we muft not expect that they will felect fuch of their own number as will take care of thofe two effential objects of our conftitution.—Equally jealous of the authority of the Crown and of the encroachments of all thofe who are not gentlemen, and even fearful of the affumptions of the Great Barons, the powerful individuals of their own order, they will always choofe fuch reprefentatives as will defend their own rights in the firft place. Such perfons are by no means fit for maintaining the proper authority of the Crown, and keeping the reprefentatives of the lower claffes within proper bounds.

But this is not the nature of our Houfe of Lords in the prefent day. It was fo formerly in a great meafure, and had the fame effects as in other countries. But fince the Revolution, the Peers of of Great-Britain have no important privileges which relate merely or chiefly to birth. These all refer to their functions as Magistrates of the Supreme Court. The King can, at any time, place in this House any eminent person whom he thinks worthy of the office of hereditary magistrate. The Peers are noble—that is, remarkable, illustrious; but are not necessarily, nor in every instance, persons of high birth. This House therefore is not, in any sort, the representative of what is called in France the Noblesse—a particular cast of the nation;—nor is it a junction of the proprietors of the great fees of the Crown, as such;—for many, very many, of the greatest baronies are in the hands of those we call Commoners.—They sit as the King's Counsellors, or as Judges.—Therefore the members of our Upper House are not swayed by the prejudices of any class of the citizens. They are hereditary magistrates, created by the Sovereign, for his counsel, to defend his prerogatives, to hold the balance between the throne and the people. The greatest part of the Nobility (in the continental sense of the word) are not called into this House, but they may be members of the Lower House, which we call the Commons; nay the sons and the brothers of the Peers are in the same situation. The Peers therefore cannot be hostile or indifferent to the liberty, the rights, or the happiness of the Commons, without being the enemies of their own families.

Nor is our House of Commons at all similar to the *Third Estate* of any of the neighbouring kingdoms. They are not the representatives of the ignobly born, or of any class of citizens. The members are the proper representatives of the *whole nation*, and consist of persons of every class, persons of the highest birth, persons of great fortune, persons of education, of knowledge, of talents.

2 Z Thus

Thus the causes of dissension which refer to the distinctive rights or prerogatives of the different classes of citizens are removed, because in each House there are many individuals selected from all the classes.

A Peer, having attained the highest honours of the state, must be an enemy to every revolution. Revolution must certainly degrade him, whether it places an absolute monarch, or a democratic junto, on the throne.

The Sovereign naturally looks for the support of the Upper House, and in every measure agreeable to the constitution, and to the public weal, exerts his influence on the House of Commons. Here the character of the monarch and his choice of ministers must appear, as in any other constitution; but with much less chance of danger to political liberty.—The great engine of monarchy in Europe, has been the jarring privileges of the different Orders; and the Sovereign, by siding with one of them, obtained accessions of prerogative and power.—It was thus that, under the House of Tudor, our constitution advanced with hasty strides to absolute monarchy; and would have attained it, had James the First been as able as he was willing to secure what he firmly believed to be the divine rights of his Crown.

I do not recollect hearing the lower ranks of the State venting much of their discontents against the Peers, and they seem to perceive pretty clearly the advantages arising from their prerogatives. They seem to look up to them as the first who will protect them against the agents of sovereignty. They know that a man may rise from the lowest station to the peerage, and that in that exaltation he remains connected with themselves by the dear-

est

est ties; and the House of Commons take no offence at the creation of new Peers, because their privileges as a Court, and their private rights, are not affected by it. Accordingly, the House has always opposed every project of limiting the King's prerogative in this respect.

How unlike is all this to the constitution consisting of the pure representatives of the Privileged Orders of the Continental States. The self-conceited constitutionalists of France saw something in the British Parliament which did not fall in with their own *hasty* notions, and prided themselves in not copying from us. This would have indicated great poverty of invention in a nation accustomed to consider itself as the teacher of mankind. The most sensible of them, however, wished to have a constitution which they called an *improvement* of ours: and this was the simple plan of a *representation* of the two or three Orders of the State. Their Upper House should contain the representatives of 100,000 noblesse. The Princes of the Blood and Great Barons should sit in it of their own right, and the rest by deputies. The Lower House, or *Tiers Etat*, should consist of deputies from those ignobly born; such as merchants, persons in the lower offices of the law, artisans, peasants, and a small number of freeholders. Surely it needs no deep reflection to teach us what sort of deliberations would occupy such a house. It would be a most useful occupation, however, to peruse the history of France, and of other nations, and see what *really did occupy* the Tiers Etat thus constructed, and what were their proceedings, their decisions, and the steps which they took to make them effectual. I have no doubt but that this study would cure most of our advocates for general eligibility, and for general suffrage. I have lately

read

read Velley and Villaret's History of France, (by the bye, the Abbé Barruel has shewn that the Club d'Holbach managed the publication of this History after the first eight or ten volumes, and slipped into it many things suited to their impious project,) and the accounts of the troublesome reigns of John, and Charles his successor, by authors who wrote long before the Revolution; and they filled me with horror. The only instance that I met with of any thing like moderation in the claims and disputes of the different Orders of their States General, and of patriotism, or regard for the general interests of the State, is in their meetings during the minority of Charles VIII.

With respect to the limitations of the eligibility into the House of Commons, I think that there can be no doubt that those should be excluded whose habits of needy and laborious life have precluded them from all opportunities of acquiring some general views of political relations. Such persons are totally unfit for deliberations, where general or comprehensive views only are to be the subjects of discussion; they can have no conceptions of the subject, and therefore no steady notions or opinions, but must change them after every speaker, and must become the dupes of every demagogue.

But there are other circumstances which make me think that, of all the classes of citizens, the land proprietors are the fittest for holding this important office. I do not infer this from their having a more real connection with the nation, and a stronger interest in its fate—I prefer them on account of their general habits of thought. Almost all their ordinary transactions are such as make them acquainted with the interests of others, cause them to consider those in general points of view; and, in short, most

of

of their occupations are, in some degree, national. They are accustomed to settle differences between those of lower stations—they are frequently in the King's commission as Justices of the Peace. All these circumstances make them much apter scholars in that political knowledge, which is absolutely necessary for a member of the House of Commons. But, besides this, I have no hesitation in saying that their turn of mind, their principles of conduct, are more generally such as become a Senator, than those of *any other class* of men. This class includes almost all men of family. I cannot help thinking that even what is called family pride is a sentiment in their favour. I am convinced that all our propensities are useful in society, and that their bad effects arise wholly from want of moderation in the indulgence of them, or sometimes from the impropriety of the occasion on which they are exerted. What propensity is more general than the desire of acquiring permanent consideration for ourselves and our families? Where is the man to be found so mean-spirited as not to value himself for being born of creditable parents, and for creditable domestic connections? Is this wrong because it has been abused? So then is every pre-eminence of office; and the directors of republican France are as criminal as her former Nobles. This propensity of the human heart should no more be rejected than the desire of power. It should be regulated—but it should certainly be made use of as one of the means of carrying on the national business. I think that we know some of its good effects—It incites to a certain propriety of conduct that is generally agreeable—its honesty is embellished by a manner that makes it more pleasing. There is something that we call the *behaviour of a Gentleman* that is immediatly and uniformly understood. The plainest peasant or labourer er will say of a man whom he esteems in a certain way, "He is a Gentleman, every bit of him,"—and he is perfectly understood by all who hear him to mean, not a rank in life, but a turn of mind, a tenor of conduct that is amiable and worthy, and the ground of confidence.—I remark, with some feeling of patriotic pride, that these are phrases almost peculiar to our language—in Russia the words would have no meaning. But there, the Sovereign is a despot, and all but the Gentry are slaves; and the Gentry are at no pains to recommend their class by such a distinction, nor to give currency to such a phrase.—I would infer from this peculiarity, that Britain is the happy land, where the wisest use has been made of this propensity of the human heart.

If therefore there be a foundation for this peculiarity, the Gentry are proper objects of our choice for filling the House of Commons.

If theoretical considerations are of any value in questions of political discussion, I would say, that we have good reasons for giving this class of citizens a great share in the public deliberations. Besides what I have already noticed of their habits of considering things in general points of view, and their *feeling* a closer connection with the nation than any other class, I would say that the power and influence which naturally attach to their being called to offices of public trust, will probably be better lodged in their hands. If they are generally selected for these offices, they come to consider them as parts of their civil condition, as situations natural to them. They will therefore exercise this power and influence with the moderation and calmness of habit,—they are no novelties to them—they are not afraid of losing them;—therefore, when in office, they do not catch at the opportunities of exercising them. This is the ordinary

nary conduct of men, and therefore is a ground of probable reasoning.—In short, I should expect from our Gentry somewhat of generosity and candour, which would temper the commercial principle, which seems to regulate the national transactions of modern Europe, and whose effects seem less friendly to the best interests of humanity, than even the Roman principle of glory.

The Reader will now believe that I would not recommend the filling the House of Commons with merchants, although they seem to be the natural Representatives of the monied interest of the nation. But I do not wish to consider that House as the Representative of any Orders whatever, or to disturb its deliberations with any debates on their jarring interests. The man of purely commercial notions disclaims all generosity—recommends honesty because it is the best policy—in short, "places the "value of a thing in as much money as 'twill bring." I should watch the conduct of such men more narrowly than that of the Nobles. Indeed, the history of Parliament will show that the Gentry have not been the most venal part of the House. The Illumination which now dazzles the world aims directly at multiplying the number of venal members, by filling the senates of Europe with men who may be bought at a low price. Ministerial corruption is the fruit of Liberty, and freedom dawned in this nation in Queen Elizabeth's time, when her minister bribed Wentworth.—A wise and free Legislation will endeavour to make this as expensive and troublesome as possible, and therefore will neither admit universal suffrage nor a very extensive eligibility. These two circumstances, besides opening a wider door to corruption, tend to destroy the very intention of all civil constitutions. The great object in them

them is, to make a great number of people happy. Some men place their chief enjoyment in meafuring their ftrength with others, and love to be continually employed in canvaffing, intriguing, and carrying on fome little pieces of a fort of public bufinefs; to fuch men univerfal fuffrage and eligibility would be paradife—but it is to be hoped that the number of fuch is not very great: for this occupation muft be accompanied by much difquiet among their neighbours, much diffenfion, and mutual offence and ill-will—and the peaceable, the indolent, the ftudious, and the half of the nation, the women, will be great fufferers by all this. In a nation poffeffing many of the comforts and pleafures of life, the happieft government is that which will leave the greateft number poffible totally unoccupied with national affairs, and at full liberty to enjoy all their domeftic and focial pleafures, and to do this with fecurity and permanency. Great limitations in the right of electing feems therefore a circumftance neceffary for this purpofe; and limitations are equally neceffary on the eligibility. When the offices of power and emolument are open to all, the fcramble becomes univerfal, and the nation is never at peace. The *road* to a feat in Parliament fhould be acceffible to all; but it fhould be long, fo that many things, which all may in time obtain, fhall be requifite for qualifying the candidate. The road fhould alfo be fuch that all fhould be induced to walk in it, in the profecution of their ordinary bufinefs; and their admiffion into public offices fhould depend on the progrefs which they have made in the advancement of their own fortunes. Such regulations would, I think, give the greateft chance of filling the offices with perfons fitteft for them, by

their

their talents, their experience, and their habits of thinking. These habits, and the views of life which a man forms in confequence of his fituation, are of the utmoft importance.

After all thefe obfervations, I muft ftill recur to a pofition which I have repeated more than once, namely, that our conftitution, which nearly embraces all thefe circumftances, has attained its prefent excellence chiefly in confequence of the innate worth of the Britifh character. About the time of the Conqueft, our conftitution hardly differed from that of France. But the clafhing of interefts between the different Orders of the fubjects was not fo rancorous and obftinate—thefe Orders melted more eafily together—the purity of the principle of Reprefentation in the States was lefs attended to; and while the French Peers gradually left off minding any bufinefs but their own, and left the High Court of Judicature to the lawyers, and the King to his Cabinet Council, the Peers of Great Britain, overlooking their own lefs important diftinctions, attended more to the State, became a permanent Council to the Sovereign in the adminiftration and legiflation; and, with a patriotifm and a patience that are unknown to the other Grandees of Europe, continued to hear and to judge in all queftions of juftice and property between the inferior citizens of the State. Britifh Liberty is the highly-prized fruit of all this worthy conduct, and moft people afcribe it to the fuperior fpirit and independence of the national character. It ftrikes me, however, as more furely indicating fuperior virtue, and more judicious patriotifm; and our happy conftitution is not more juftly entitled to the admiration and refpect that is paid to it by all Europe,

3 A   than

than to the affectionate and grateful attachment of every true-hearted Briton.

Since the publication of this volume I have seen a very remarkable work indeed, on the same subject, *Memoires pour servir a l'Histoire du Jacobinisme, par M. l'Abbé Barruel*. This author confirms all that I have said of the *Enlighteners*, whom he very aptly calls *Philosophists;* and of the abuses of Free Masonry in France. He shows, unequestionably, that a formal and systematic conspiracy against Religion was formed and zealously prosecuted by Voltaire, d'Alembert, and Diderot, assisted by Frederic II. King of Prussia; and I see that their principles and their manner of procedure have been the same with those of the German atheists and anarchists. Like them they hired an Army of Writers; they industriously pushed their writings into every house and every cottage. Those writings were equally calculated for inflaming the sensual appetites of men, and for perverting their judgments. They endeavoured to get the command of the Schools, particularly those for the lower classes; and they erected and managed a prodigious number of Circulating Libraries and Reading Societies. M. Barruel says, that this gang of public corruptors have held their meetings for many years in the *Hotel de Holbach* at Paris, and that Voltaire was their honorary President. The most eminent members were *d'Alembert, Diderot, Condorcet, La Harpe, Turgot, Lamoignon*. They took the name of ŒCONOMISTS, and affected to be continually occupied with plans for improving Commerce, Manufactures, Agriculture, Finance, &c. and published from time to time respectable performances on those subjects.— But their darling project was to destroy Christianity and all Religion, and to bring about a total change of Government. They employed writers to compose corrupting and impious books—these were revised by the Society, and corrected till they suited their purpose. A number were printed in a handsome manner, to defray the expence; and then a much greater number were printed in the cheapest form possible, and given for nothing, or at very low prices, to hawkers and pedlars, with injunctions to distribute them secretly through the cities and villages. They even hired persons to read them to conventicles of those who had not learned to read.* (See vol. i. 343—355.)

I am particularly struck by a position of Abbé Barruel, " *That Irreligion and unqualified Liberty and* " *Equality are the genuine and original Secrets of Free* " *Masonry, and the ultimatum of a regular progress* " *through all its degrees.*" He supports this remarkable position with great ingenuity, and many very pertinent facts. I confess that now, when I have got this impression, I shall find it very difficult to efface it. But I must also say, that this thought never struck me, during all the time that I have been

---

* The author makes an observation which is as just as it is agreeable. This atrocious gang solicited, with the most anxious assiduity, the participation and patronage of the great ones of the world, and boast of several very exalted names; Frederic II. of Prussia, whom they call the Solomon of the North, Catharine II. Gustavus King of Sweden, the King of Denmark, &c. &c. But in the whole series of their correspondence there is not the least trace of any encouragement or any hopes from our excellent Sovereign George III. Despising the incense of such wretches, and detesting their science, he has truly merited the title of *Philosopher*, by having done more for the real Illumination of the World, by the promotion of true Science, than Louis XIV. with his pensioned Academicians, or than all the present Sovereigns of Europe united; and has uniformly distinguished himself by his regard for true Religion, and every thing that is venerable and sacred. This omission is above all praise!

been occupied with it; nor have I ever heard it expressed by any Brother, except such as had been illuminated; and such Brethren always considered this as an innovation or improvement on genuine British Free Masonry. I recollect, indeed, that Nicholai, in his account of the German Rosycrucians, says, that the object of Free Masonry in England, since the time of James II. is *Toleration* in *Religious Opinions*, as *Royalism* had been the object before that time.

The account which the Abbé gives of the *Chevalerie du Soleil* is very conformable to one of the three rituals in my possession. His account of the *Chevalerie de Rose Croix*, and some others, differs considerably from those in my box. I have reason to think that my materials are transcripts from the rituals,* &c. which Rosa introduced into the German Lodges, because the writer of the greatest part of them is an inhabitant of that city.

I think that the Abbé Barruel's account of this matter suggests a pleasing reflection. All the Brethren on the Continent agree in saying, that Free Masonry was imported from Great Britain about the beginning of this century, and this in the form of a Mystical Society. It has been assiduously cultivated in Britain ever since that time, and I believe that the Fraternity is more numerous here, in proportion to the population of the country, than in any other kingdom; yet in Britain the Brethren have never suspected that its principles were seditious or atheistical. While the Free Masonry of the Continent was tricked up with all the frippery of stars and ribands, or was perverted to the most profligate and impious purposes, and the Lodges became seminaries of Foppery, of Sedition, and Impiety, it has retained in Britain its original form,

simple

simple and unadorned, and the Lodges have remained the scenes of innocent merriment, or meetings of Charity and Beneficence. As the good sense and sound judgments of Britons have preserved them from the absurd follies of Transmutation, of Ghost-raising, and of Magic, so their honest hearts and their innate good dispositions have made them detest and reject the mad projects and impious doctrines of Cosmopolites, Epicurists, and Atheists.

*O fortunatos nimium, sua si bona norint
Anglicolas!*

I have more confidence than ever in the sentiment which I expressed as an encouragement for our moral instructors; and with greater earnestness do I call on them to rescue from corruption and impending ruin a nation so highly deserving of their care.

Mr. Barruel, in the eighteenth chapter of his work, has suggested some reflections, which highly merit attention, and greatly tend to efface the impression which is naturally made on the minds of the unthinking and precipitant, when they observe such a list of authors, whom they have been accustomed to admire, all leagued against Religion. I think, however, that nothing can more effectually remove it, than what I have already shown of the vile and disgraceful tricks which these sophists have been guilty of to support their cause. The cause of this numerous association is distinctly seen in their very procedure. The very first step in their progress is *depravation of manners*. In this they have laboured with as much earnestness as either Spartacus, or Minos, or Bahrdt. It was a treat to me to learn that La Close's abominable book *Les Liaisons Dangereuses,*

Dangereufes, was not merely pandering for his patron Orleans, but alſo working for his maſters at the Hotel d'Holbach. Nothing gives ſuch certain bread to thoſe authors, in the beginning of their career, as immoral and impure writings;—and with ſuch did even their chief ſet out, and fill his pockets; witneſs his *Pucelle d'Orleans*; and even after they became the *ſages of France*, they continued, either from coarſe taſte or from ſerious principle, for the diabolical purpoſe of inflaming the paſſions of others, to interlard their graveſt performances with impure thoughts and ſentiments. Nay, the ſecret of the Hotel d'Holbach ſhews us that, for any thing we know to the contrary, the vileſt productions of their preſs may have been the compoſitions of the octogenary Voltaire, of the ſly d'Alembert, or of the author of the *Pere de Famille*. What a pity it is that the *Decline of the Roman Empire* was not all written in England, and that its learned and elegant author, by going into their ſociety, has allowed himſelf to be drawn into this muddy and degrading vortex!

I ſhould ſcarcely aſk for more to diſguſt me with the philoſophy of theſe ſages, and to make me diſtruſt all their pretenſions to knowledge. The meanneſs of the conduct ſuited the original poverty of the whole of them; but its continuance ſtrips them of all claims to the name of philoſophers. Their pretended wiſdom is only cunning,—and we muſt acknowledge that their conduct was clever: for this mean of corruption, concealed or embelliſhed by their talents for ſentimental ſlang, (I can give it no better name,) made their converſation and their writings moſt acceptable to their noble patrons.—Now it is that Religion, of neceſſity, comes on the field; for Religion tells us, that theſe

are

are mean pleasures for creatures born to our prospects; and Christianity tells us, that they are gross transgressions of *the only just morality*. The progress of the pupil will now be rapid; for he will listen with willing ears to lessons which flatter his passions. Yet Voltaire thinks it necessary to enliven the lessons by a little of the *salaison, quelques bons mots à-propos auprès des femmes*, which he recommends to d'Alembert, who, it seems, was deficient in this kind of small talk.

Surely all this is very unlike to wisdom; and when we see that it is part of a plan, and this an obvious one, it should greatly lessen our wonder at the number of these admired infidels. If we would now proceed to examine their pretensions to science, on which they found their claim to the name of philosophers, we must be careful to take the word in a sense that is unequivocal. Its true meaning is by no means what is commonly assigned to it, a lover of knowledge. It is a lover of wisdom; and philosophy professes to teach us what are the constituents of human felicity, and what are the means of attaining it; what are our duties, and the general rules for our conduct. The stoics were philosophers. The Christians are also philosophers. The Epicureans and the Sophists of France would also be called philosophers. I have put in my objection to this claim already, and need not repeat my reasons for saying that their doctrines are not dictates of wisdom. I shall only add, that their own conduct shows plainly that their principles had no effect on themselves, because we see, from the series of correspondence which Mr. Barruel has laid before us, that they do not scruple to practise villanous and hypocritical tricks, which never fail to disgrace a man, and are totally irreconcilable with
our

our notions of human dignity. Voltaire patiently took a caning from an officer at Frankfort, for having wittily told lies of his scholar Frederic, and his wisdom told him that his honour was cleared by offering to meet the Major, each of them provided with an injection syringe. This was thought sublime wit at Ferney. I do not suppose that the slave Epictetus, or the soldier Digby, would have ended the affair in this manner. Many of the deeds of wisdom of the club d'Holbach were more degrading than even this; and I am confident that the whole of this phalanx of sages were conscious that they were treated by their patrons and pupils as Voltaire was treated by the Solomon of the North, and that their notions of the *vraie sagesse* were also the same with his. He gives this account of it in his letter to his niece: " Le Roi lui avoit repondu; ' j'aurai " besoin de Voltaire un an tout au plus—On presse " l'orange, et on jette l'écorce.' Je me suis fait " repeter ces douces paroles"—(How poor Voltaire would grin!)—" Je vois bien qu'on a pressé " l'orange—il faut penser à sauver l'ecorce."

But, as things stand at present, philosopher means a man of science, and in this sense of the word our sages claim great respect. No claim can be worse founded. It is amusing to observe the earnestness with which they recommend the study of natural history. One does not readily see the connection of this with their ostensible object, the happiness of man. A perusal of Voltaire's letters betrays the secret. Many years ago he heard that some observations on the formation of strata, and the fossils found in them, were incompatible with the age which the Mosaic history seems to assign to this globe. He mentions this with great exultation in some of his early letters; and, from that time

forward,

forward, never ceases to enjoin his colleagues to press the study of natural history and cosmogony, and carefully to bring forward every fact which was hostile to the Mosaic accounts. It became a serious part of the exercises of their wealthy pupils, and their perplexing discoveries were most ostentatiously displayed. M. de Luc, a very eminent naturalist, has shewn, in a letter to the Chevalier Dr. Zimmermann, (published, I think, about the year 1790,) how very scanty the knowledge of these observers has been, and how precipitate have been their conclusions. For my own part, I think the affair is of little consequence. Moses writes the history, not of this globe, but of the race of Adam.

The science of these philosophers is not remarkable in other branches, if we except M. d'Alembert's mathematics*. Yet the imposing confidence of Voltaire was such, that he passes for a person fully informed, and he pronounces on every subject with so much authority, with such a force of expression, and generally with so much wit or pleasantry, that his hearers and readers are fascinated, and soon convinced of what they wish to be true.

It is not by the wisdom nor by the profound knowledge which these writers display, that they

---

* Never was there any thing more contemptible than the physical and mechanical positions in Diderot's great work, the *Systeme de la Nature*, (Barruel affirms, that he was the author, and got 100 pistoles for the copy, from the person who related the story to him,) that long ago found that Diderot had assisted Robinet to make a book out of his Masonic Oration, which I mentioned in page 41. Robinet trusted to Diderot's knowledge in natural philosophy. But the Junto were ashamed of the book *De la Nature*. Diderot seems to have, after this, read Dr. Hartley's book, and has greatly refined on the crude system of Robinet. But after all, the *Systeme de la Nature* is contemptible, if it be considered as pretending to what is received as science by a mechanical philosopher.

have acquired celebrity, a fame which has been so pernicious. It is by fine writing, by works addressed to the imagination and to the affections, by excellent dramas, by affecting moral essays, full of expressions of the greatest respect for virtue, the most tender benevolence, and the highest sentiments of honour and dignity.—By these means they fascinate all readers; they gain the esteem of the worthy, who imagine them sincere, and their pernicious doctrines are thus spread abroad, and steal into the minds of the dissolute, the licentious, and the unwary.

But I am writing to Britons, who are considered by our neighbours on the Continent as a nation of philosophers—to the countrymen of Bacon, of Locke, of Newton—who are not to be wheedled like children, but must be reasoned with as men.— Voltaire, who decides without hesitation on the character of the most distant nations in the most remote antiquity, did not know us: he came among us, in the beginning of his career, with the highest expectations of our support, and hoped to make his fortune by his Pucelle d'Orleans. It was rejected with disdain—but we published his Henriade for him: and, notwithstanding his repeated disappointments of the same kind, he durst not offend his countrymen by slandering us, but joined in the profound respect paid by all to British science.—Our writers, whether on natural or moral science, are still regarded as standard classics, and are studied with care. Lord Verulam is acknowledged by every man of science to have given the first just description of true philosophy, pointed out its objects, and ascertained its mode of procedure—And Newton is equally allowed to have evinced the propriety of the Baconian precepts by his unequalled success,

sud

suâ Mathesi facem preferente.—The most celebrated philosophers on the Continent are those who have completed by demonstration the wonderful guesses of his penetrating genius. Bailli, or Condorcet, (I forget which,) struck with the inconceivable reaches of Newton's thoughts, breaks out, in the words of Lucretius,

Te sequor, O magnæ gentis decus, inque tuis nunc
Fixa pedum pono pressis vestigia signis.
Tu pater et rerum inventor, tu patria nobis
Suppeditas precepta, tuisque ex inclute chartis,
Floriferis ut apes in saltibus omnia libant,
Omnia nos itidem depascimur aurea dicta;
Aurea, perpetuâ semper dignissima vitâ.

After such avowals of our capacity to instruct ourselves, shall we still fly to those disturbers of the world for our lessons? No—Let us rally round our own standards—let us take the path pointed out by Bacon—let us follow the steps of Newton—and, to conclude, let us seriously consider a most excellent advice by the highest authority:

" Beware of false prophets, who come to you
" in sheep's cloathing, but inwardly they are ra
" vening wolves—BY THEIR FRUITS YE SHA
" KNOW THEM—Do men gather grapes of thorns,
" or figs of thistles?"

THE END.

To the Binder.

* 2 B, and * 2 C, are to be placed before 2 B, these pages being repeated.

www.ingramcontent.com/pod-product-compliance
Lightning Source LLC
Chambersburg PA
CBHW030428300426
44112CB00009B/905